OREGON'S
BEST FISHING WATERS™

179 Detailed Maps of 33 of the Best Rivers, Bays, and Streams

BEST FISHING WATERS™

Wilderness
Adventures
Press, Inc.™

Belgrade, Montana

© 2007 Text, Wilderness Adventures Press, Inc.™
Cover photograph (Grande Ronde River) © 2007 John Shewey

Maps, book and cover design © 2007 Wilderness Adventures Press, Inc.™
Best Fishing Waters™

Published by Wilderness Adventures Press, Inc.™
45 Buckskin Road
Belgrade, MT 59714
866-400-2012
Website: www.wildadvpress.com
Email: books@wildadvpress.com

First Edition

Printed in Singapore

ISBN 9-781932-09838-9 (1-932098-38-0)

TABLE OF CONTENTS

WATERS

FEATURED WATERS

28. Siletz River
29. Tillamook River
30. Trask River
31. Umpqua River
32. Willamette River
33. Wilson River

19. McKenzie River
20. Miami River
21. Molalla River
22. Necanicum River
23. Nehalem River
24. Nestucca River
25. Rogue River
26. Sandy River
27. Santiam River

10. Crooked River
11. Deschutes River
12. Elk River
13. Fall River
14. Grande Ronde River
15. Hood River
16. John Day River
17. Kilchis River
18. Klamath River

1. Alsea River
2. Ana River
3. Applegate River
4. Chetco River
5. Chewaucan River
6. Clackamas River
7. Columbia River
8. Coos Bay
9. Coquille River

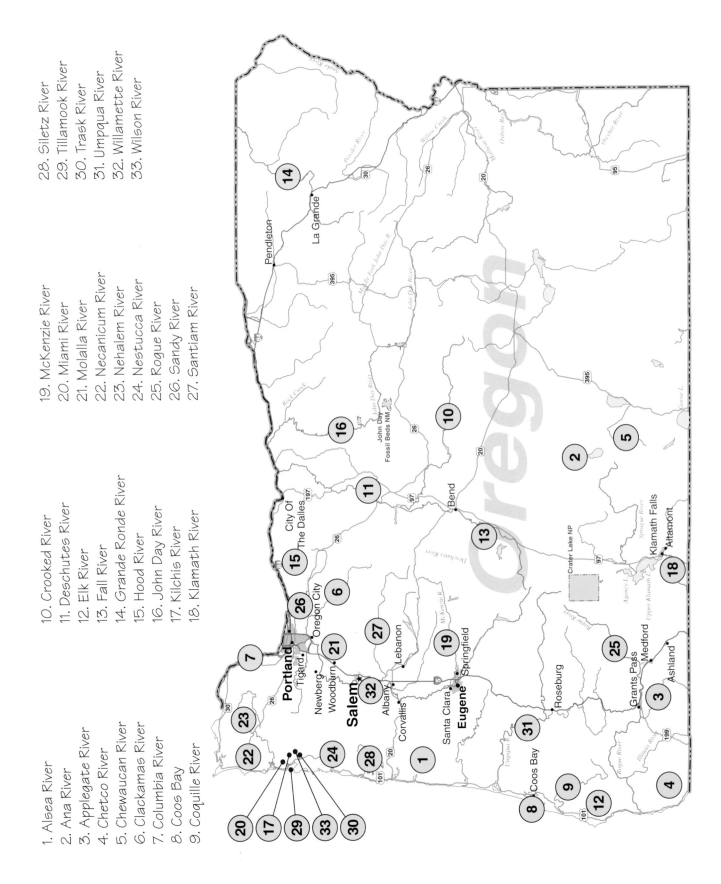

INTRODUCTION

Oregon hosts some of the most sought-after fisheries in the world. In a state with some of the nation's best steelhead and salmon fishing, you have opportunities to fish for either year-round. You can fish for tiny cutthroat in a high mountain stream one day and find yourself hooked up with a giant steelhead the next. You can bump elbows with fly fishers on the Deschutes or be the only soul for miles on some of Oregon's more remote fisheries. Finally you can spend months, maybe years, fishing the Umpqua, Willamette, Rogue or the giant Columbia and never see the same water twice. *Oregon's Best Fishing Waters* is the fifth book in our great map book series. Chris Camuto of *Gray's Sporting Journal* wrote of our first book, *Colorado's Best Fishing Waters*, "This book has by far the clearest road and river maps I've ever seen in a guide book, all in a decent scale so that you can get on good water, off state highways and local roads, with a minimum of fuss and second guessing."

This comprehensive map book contains 179 full-page maps and covers 33 rivers, bays, and streams. Our maps are based on the U.S. Geological Survey maps and include a wealth of useful angling information, along with an overview of the fishing opportunities and the fish found in each water. Access points are clearly indicated, along with boat ramps and campgrounds. Most access points have corresponding GPS coordinates. We also show roads, trails, and public access in the National Forest and State Lands. The information in this book enables you to get to many overlooked areas and waters that result in a better overall angling experience. Each of the waters has an overview map showing the entire river. Then we break the river down into more detailed maps, each showing a smaller section of the river; giving you a more comprehensive view than you will find in other map books.

The waters are listed in alphabetical order for easy reference without the need to consult an index. As with anywhere you fish, always make sure you have a copy of the most current regulations. Copies of regulations are available at most sporting goods shops or online at http://www.dfw.state.or.us/.

OREGON RESOURCES

ODFW Headquarters
Phone: (503) 872-5268
2501 Southwest First Ave
Portland, OR 97207
http://www.dfw.state.or.us/

Northwest Region
7118 Northeast Vandenburg Ave Adair Village
Corvallis, OR 97330
Phone: (541) 757-4186

High Desert Region
61374 Parrell Road
Bend, OR 97702
(541) 388-6363
(541) 573-6582

Columbia Region
17330 Southeast Evelyn St.
Clackamas, OR 97015
(503) 657-2000

Southwest Region
4192 North Umpqua HWY
Roseburg, OR 97470
(541) 440-3353

Northeast Region
107 20th St.
LaGrande, OR 97850

Marine Program
2040 Southeast Marine Science Drive
Newport, OR 97365
(541) 867-4741

LEGEND

—— Interstate	State - Public Land	🐟 Marina / Moorage	Wild & Scenic River
═══ Primary Highway	Indian Reservation	🛏 Picnic Area	Recreation Area
— Road or Street	National Forest	✈ Airport	Oregon State Park
.... Trails	BLM - Public Land	〰 Rapids	Forest/Grass Lands
+—+ Railroad	Boat Launch	○ Locale	Wilderness Lands
15 Interstate Route	▲ Campsite	▽ Danger	Parking
216 State Route	🚐 RV Access	GPS GPS Coordinates	
287 U.S. Route	🎣 Fishing Access	99 Forest Route	

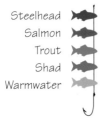

Steelhead
Salmon
Trout
Shad
Warmwater

Easily flip through the pages to locate the species you wish to target. Our new fish indicators tell you with the flip of a page what kind of fish are primarily targeted in that particular stream. A blue fish indicates steelhead, a red fish a salmon. A green fish is for trout, and the brown is for shad. Finally the orange fish indicator is for warm water species. These fish indicators are not suggesting quality of fishing, or that there are not other species in the stream. They are simply a guide to help you find the type of fish you would like to hook up with. Overview maps contain more specifics on which species are hosted by that stream. Read more on the stream maps themselves to learn about the quality of fishing and access provided.

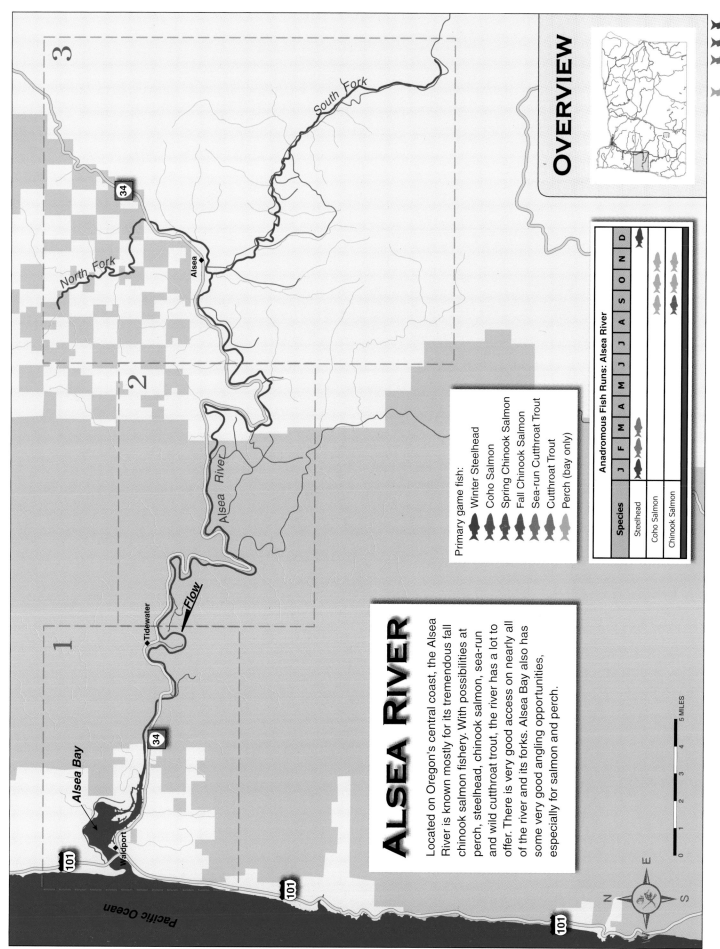

ALSEA RIVER

Located on Oregon's central coast, the Alsea River is known mostly for its tremendous fall chinook salmon fishery. With possibilities at perch, steelhead, chinook salmon, sea-run and wild cutthroat trout, the river has a lot to offer. There is very good access on nearly all of the river and its forks. Alsea Bay also has some very good angling opportunities, especially for salmon and perch.

OVERVIEW

Primary game fish:
Winter Steelhead
Coho Salmon
Spring Chinook Salmon
Fall Chinook Salmon
Sea-run Cutthroat Trout
Cutthroat Trout
Perch (bay only)

Anadromous Fish Runs: Alsea River

Species	J	F	M	A	M	J	J	A	S	O	N	D
Steelhead												
Coho Salmon												
Chinook Salmon												

Pacific Ocean

Alsea Bay

Waldport

Tidewater

Flow

Alsea River

North Fork

Alsea

South Fork

N E S W

0 1 2 3 4 5 MILES

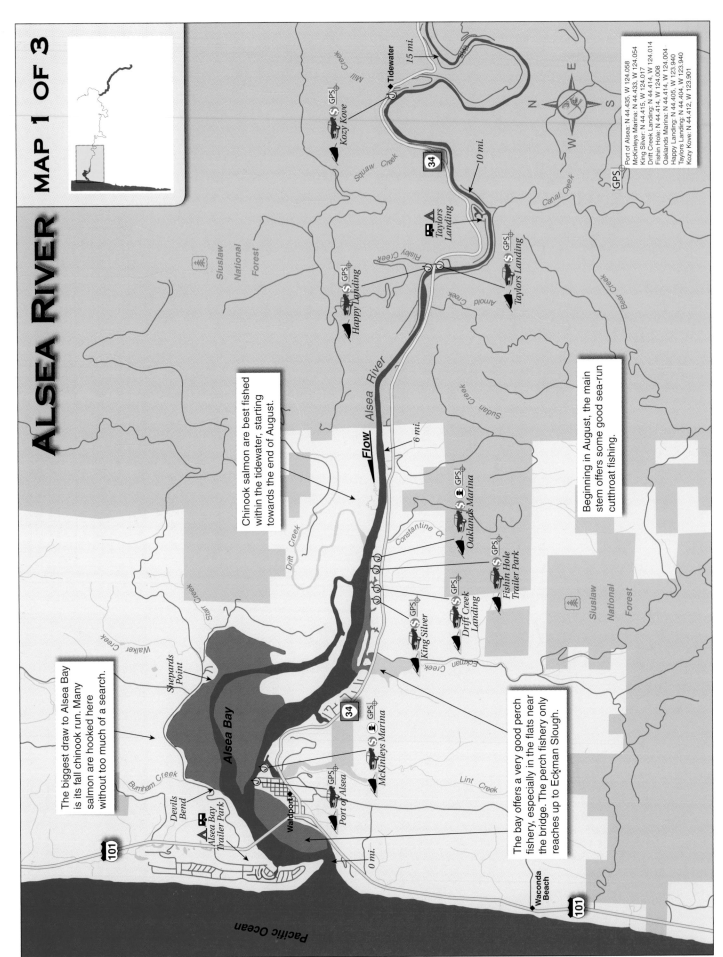

ALSEA RIVER

MAP 1 OF 3

Pacific Ocean

Alsea Bay

Alsea River

Flow

Siuslaw National Forest

Siuslaw National Forest

Tidewater

Kozy Kove

Taylors Landing

Happy Landing

Taylors Landing

Oaklands Marina

Fishin Hole Trailer Park

Drift Creek Landing

King Silver

McKinleys Marina

Port of Alsea

Alsea Bay Trailer Park

Devils Bend

Shepards Point

Waldport

Waconda Beach

Squaw Creek

Mill Creek

Risley Creek

Canal Creek

Arnold Creek

Bear Creek

Sudan Creek

Constantine Cr.

Eckman Creek

Lint Creek

Drift Creek

Star Creek

Walker Creek

Burnham Creek

15 mi.

10 mi.

6 mi.

0 mi.

34

34

101

101

The biggest draw to Alsea Bay is its fall chinook run. Many salmon are hooked here without too much of a search.

Chinook salmon are best fished within the tidewater, starting towards the end of August.

Beginning in August, the main stem offers some good sea-run cutthroat fishing.

The bay offers a very good perch fishery, especially in the flats near the bridge. The perch fishery only reaches up to Eckman Slough.

Port of Alsea: N 44.435, W 124.058
McKinleys Marina: N 44.433, W 124.054
King Silver: N 44.415, W 124.017
Drift Creek Landing: N 44.414, W 124.014
Fishin Hole: N 44.414, W 124.008
Oaklands Marina: N 44.414, W 124.004
Happy Landing: N 44.405, W 123.940
Taylors Landing: N 44.404, W 123.940
Kozy Kove: N 44.412, W 123.901

© 2007 Wilderness Adventures Press, Inc.

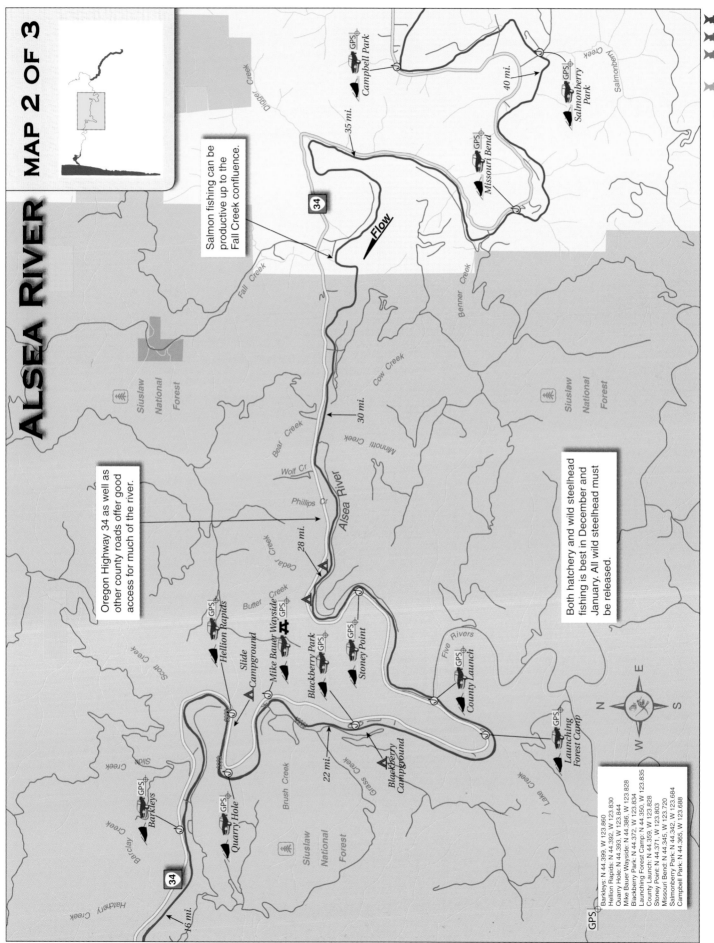

ALSEA RIVER

MAP 2 OF 3

Salmon fishing can be productive up to the Fall Creek confluence.

Oregon Highway 34 as well as other county roads offer good access for much of the river.

Both hatchery and wild steelhead fishing is best in December and January. All wild steelhead must be released.

Siuslaw National Forest

Siuslaw National Forest

Siuslaw National Forest

Flow

Campbell Park

Salmonberry Park

Missouri Bend

40 mi.

35 mi.

30 mi.

28 mi.

22 mi.

16 mi.

Digger Creek

Fall Creek

Bear Creek

Wolf Cr

Phillips Cr

Cedar Creek

Butter

Mike Bauer Wayside

Blackberry Park

Stoney Point

County Launch

Five Rivers

Launching Forest Camp

Blackberry Campground

Grass Creek

Brush Creek

Scott Creek

Slide Campground

Hellion Rapids

Quarry Hole

Barkleys

Slide Creek

Barclay Creek

Hatchery Creek

Lake Creek

Benner Creek

Cow Creek

Mennotti Creek

Salmonberry Creek

Alsea River

Barkleys: N 44.399, W 123.860
Hellion Rapids: N 44.392, W 123.830
Quarry Hole: N 44.393, W 123.844
Mike Bauer Wayside: N 44.386, W 123.828
Blackberry Park: N 44.372, W 123.834
Launching Forest Camp: N 44.350, W 123.835
County Launch: N 44.359, W 123.828
Stoney Point: N 44.371, W 123.803
Missouri Bend: N 44.345, W 123.720
Salmonberry Park: N 44.342, W 123.684
Campbell Park: N 44.365, W 123.688

© 2007 Wilderness Adventures Press, Inc.

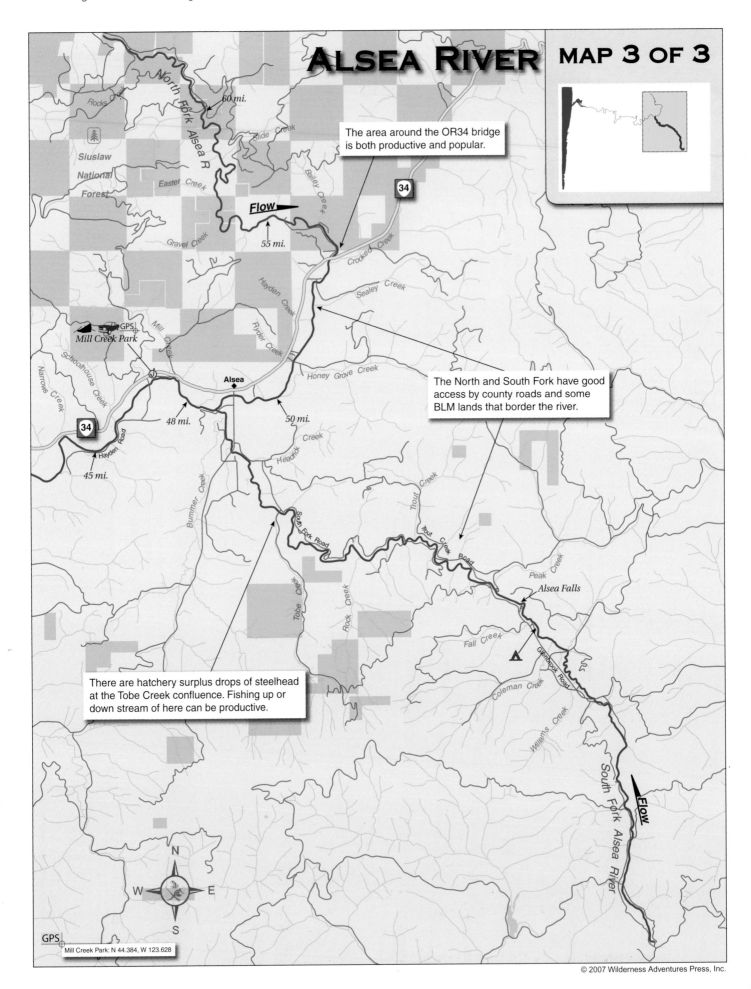

ALSEA RIVER MAP 3 OF 3

The area around the OR34 bridge is both productive and popular.

The North and South Fork have good access by county roads and some BLM lands that border the river.

There are hatchery surplus drops of steelhead at the Tobe Creek confluence. Fishing up or down stream of here can be productive.

Mill Creek Park: N 44.384, W 123.628

© 2007 Wilderness Adventures Press, Inc.

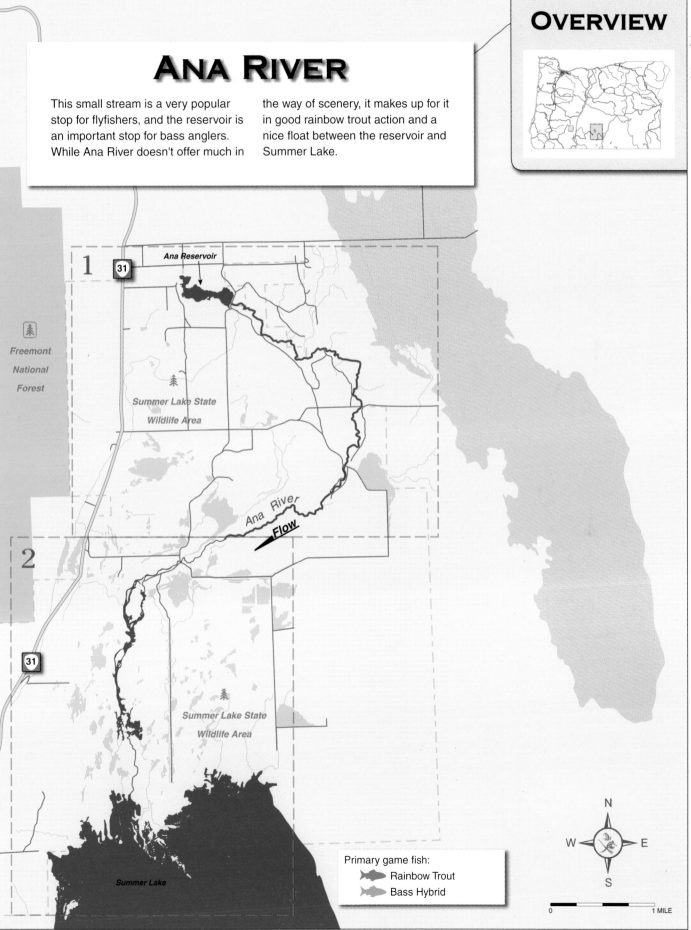

ANA RIVER

This small stream is a very popular stop for flyfishers, and the reservoir is an important stop for bass anglers. While Ana River doesn't offer much in the way of scenery, it makes up for it in good rainbow trout action and a nice float between the reservoir and Summer Lake.

OVERVIEW

Ana Reservoir

1 31

Freemont National Forest

Summer Lake State Wildlife Area

Ana River

Flow

2 31

Summer Lake State Wildlife Area

Primary game fish:
Rainbow Trout
Bass Hybrid

N
W E
S

Summer Lake

0   1 MILE

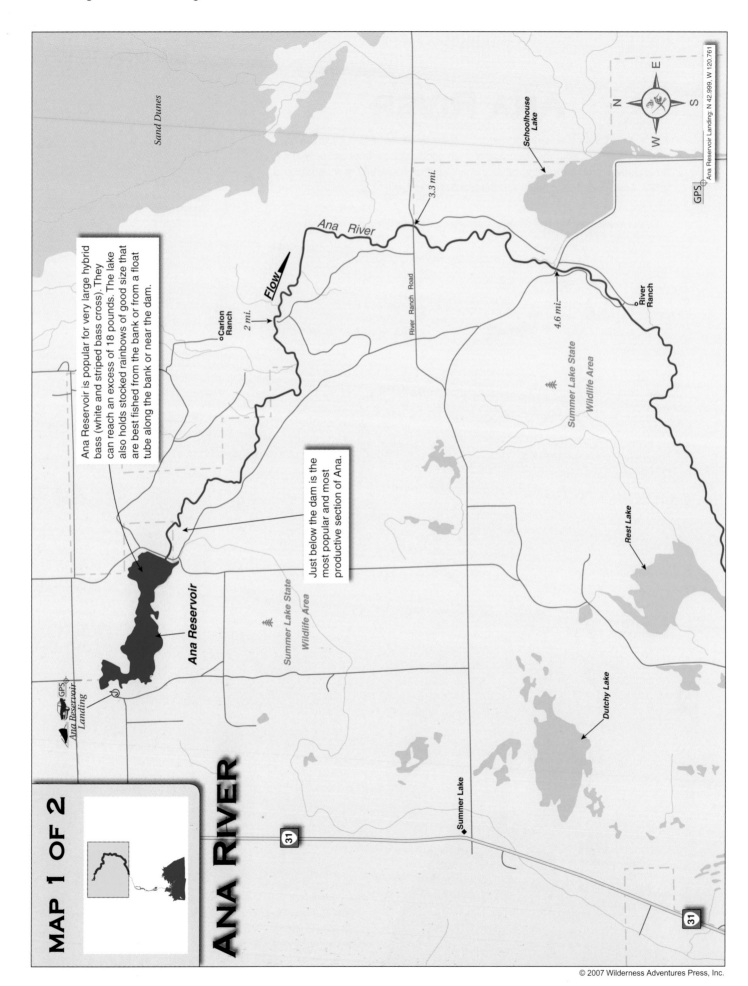

MAP 1 OF 2

ANA RIVER

Ana Reservoir is popular for very large hybrid bass (white and striped bass cross). They can reach an excess of 18 pounds. The lake also holds stocked rainbows of good size that are best fished from the bank or from a float tube along the bank or near the dam.

Just below the dam is the most popular and most productive section of Ana.

Sand Dunes

Ana River

Flow

Schoolhouse Lake

3.3 mi.

4.6 mi.

River Ranch

Carlon Ranch

2 mi.

River Ranch Road

Ana Reservoir

Ana Reservoir Landing

GPS

Summer Lake State Wildlife Area

Summer Lake State Wildlife Area

Rest Lake

Dutchy Lake

Summer Lake

31

31

GPS

Ana Reservoir Landing: N 42.999, W 120.761

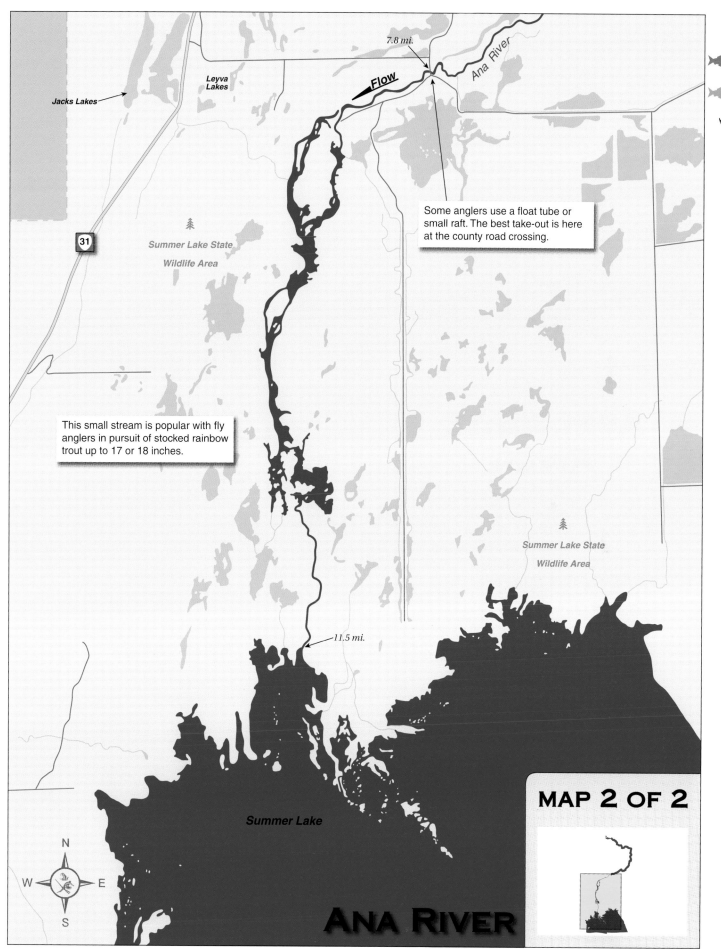

7.8 mi.

Ana River

Flow

Jacks Lakes

Leyva Lakes

31

Summer Lake State Wildlife Area

Some anglers use a float tube or small raft. The best take-out is here at the county road crossing.

This small stream is popular with fly anglers in pursuit of stocked rainbow trout up to 17 or 18 inches.

Summer Lake State Wildlife Area

11.5 mi.

Summer Lake

MAP 2 OF 2

ANA RIVER

N W E S

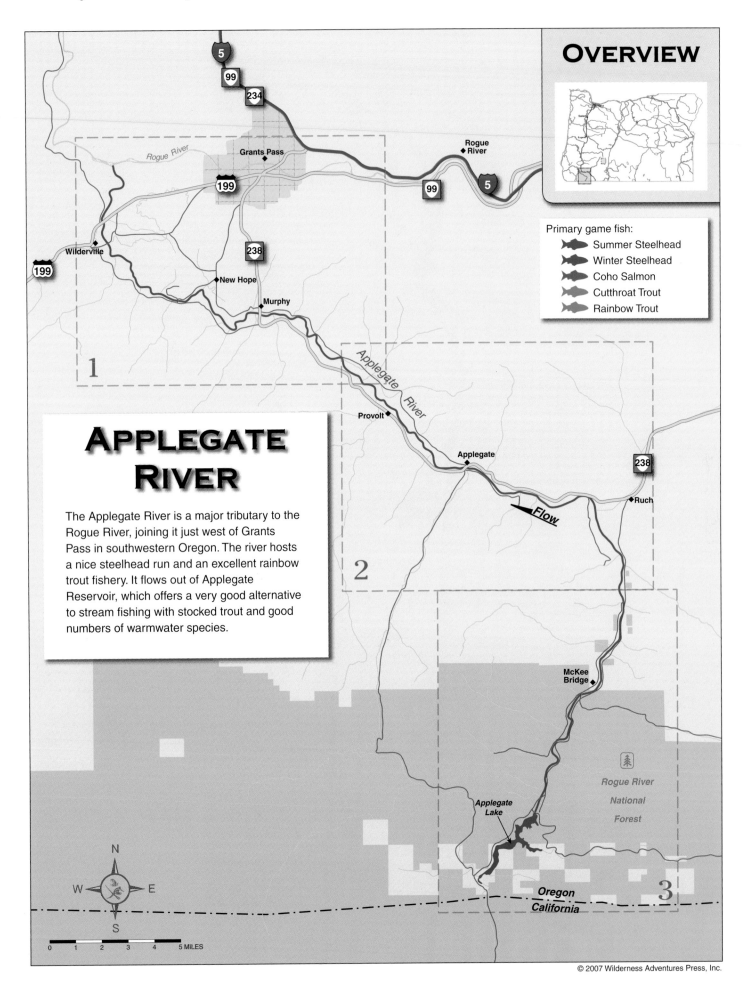

OVERVIEW

Primary game fish:
- Summer Steelhead
- Winter Steelhead
- Coho Salmon
- Cutthroat Trout
- Rainbow Trout

APPLEGATE RIVER

The Applegate River is a major tributary to the Rogue River, joining it just west of Grants Pass in southwestern Oregon. The river hosts a nice steelhead run and an excellent rainbow trout fishery. It flows out of Applegate Reservoir, which offers a very good alternative to stream fishing with stocked trout and good numbers of warmwater species.

Rogue River

Grants Pass

Rogue River

Wilderville

New Hope

Murphy

Provolt

Applegate River

Applegate

Flow

Ruch

McKee Bridge

Applegate Lake

Rogue River National Forest

Oregon
California

1

2

3

N
W E
S

0 1 2 3 4 5 MILES

© 2007 Wilderness Adventures Press, Inc.

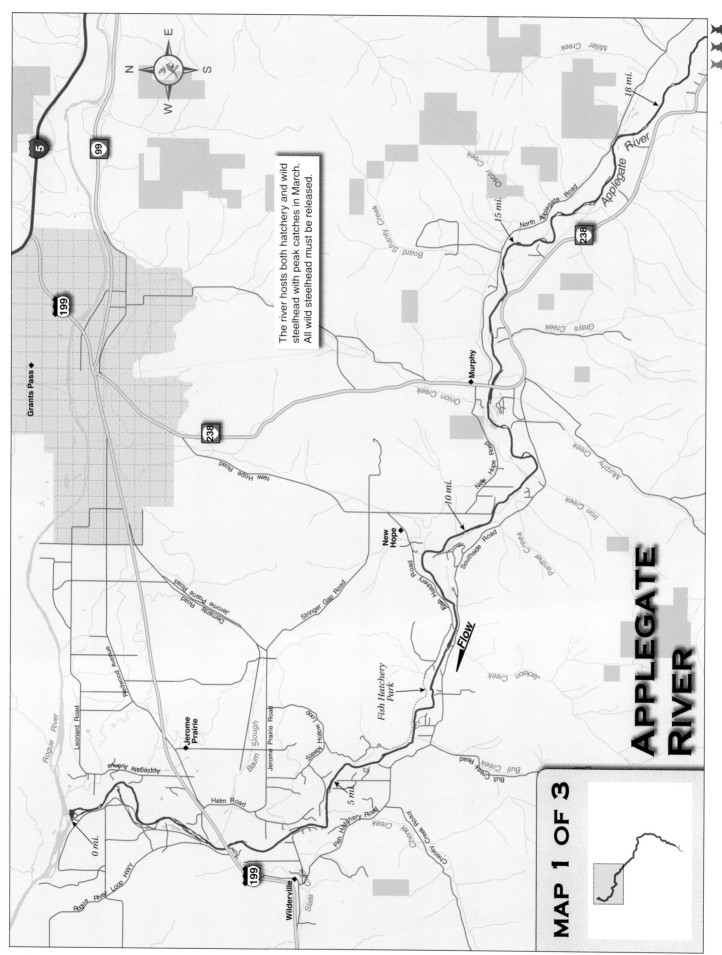

The river hosts both hatchery and wild steelhead with peak catches in March. All wild steelhead must be released.

APPLEGATE RIVER

MAP 1 OF 3

© 2007 Wilderness Adventures Press, Inc.

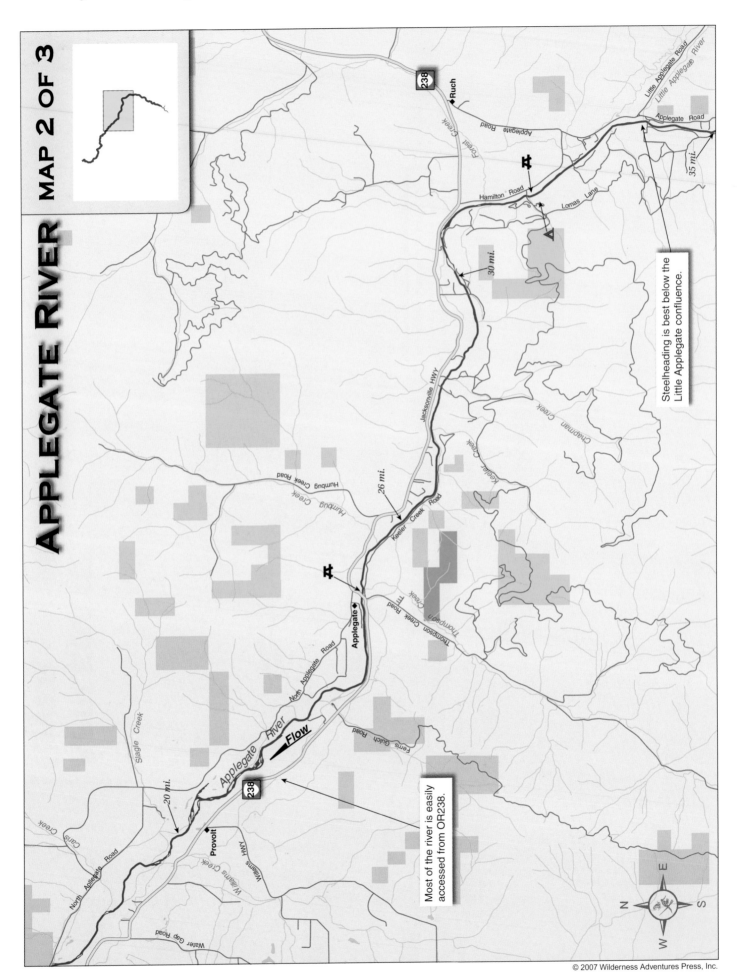

APPLEGATE RIVER MAP 2 OF 3

Steelheading is best below the Little Applegate confluence.

Most of the river is easily accessed from OR238.

35 mi.

30 mi.

26 mi.

20 mi.

Ruch

238

Applegate Road

Little Applegate River

Forest Creek

Hamilton Road

Lomas Lane

Chapman Creek

Keeler Creek

Jacksonville Hwy

Humbug Creek Road

Humbug Creek

Keeler Creek Road

Thompson Creek

Thompson Creek Road

Applegate

North Applegate Road

Ferris Gulch Road

Applegate River

Flow

238

Provolt

Williams Creek

Williams Hwy

Slagle Creek

Cans Creek

North Applegate Road

Water Gap Road

N E S W

© 2007 Wilderness Adventures Press, Inc.

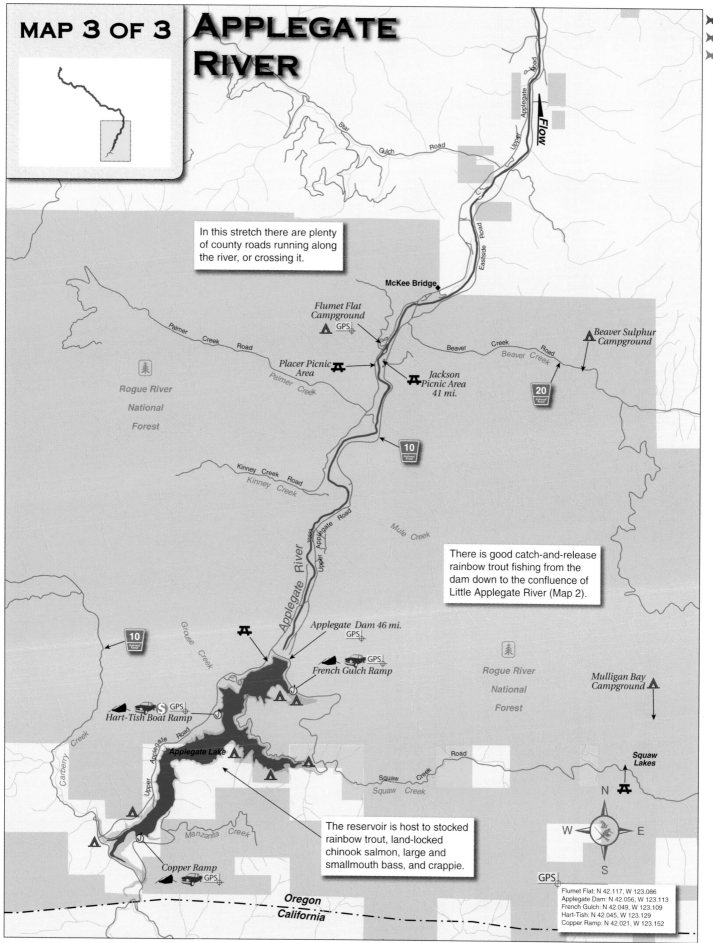

MAP 3 OF 3 APPLEGATE RIVER

In this stretch there are plenty of county roads running along the river, or crossing it.

Flumet Flat Campground GPS

McKee Bridge

Beaver Sulphur Campground

Beaver Creek Road

Placer Picnic Area

Jackson Picnic Area 41 mi.

Rogue River National Forest

Palmer Creek Road

Kinney Creek Road

Mule Creek

There is good catch-and-release rainbow trout fishing from the dam down to the confluence of Little Applegate River (Map 2).

Applegate Dam 46 mi. GPS

French Gulch Ramp GPS

Hart-Tish Boat Ramp GPS

Rogue River National Forest

Mulligan Bay Campground

Applegate River

Grouse Creek

Carberry Creek

Applegate Lake

Squaw Creek Road

Squaw Lakes

N

W E

S

GPS

Copper Ramp GPS

Manzanita Creek

The reservoir is host to stocked rainbow trout, land-locked chinook salmon, large and smallmouth bass, and crappie.

Oregon
California

Flumet Flat: N 42.117, W 123.086
Applegate Dam: N 42.056, W 123.113
French Gulch: N 42.049, W 123.109
Hart-Tish: N 42.045, W 123.129
Copper Ramp: N 42.021, W 123.152

© 2007 Wilderness Adventures Press, Inc.

OVERVIEW

CHETCO RIVER

The Chetco is located near the California border on the southern coast of Oregon. It is well known for hosting very large fish, and that is a huge draw for anglers that show up on the river's banks. Most of the fishing takes place in the lower river, where there is productive water and plenty of access. The river hosts chinook salmon, steelhead, and both sea-run and wild cutthroat trout.

Primary game fish:
- Winter Steelhead
- Coho Salmon
- Fall Chinook Salmon
- Sea-run Cutthroat Trout
- Cutthroat Trout

Anadromous Fish Runs: Chetco River

Species	J	F	M	A	M	J	J	A	S	O	N	D
Steelhead												
Chinook Salmon												

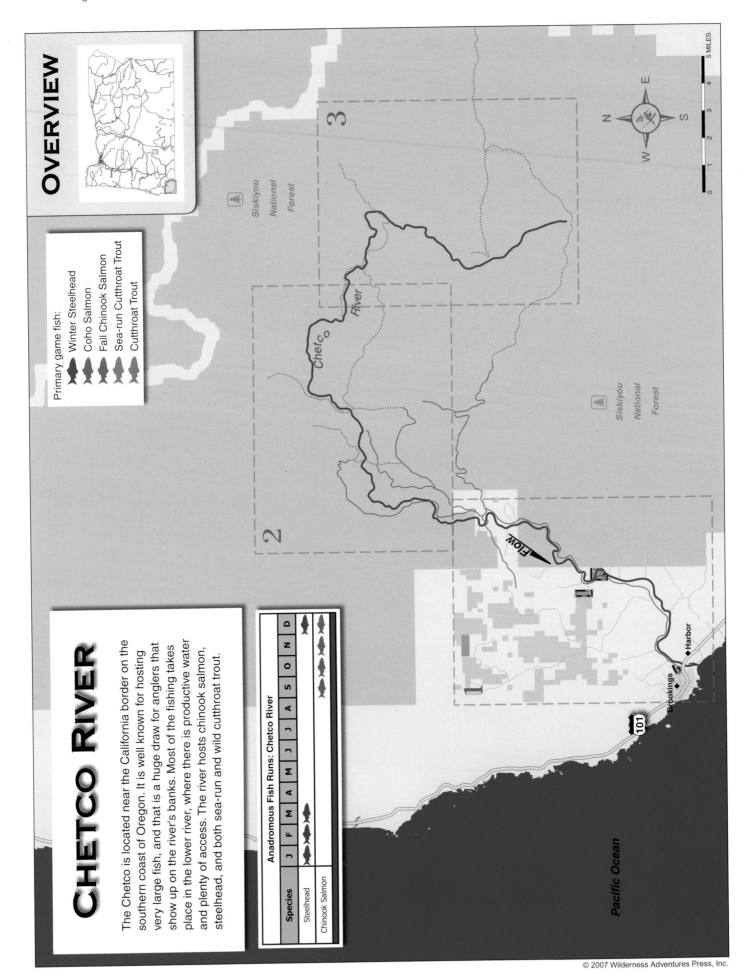

Siskiyou National Forest

Chetco River

Siskiyou National Forest

Flow

Harbor

Brookings

101

Pacific Ocean

5 MILES

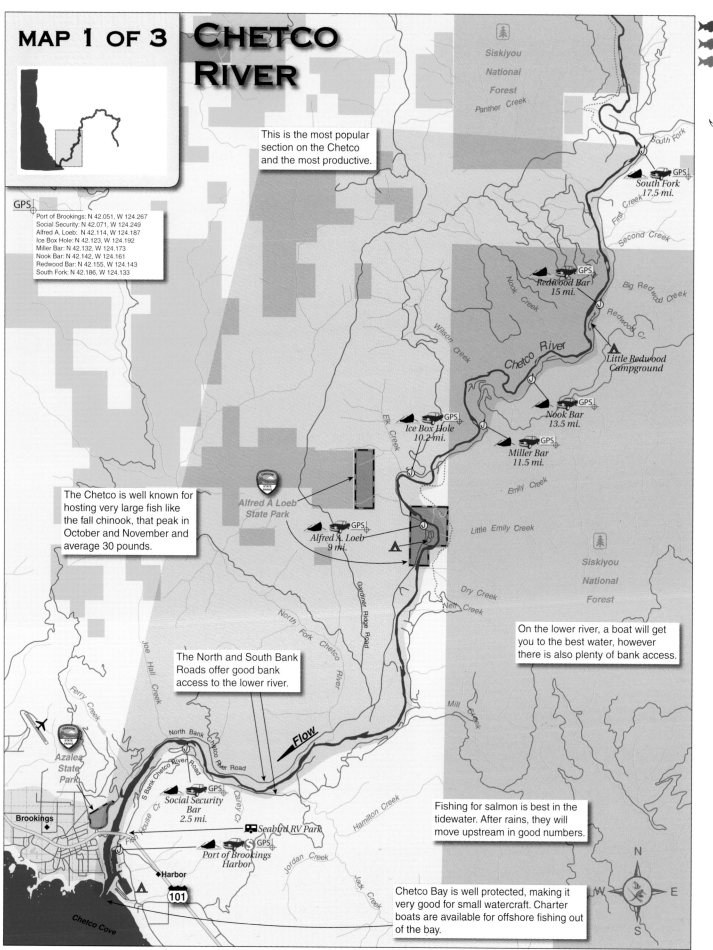

MAP 1 OF 3 CHETCO RIVER

GPS
Port of Brookings: N 42.051, W 124.267
Social Security: N 42.071, W 124.249
Alfred A. Loeb: N 42.114, W 124.187
Ice Box Hole: N 42.123, W 124.192
Miller Bar: N 42.132, W 124.173
Nook Bar: N 42.142, W 124.161
Redwood Bar: N 42.155, W 124.143
South Fork: N 42.186, W 124.133

This is the most popular section on the Chetco and the most productive.

Siskiyou National Forest

Panther Creek

South Fork 17.5 mi.

First Creek

Second Creek

Redwood Bar 15 mi.

Big Redwood Creek

Nook Creek

Redwood Cr.

Chetco River

Little Redwood Campground

Wilson Creek

Nook Bar 13.5 mi.

Elk Creek

Ice Box Hole 10.2 mi.

Miller Bar 11.5 mi.

Emily Creek

The Chetco is well known for hosting very large fish like the fall chinook, that peak in October and November and average 30 pounds.

OREGON STATE PARKS

Alfred A Loeb State Park

Alfred A. Loeb 9 mi.

Little Emily Creek

Siskiyou National Forest

Dry Creek

Nell Creek

Gardner Ridge Road

On the lower river, a boat will get you to the best water, however there is also plenty of bank access.

North Fork Chetco River

The North and South Bank Roads offer good bank access to the lower river.

Flow

Joe Hall Creek

Ferry Creek

Mill Creek

OREGON STATE PARKS

Azalea State Park

North Bank Chetco River Road

S Bank Chetco River Road

Fish House Cr.

Social Security Bar 2.5 mi.

Carey Cr.

Brookings

Seabird RV Park

Port of Brookings Harbor

Hamilton Creek

Fishing for salmon is best in the tidewater. After rains, they will move upstream in good numbers.

Harbor

Jordan Creek

Jack Creek

101

N
W E
S

Chetco Bay is well protected, making it very good for small watercraft. Charter boats are available for offshore fishing out of the bay.

Chetco Cove

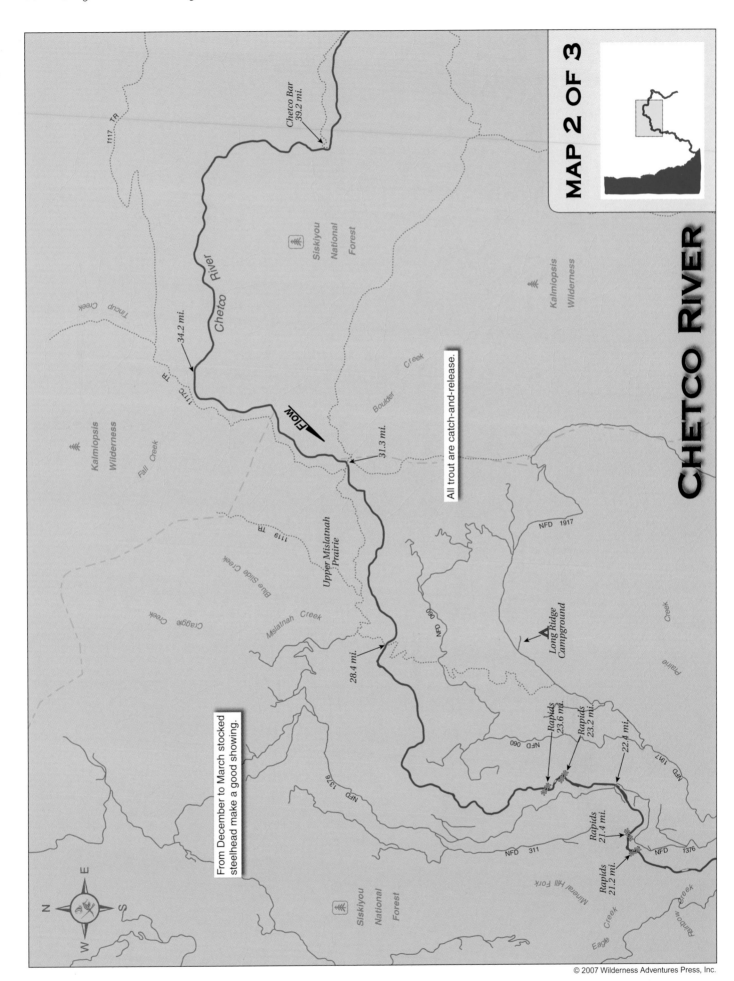

MAP 2 OF 3

CHETCO RIVER

Chetco Bar
39.2 mi.

34.2 mi.

Siskiyou
National
Forest

Kalmiopsis
Wilderness

Tincup Creek

1117 TR

Chetco River

1117 TR

Kalmiopsis
Wilderness

Fall Creek

Boulder Creek

Flow

31.3 mi.

All trout are catch-and-release.

NFD 1917

Upper Mislatnah
Prairie

1119 TR

Blue Slide Creek

Craggie Creek

Mislatnah Creek

NFD 060

Long Ridge
Campground

Prairie Creek

28.4 mi.

From December to March stocked
steelhead make a good showing.

NFD 1376

Rapids
23.6 mi.

Rapids
23.2 mi.

NFD 060

22.4 mi.

NFD 1917

Rapids
21.4 mi.

NFD 311

Rapids
21.2 mi.

NFD 1376

Mineral Hill Fork

Siskiyou
National
Forest

N
E
S
W

Eagle Creek

Rainbow Creek

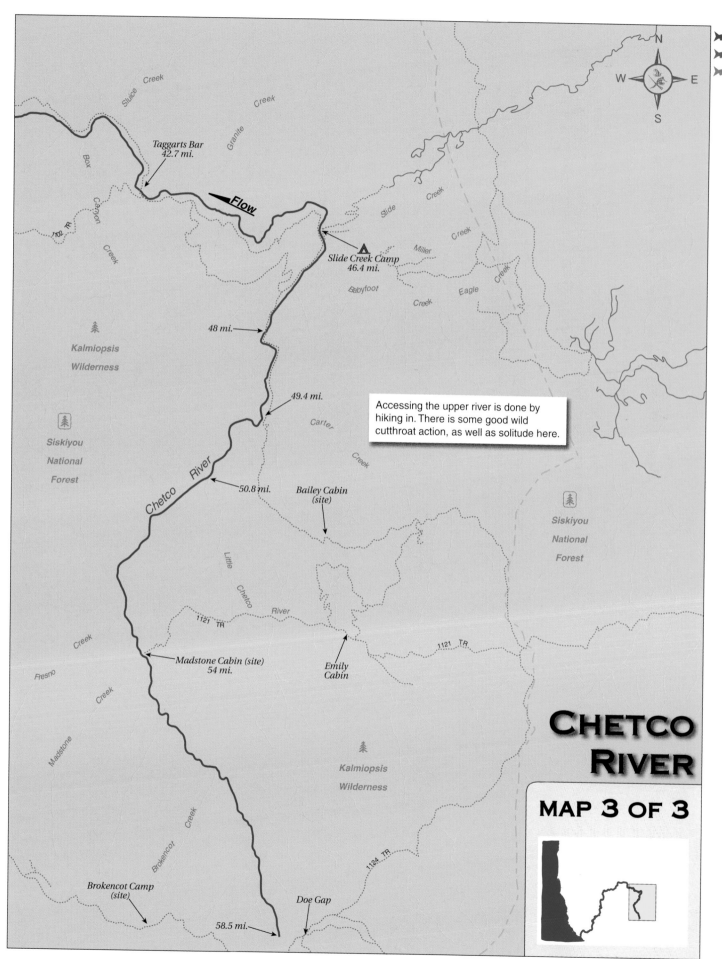

Taggarts Bar
42.7 mi.

Flow

Slide Creek Camp
46.4 mi.

48 mi.

49.4 mi.

Accessing the upper river is done by
hiking in. There is some good wild
cutthroat action, as well as solitude here.

50.8 mi.

Bailey Cabin
(site)

Kalmiopsis
Wilderness

Siskiyou
National
Forest

Siskiyou
National
Forest

Madstone Cabin (site)
54 mi.

Emily
Cabin

CHETCO
RIVER

Kalmiopsis
Wilderness

MAP 3 OF 3

Brokencot Camp
(site)

Doe Gap

58.5 mi.

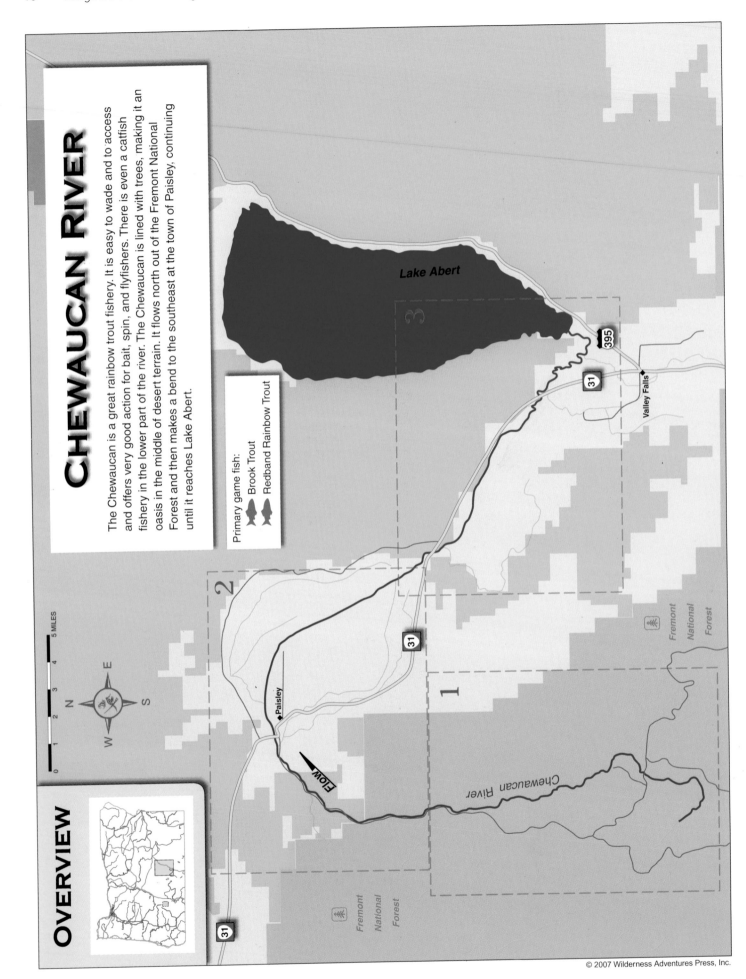

CHEWAUCAN RIVER

The Chewaucan is a great rainbow trout fishery. It is easy to wade and to access and offers very good action for bait, spin, and flyfishers. There is even a catfish fishery in the lower part of the river. The Chewaucan is lined with trees, making it an oasis in the middle of desert terrain. It flows north out of the Fremont National Forest and then makes a bend to the southeast at the town of Paisley, continuing until it reaches Lake Abert.

Primary game fish:
Brook Trout
Redband Rainbow Trout

Lake Abert

Valley Falls

Paisley

Flow

Chewaucan River

Fremont National Forest

OVERVIEW

© 2007 Wilderness Adventures Press, Inc.

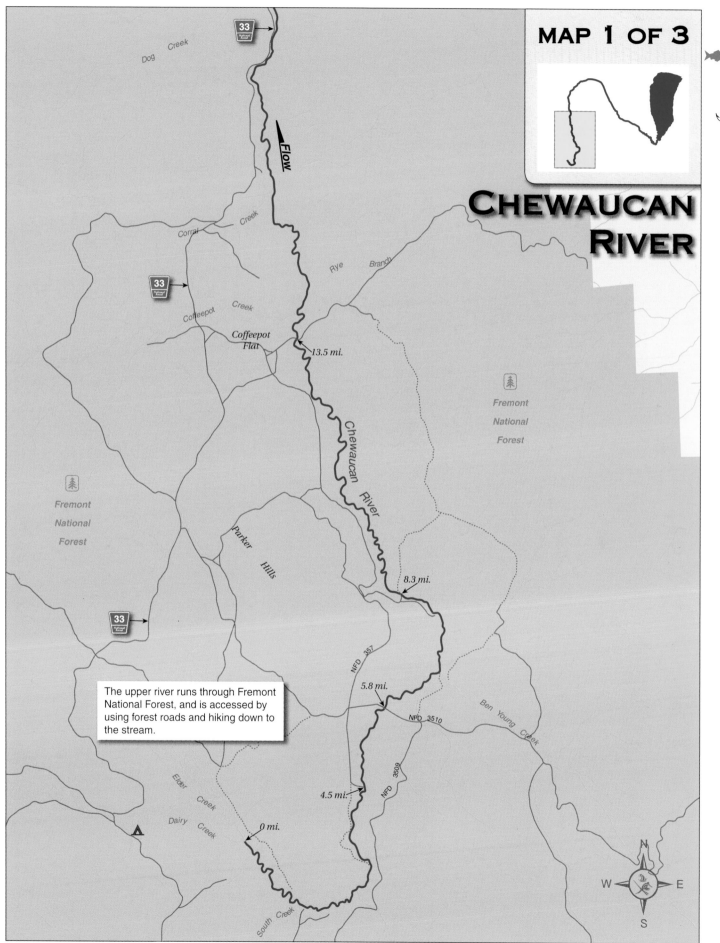

MAP **1** OF **3**

CHEWAUCAN RIVER

Dog Creek

Flow

Corral Creek

Rye Branch

Coffeepot Creek

Coffeepot Flat

13.5 mi.

Chewaucan River

Fremont National Forest

Fremont National Forest

Parker Hills

8.3 mi.

NFD 357

The upper river runs through Fremont National Forest, and is accessed by using forest roads and hiking down to the stream.

5.8 mi.

NFD 3510

Ben Young Creek

NFD 3509

4.5 mi.

Elder Creek

Dairy Creek

0 mi.

South Creek

N
W   E
S

© 2007 Wilderness Adventures Press, Inc.

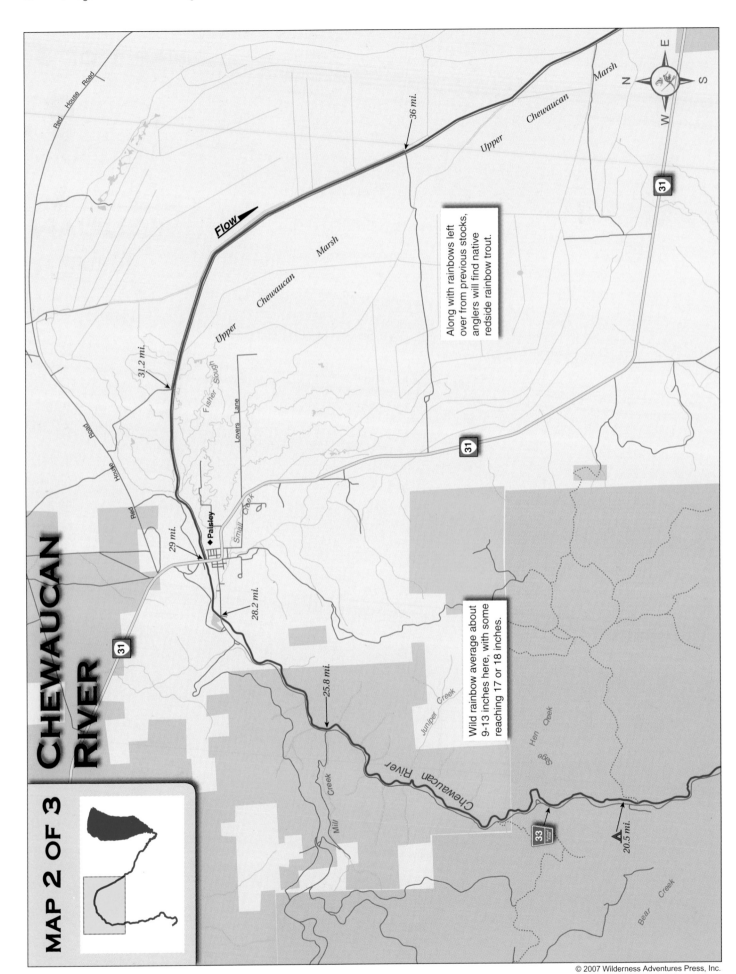

Along with rainbows left over from previous stocks, anglers will find native redside rainbow trout.

Wild rainbow average about 9-13 inches here, with some reaching 17 or 18 inches.

CHEWAUCAN RIVER

MAP 2 OF 3

© 2007 Wilderness Adventures Press, Inc.

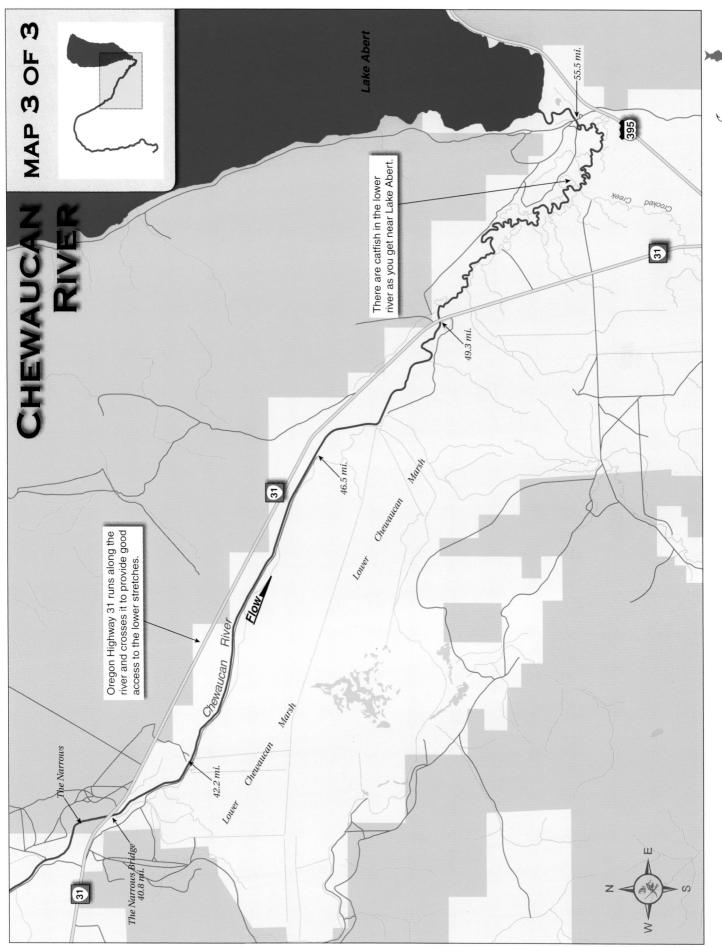

MAP 3 OF 3

CHEWAUCAN RIVER

Lake Abert

55.5 mi.

395

Crooked Creek

31

There are catfish in the lower river as you get near Lake Abert.

49.3 mi.

Lower Chewaucan Marsh

46.5 mi.

31

Oregon Highway 31 runs along the river and crosses it to provide good access to the lower stretches.

Chewaucan River

Flow

Lower Chewaucan Marsh

42.2 mi.

Lower Chewaucan Marsh

The Narrows

The Narrows Bridge 40.8 mi.

31

N E W S

OVERVIEW

10 MILES

0

CLACKAMAS RIVER

The Clackamas River is a quality fishery that is just an hour's drive from Oregon's largest metropolitan area, Portland. The river can get very crowded but, with a little work, a trout fisher can find some solitude. If you are fishing for salmon or steelhead on the river, then be prepared for some crowds. Steelhead are in the river all year offering both winter and summer runs of hatchery and wild fish. The Clackamas joins the Willamette just south of Portland as it flows northwest from Mount Hood National Forest.

Primary game fish:

Winter Steelhead
Summer Steelhead
Coho Salmon
Spring Chinook Salmon
Rainbow Trout
Cutthroat Trout
Brook Trout
Brown Trout

Clackamas River

Three Lynx
Ripplebrook

Flow

Sandy

Estacada
Faraday

Eagle Creek

Barton

Logan

Redland

Clackamas

Gladstone

Lake Oswego

Canby

Anadromous Fish Runs: Clackamas River

Species	J	F	M	A	M	J	J	A	S	O	N	D
Steelhead												
Coho Salmon												
Chinook Salmon												

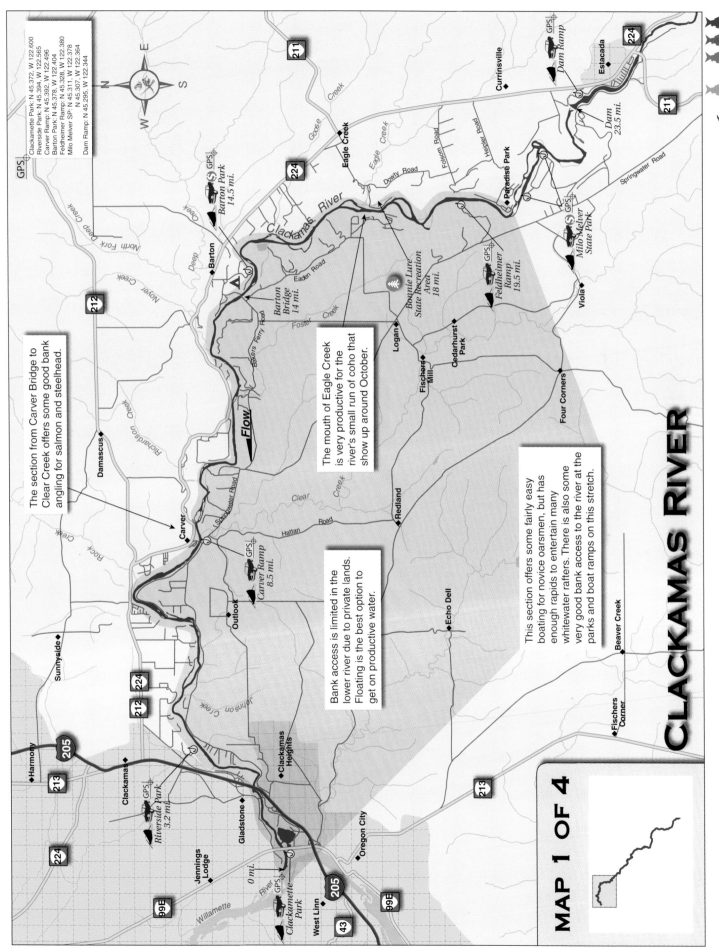

GPS

Clackamette Park: N 45.372, W 122.600
Riverside Park: N 45.394, W 122.565
Carver Ramp: N 45.392, W 122.496
Barton Park: N 45.378, W 122.404
Feldheimer Ramp: N 45.328, W 122.380
Milo Melver SP: N 45.311, W 122.378
Dam Ramp: N 45.307, W 122.364
Dam Ramp: N 45.295, W 122.344

The section from Carver Bridge to Clear Creek offers some good bank angling for salmon and steelhead.

The mouth of Eagle Creek is very productive for the river's small run of coho that show up around October.

Bank access is limited in the lower river due to private lands. Floating is the best option to get on productive water.

This section offers some fairly easy boating for novice oarsmen, but has enough rapids to entertain many whitewater rafters. There is also some very good bank access to the river at the parks and boat ramps on this stretch.

Barton Park
14.5 mi.

Barton Bridge
14 mi.

Bonnie Lure State Recreation Area

Feldheimer Ramp
19.5 mi.

Milo Melver State Park

Dam
23.5 mi.

Carver Ramp
8.5 mi.

Riverside Park
3.2 mi.

Clackamette Park

0 mi.

Flow

CLACKAMAS RIVER

MAP 1 OF 4

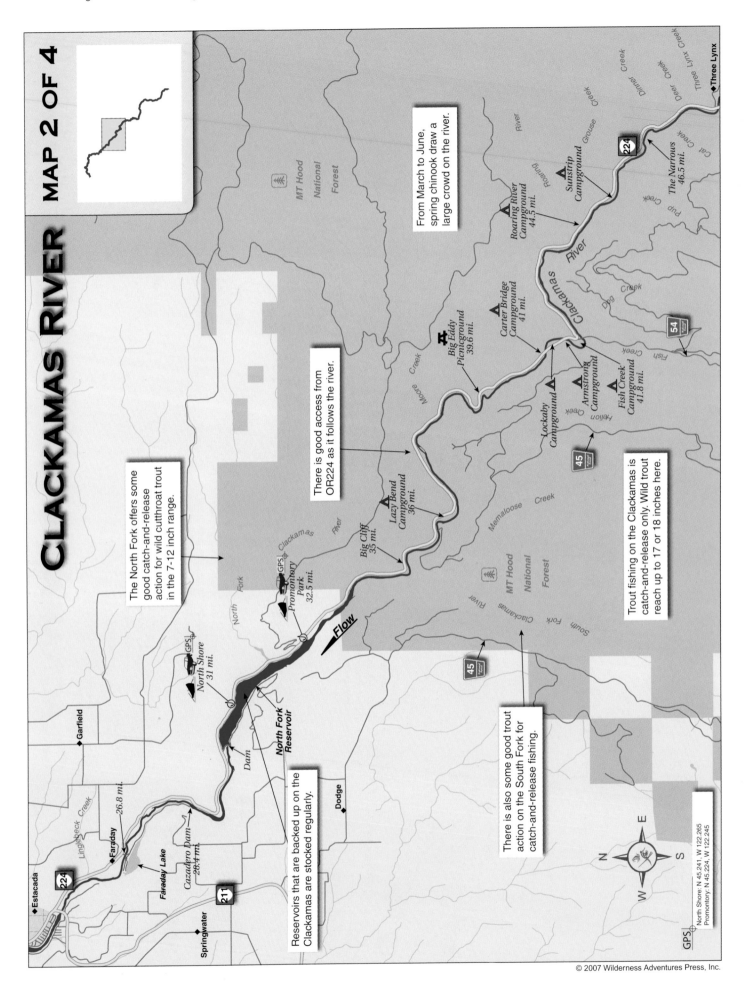

CLACKAMAS RIVER

MAP 2 OF 4

The North Fork offers some good catch-and-release action for wild cutthroat trout in the 7-12 inch range.

There is good access from OR224 as it follows the river.

From March to June, spring chinook draw a large crowd on the river.

Trout fishing on the Clackamas is catch-and-release only. Wild trout reach up to 17 or 18 inches here.

There is also some good trout action on the South Fork for catch-and-release fishing.

Reservoirs that are backed up on the Clackamas are stocked regularly.

MT Hood National Forest

Three Lynx

Three Lynx Creek
Deer Creek
Dinner Creek
Cat Creek

The Narrows 46.5 mi.

Sunstrip Campground

Roaring River Campground 44.5 mi.

Grouse Creek
Roaring River

Clackamas River

Pup Creek
Dog Creek

Fish Creek

Carter Bridge Campground 41 mi.

Big Eddy Picnicground 39.6 mi.

Armstrong Campground
Fish Creek Campground 41.8 mi.
Lockaby Campground
Fallon Creek

Moore Creek

Memaloose Creek

Lazy Bend Campground 36 mi.

Big Cliff 35 mi.

Clackamas River

North Fork

Promontory Park 32.5 mi.

GPS

Flow

North Shore 31 mi.
GPS

North Fork Reservoir

Dam

Faraday Lake

Cazadero Dam 28.4 mi.

Faraday 26.8 mi.

Lingbeck Creek

Garfield

Estacada

Springwater

Dodge

MT Hood National Forest

South Fork Clackamas River

GPS North Shore: N 45.241, W 122.265
Promontory: N 45.224, W 122.245

© 2007 Wilderness Adventures Press, Inc.

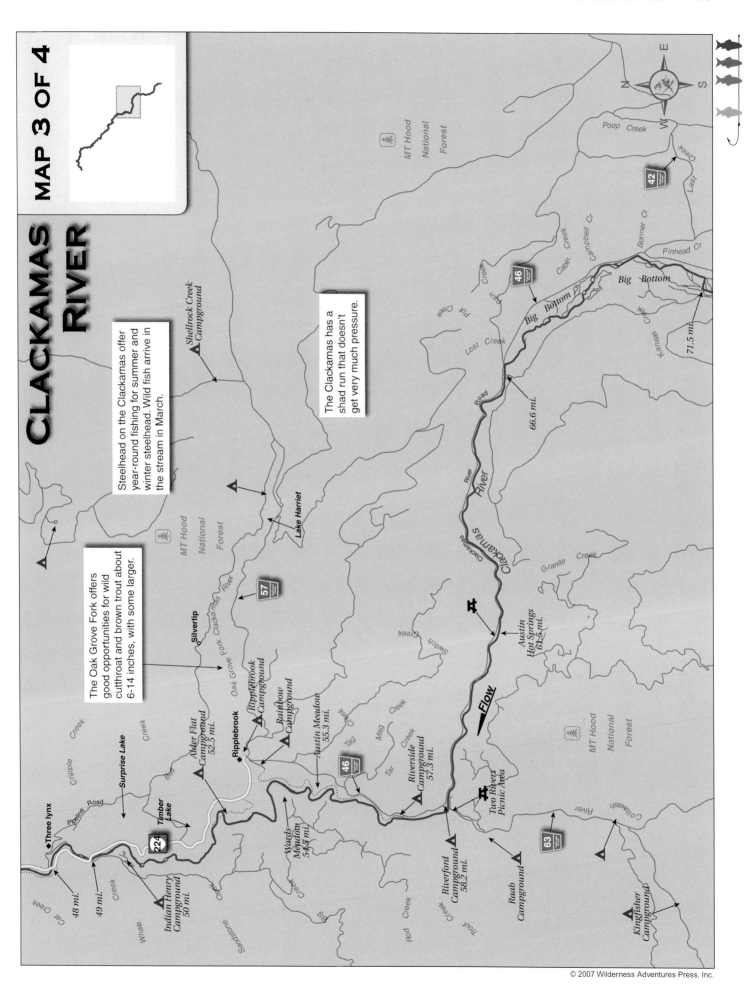

MAP 3 OF 4

CLACKAMAS RIVER

Steelhead on the Clackamas offer year-round fishing for summer and winter steelhead. Wild fish arrive in the stream in March.

The Clackamas has a shad run that doesn't get very much pressure.

The Oak Grove Fork offers good opportunities for wild cutthroat and brown trout about 6-14 inches, with some larger.

Shellrock Creek Campground

Lake Harriet

Silvertip

Ripplebrook

Alder Flat Campground 52.5 mi.

Ripplebrook Campground

Rainbow Campground

Austin Meadow 55.3 mi.

Wash Meadow 54.5 mi.

Surprise Lake

Timber Lake

Three lynx

Pipeline Road

Indian Henry Campground 50 mi.

48 mi.

49 mi.

Cripple Creek

Cat Creek

Sandstone

Whale Creek

Big Creek

Rod Creek

Trout Creek

Tag Creek

Switch Creek

Mag Creek

Tar Creek

Riverside Campground 57.3 mi.

Riverford Campground 58.2 mi.

Raab Campground

Kingfisher Campground

Two Rivers Picnic Area

Flow

Austin Hot Springs 61.5 mi.

Collawash River

Granite Creek

Clackamas River

Road

River

66.6 mi.

71.5 mi.

Big Bottom

Big Bottom

Lost Creek

Fan Creek

Pot Creek

Cabin Creek

Campbell Cr.

Bonner Cr.

Kansas Creek

Pinhead Cr

Poop Creek

Last Creek

MT Hood National Forest

MT Hood National Forest

MT Hood National Forest

Oak Grove Fork Clackamas River

224

57

46

46

63

42

N E S W

© 2007 Wilderness Adventures Press, Inc.

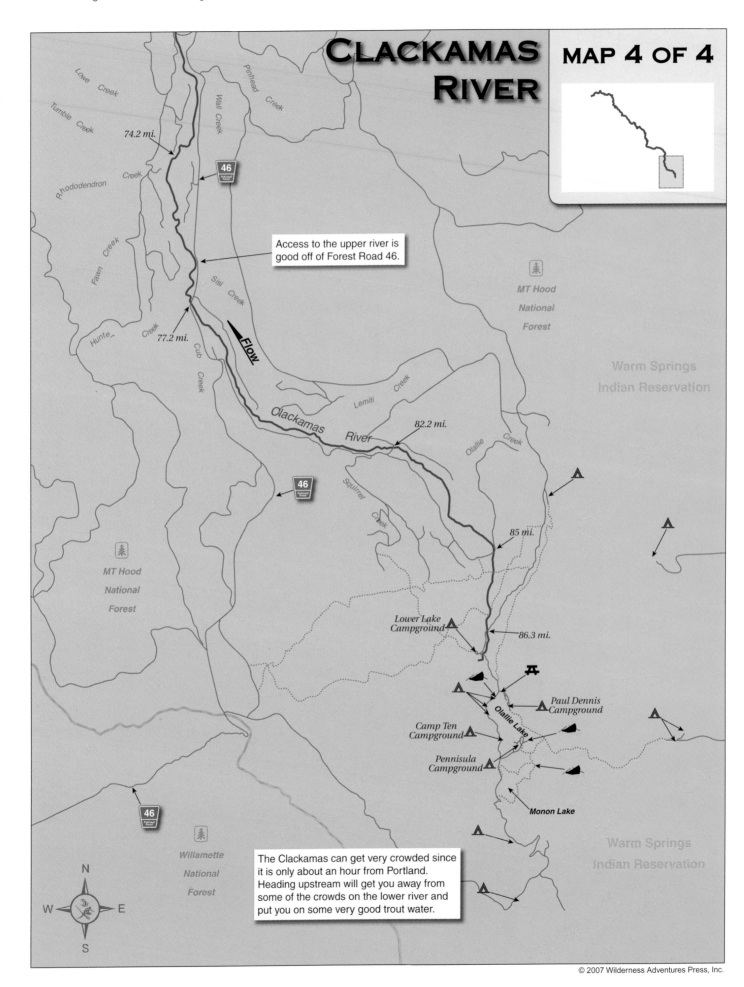

CLACKAMAS RIVER

MAP 4 OF 4

74.2 mi.

46

Access to the upper river is good off of Forest Road 46.

77.2 mi.

Flow

MT Hood National Forest

Warm Springs Indian Reservation

Lemiti Creek

Clackamas River

82.2 mi.

Olallie Creek

46

Squirrel Creek

85 mi.

MT Hood National Forest

86.3 mi.

Lower Lake Campground

Paul Dennis Campground

Olallie Lake

Camp Ten Campground

Pennisula Campground

Monon Lake

Warm Springs Indian Reservation

46

Willamette National Forest

N
W   E
S

The Clackamas can get very crowded since it is only about an hour from Portland. Heading upstream will get you away from some of the crowds on the lower river and put you on some very good trout water.

© 2007 Wilderness Adventures Press, Inc.

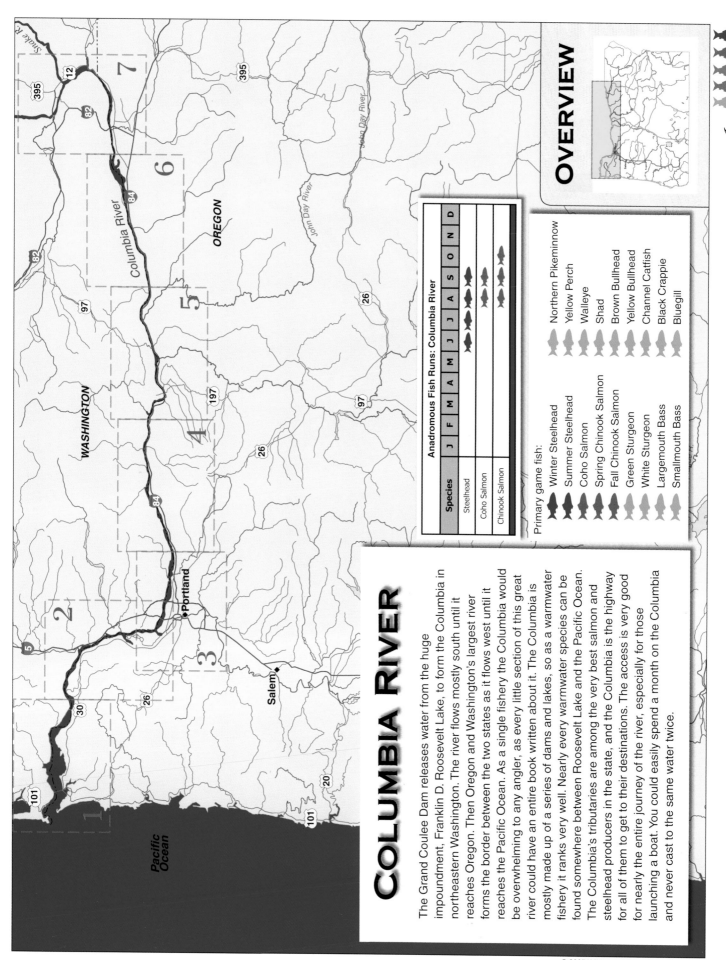

OVERVIEW

Snake R.

WASHINGTON

OREGON

John Day River

Columbia River

Portland

Salem

Pacific Ocean

COLUMBIA RIVER

The Grand Coulee Dam releases water from the huge impoundment, Franklin D. Roosevelt Lake, to form the Columbia in northeastern Washington. The river flows mostly south until it reaches Oregon. Then Oregon and Washington's largest river forms the border between the two states as it flows west until it reaches the Pacific Ocean. As a single fishery the Columbia would be overwhelming to any angler, as every little section of this great river could have an entire book written about it. The Columbia is mostly made up of a series of dams and lakes, so as a warmwater fishery it ranks very well. Nearly every warmwater species can be found somewhere between Roosevelt Lake and the Pacific Ocean. The Columbia's tributaries are among the very best salmon and steelhead producers in the state, and the Columbia is the highway for all of them to get to their destinations. The access is very good for nearly the entire journey of the river, especially for those launching a boat. You could easily spend a month on the Columbia and never cast to the same water twice.

Anadromous Fish Runs: Columbia River

Species	J	F	M	A	M	J	J	A	S	O	N	D
Steelhead												
Coho Salmon												
Chinook Salmon												

Primary game fish:

Winter Steelhead
Summer Steelhead
Coho Salmon
Spring Chinook Salmon
Fall Chinook Salmon
Green Sturgeon
White Sturgeon
Largemouth Bass
Smallmouth Bass

Northern Pikeminnow
Yellow Perch
Walleye
Shad
Brown Bullhead
Yellow Bullhead
Channel Catfish
Black Crappie
Bluegill

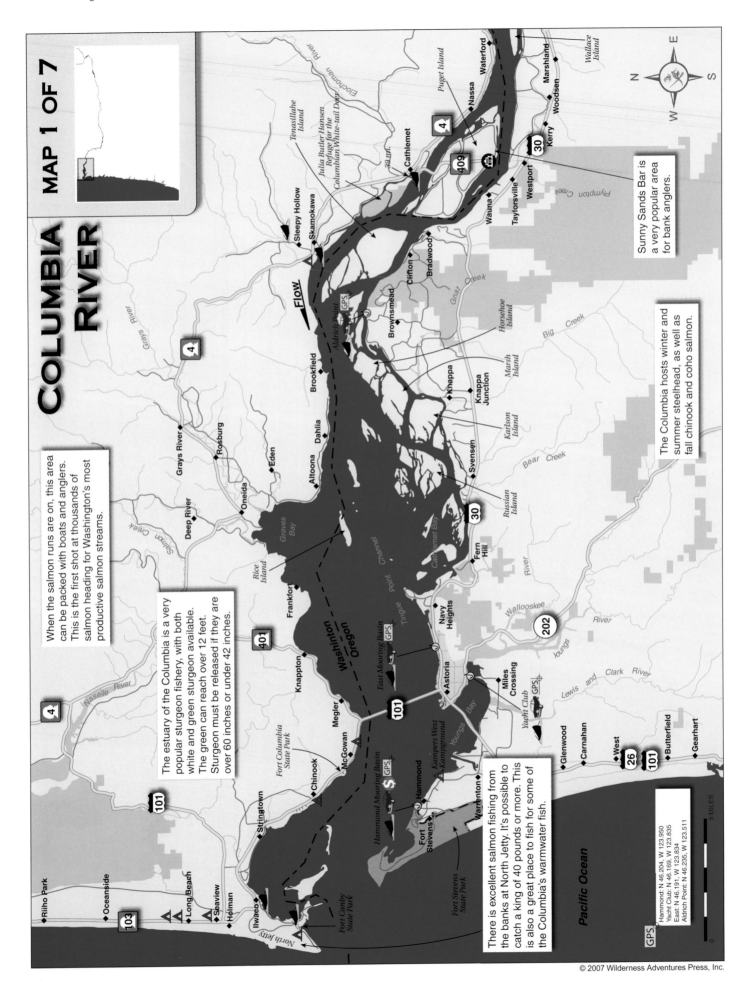

MAP 1 OF 7

COLUMBIA RIVER

Flow

When the salmon runs are on, this area can be packed with boats and anglers. This is the first shot at thousands of salmon heading for Washington's most productive salmon streams.

The estuary of the Columbia is a very popular sturgeon fishery, with both white and green sturgeon available. The green can reach over 12 feet. Sturgeon must be released if they are over 60 inches or under 42 inches.

There is excellent salmon fishing from the banks at North Jetty. It's possible to catch a king of 40 pounds or more. This is also a great place to fish for some of the Columbia's warmwater fish.

Sunny Sands Bar is a very popular area for bank anglers.

The Columbia hosts winter and summer steelhead, as well as fall chinook and coho salmon.

GPS
Hammond: N 46.204, W 123.950
Yacht Club: N 46.169, W 123.835
East: N 46.191, W 123.834
Aldrich Point: N 46.235, W 123.511

Pacific Ocean

Washington
Oregon

0   5 MILES

© 2007 Wilderness Adventures Press, Inc.

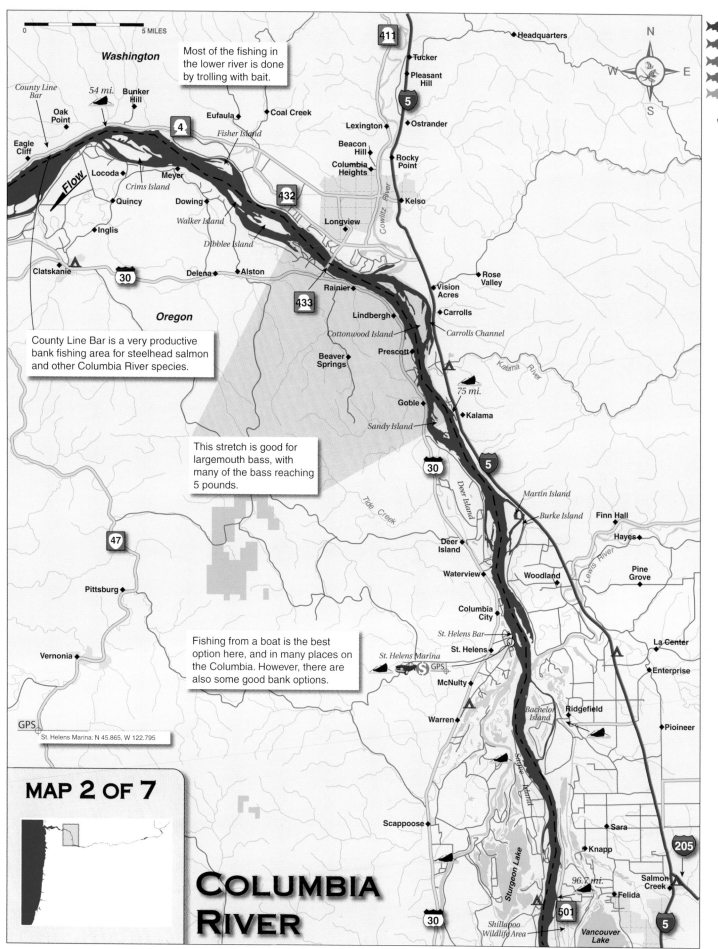

MAP 2 OF 7

COLUMBIA RIVER

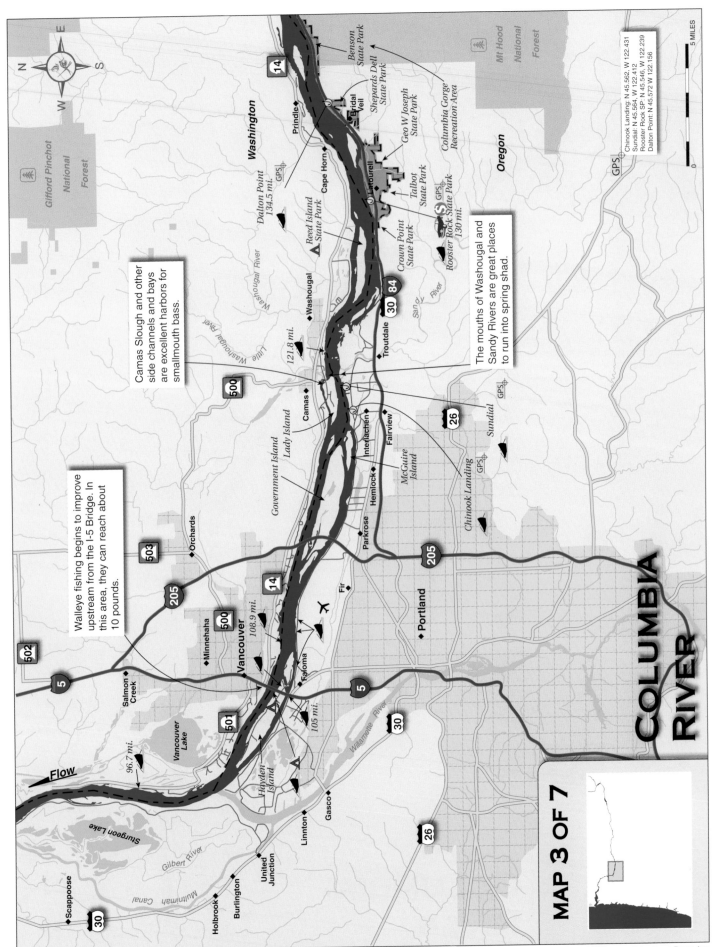

Chinook Landing: N 45.562, W 122.431
Sundial: N 45.564, W 122.412
Rooster Rock SP: N 45.546, W 122.239
Dalton Point: N 45.572 W 122.156

5 MILES

Benson State Park

Shepards Dell State Park

Geo W Joseph State Park

Columbia Gorge Recreation Area

Mt Hood National Forest

Bridal Veil

Prindle

Cape Horn

Dalton Point 134.5 mi.

Reed Island State Park

Talbot State Park

Latourell

Crown Point State Park

Rooster Rock State Park 130 mi.

Sandy River

Washougal

30 84

Camas Slough and other side channels and bays are excellent harbors for smallmouth bass.

Troutdale

121.8 mi.

The mouths of Washougal and Sandy Rivers are great places to run into spring shad.

Little Washougal River

Washougal River

Gifford Pinchot National Forest

500

Camas

Lady Island

Interlachen

Fairview

26

Sundial

Government Island

Hemlock

McGuire Island

Parkrose

Chinook Landing

Walleye fishing begins to improve upstream from the I-5 Bridge. In this area, they can reach about 10 pounds.

Orchards

503

205

Minnehaha

500

Vancouver

108.9 mi.

14

Fir

205

Portland

502

5

Salmon Creek

Faloma

501

105 mi.

5

30

Willamette River

Vancouver Lake

96.7 mi.

Hayden Island

Gasco

Linnton

26

Flow

Sturgeon Lake

Gilbert River

United Junction

Burlington

Holbrook

Multnomah Canal

Scappoose

30

Washington

Oregon

COLUMBIA RIVER

MAP 3 OF 7

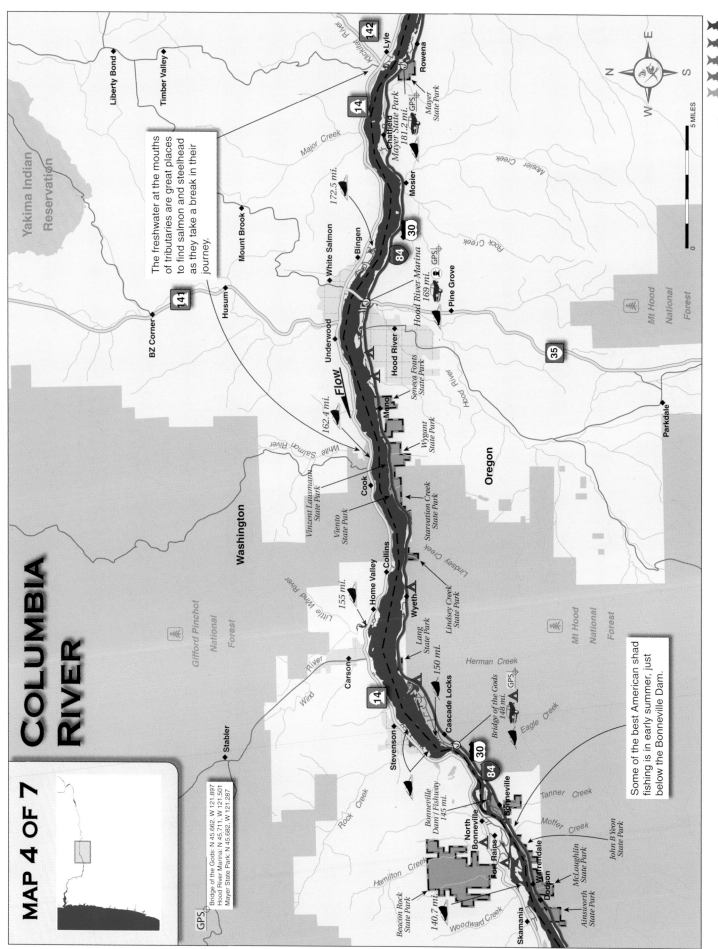

MAP 4 OF 7

COLUMBIA RIVER

GPS
Bridge of the Gods: N 45.662, W 121.897
Hood River Marina: N 45.711, W 121.501
Mayer State Park: N 45.682, W 121.287

The freshwater at the mouths of tributaries are great places to find salmon and steelhead as they take a break in their journey.

Some of the best American shad fishing is in early summer, just below the Bonneville Dam.

Yakima Indian Reservation

Liberty Bond

Timber Valley

Mount Brook

Klickitat River

142

Lyle

Rowena

14

Chatfield
Mayer State Park
181.2 mi.

GPS

Mayer State Park

Major Creek

Mosier

Mosier Creek

172.5 mi.

30

84

Husum

141

BZ Corner

White Salmon

Bingen

Underwood

Hood River Marina
169 mi.

GPS

Pine Grove

Rock Creek

Mt Hood National Forest

35

Hood River

Seneca Fouts State Park

Hood River

FLOW

162.4 mi.

Menol

Wygant State Park

Parkdale

Washington

White Salmon River

Little Wind River

Cook

Vinzent Lausmann State Park

Viento State Park

Starvation Creek State Park

Oregon

Collins

Home Valley

155 mi.

Wyeth

Lindsey Creek

Lindsey Creek State Park

Gifford Pinchot National Forest

Lang State Park

150 mi.

Herman Creek

Mt Hood National Forest

Carson

Wind River

14

Cascade Locks

Bridge of the Gods
146 mi.

GPS

Eagle Creek

Stabler

Stevenson

30

84

Rock Creek

Bonneville
Dam / Fishway
145 mi.

Bonneville

Tanner Creek

Moffet Creek

North Bonneville

Fort Rains

Warrendale

McLoughlin State Park

John B Yeon State Park

Hamilton Creek

Beacon Rock State Park

140.7 mi.

Dodson

Woodward Creek

Skamania

Ainsworth State Park

N E S W

5 MILES

0

© 2007 Wilderness Adventures Press, Inc.

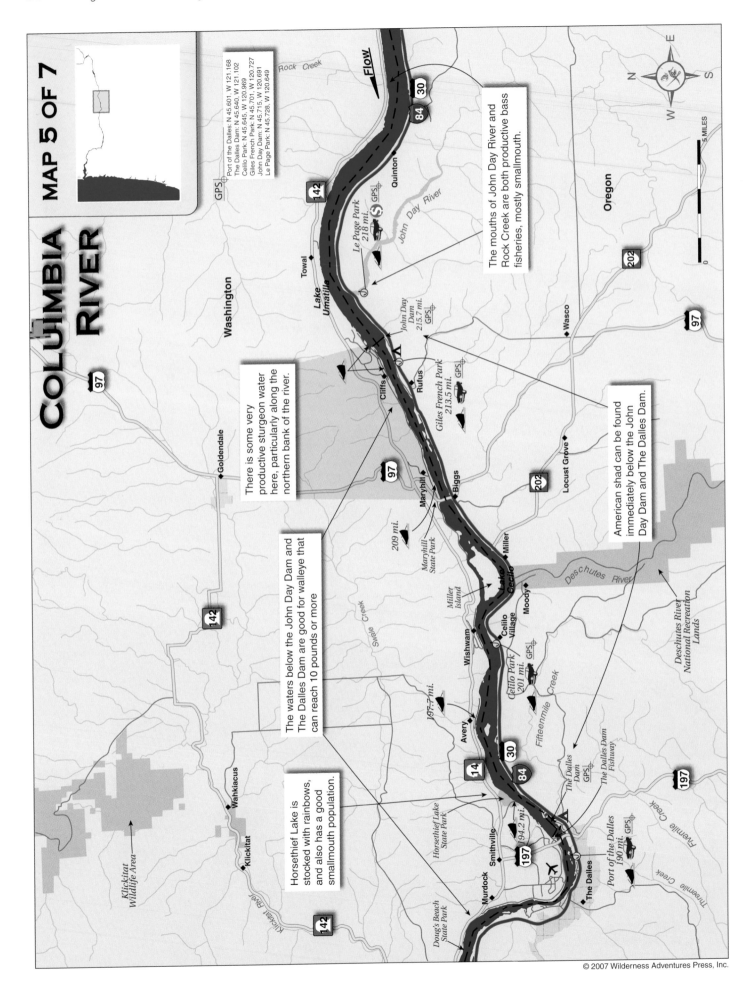

MAP 5 OF 7

COLUMBIA RIVER

GPS
Port of the Dalles: N 45.601, W 121.168
The Dalles Dam: N 45.640, W 121.102
Celilo Park: N 45.645, W 120.969
Giles French Park: N 45.701, W 120.727
John Day Dam: N 45.715, W 120.691
Le Page Park: N 45.728, W 120.649

FLOW

Rock Creek

Quinton

John Day River

Le Page Park
218 mi.

Towal

Lake
Umatilla

The mouths of John Day River and
Rock Creek are both productive bass
fisheries, mostly smallmouth.

Oregon

Washington

Goldendale

John Day
Dam
215.7 mi.

Cliffs

Rufus

Giles French Park
213.5 mi.

Wasco

There is some very
productive sturgeon water
here, particularly along the
northern bank of the river.

Maryhill

Biggs

209 mi.

Maryhill
State Park

Locust Grove

American shad can be found
immediately below the John
Day Dam and The Dalles Dam.

The waters below the John Day Dam and
The Dalles Dam are good for walleye that
can reach 10 pounds or more

Miller Island

Lake
Celilo

Miller

Moody

Deschutes River

Swale Creek

197.7 mi.

Avery

Wishram

Celilo
Village

Celilo Park
201 mi.

Fifteenmile Creek

Deschutes River
National Recreation
Lands

Klickitat
Wildlife Area

Wahkiacus

Horsethief Lake is
stocked with rainbows,
and also has a good
smallmouth population.

Horsethief Lake
State Park

Smithville

Murdock

194.2 mi.

The Dalles Dam

The Dalles Dam
Fishway

The Dalles

Port of the Dalles
190 mi.

Fivemile Creek

Threemile Creek

Doug's Beach
State Park

Klickitat

Klickitat River

5 MILES

0

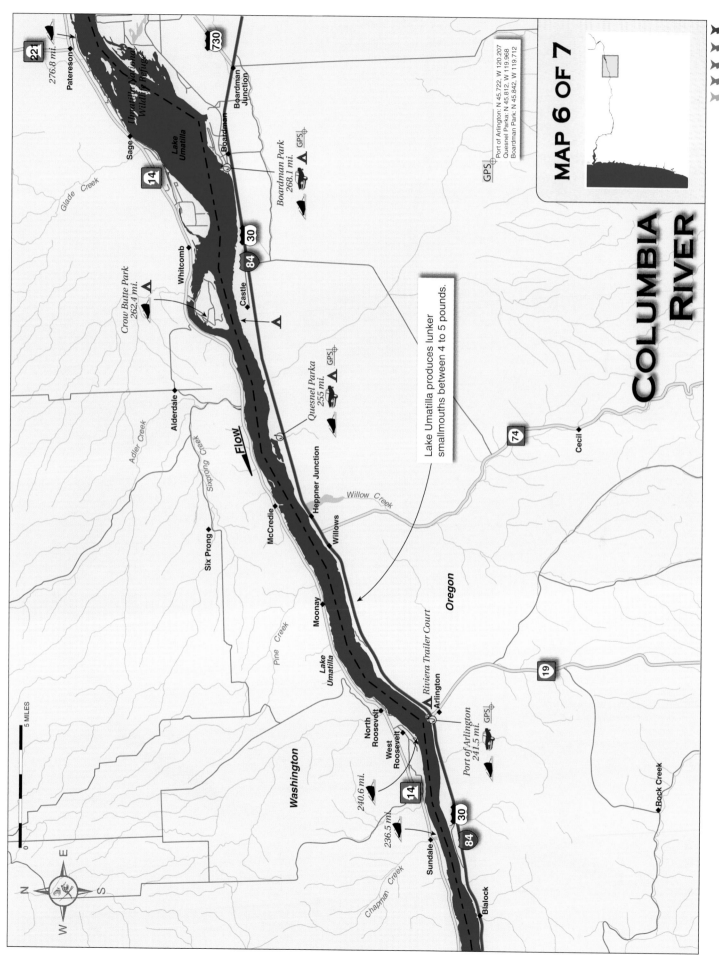

Lake Umatilla produces lunker smallmouths between 4 to 5 pounds.

Port of Arlington: N 45.722, W 120.207
Quesnel Parka: N 45.812, W 119.968
Boardman Park: N 45.842, W 119.712

MAP 6 OF 7

COLUMBIA RIVER

© 2007 Wilderness Adventures Press, Inc.

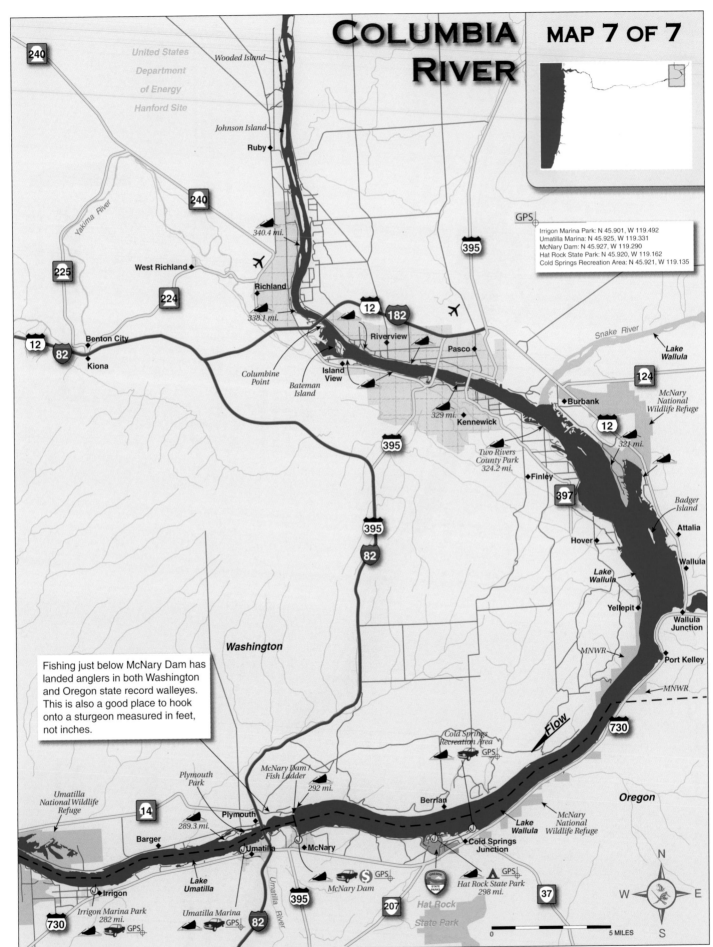

COLUMBIA RIVER

MAP 7 OF 7

240

United States
Department
of Energy
Hanford Site

Wooded Island

Johnson Island

Ruby

240

Yakima River

340.4 mi.

225

West Richland

224

Richland

338.1 mi.

12

12   182

Benton City

82

Kiona

Columbine
Point

Bateman
Island

Island
View

Riverview

Pasco

329 mi.

Kennewick

395

395

82

Washington

Fishing just below McNary Dam has
landed anglers in both Washington
and Oregon state record walleyes.
This is also a good place to hook
onto a sturgeon measured in feet,
not inches.

GPS

Irrigon Marina Park: N 45.901, W 119.492
Umatilla Marina: N 45.925, W 119.331
McNary Dam: N 45.927, W 119.290
Hat Rock State Park: N 45.920, W 119.162
Cold Springs Recreation Area: N 45.921, W 119.135

395

Snake River

Lake
Wallula

124

Burbank

12

321 mi.

McNary
National
Wildlife Refuge

Two Rivers
County Park
324.2 mi.

Finley

397

Badger
Island

Attalia

Hover

Wallula

Lake
Wallula

Yellepit

Wallula
Junction

MNWR

Port Kelley

MNWR

Flow

730

Plymouth
Park

McNary Dam /
Fish Ladder
292 mi.

Cold Springs
Recreation Area

GPS

Berrian

Oregon

McNary
National
Wildlife Refuge

Umatilla
National Wildlife
Refuge

14

289.3 mi.

Plymouth

Barger

Umatilla

McNary

Lake
Umatilla

Umatilla River

395

McNary Dam

S   GPS

207

Cold Springs
Junction

Lake
Wallula

OREGON
STATE
PARKS

Hat Rock State Park
298 mi.

GPS

37

Hat Rock
State Park

Irrigon

730

Irrigon Marina Park
282 mi.

GPS

Umatilla Marina

GPS

82

N

W   E

S

0   5 MILES

© 2007 Wilderness Adventures Press, Inc.

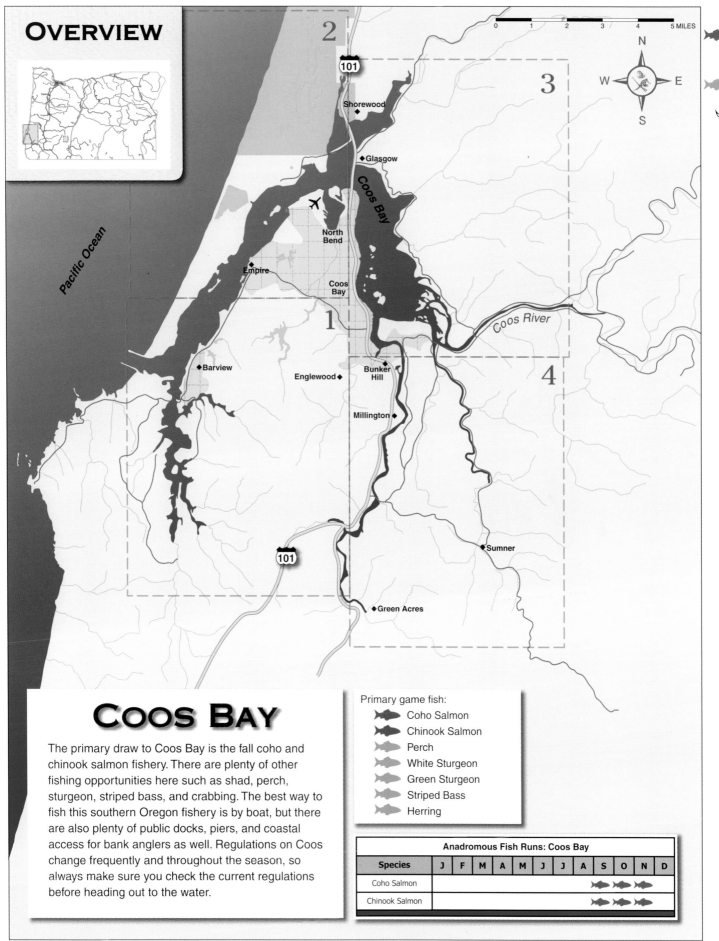

OVERVIEW

COOS BAY

The primary draw to Coos Bay is the fall coho and chinook salmon fishery. There are plenty of other fishing opportunities here such as shad, perch, sturgeon, striped bass, and crabbing. The best way to fish this southern Oregon fishery is by boat, but there are also plenty of public docks, piers, and coastal access for bank anglers as well. Regulations on Coos change frequently and throughout the season, so always make sure you check the current regulations before heading out to the water.

Primary game fish:
- Coho Salmon
- Chinook Salmon
- Perch
- White Sturgeon
- Green Sturgeon
- Striped Bass
- Herring

Anadromous Fish Runs: Coos Bay												
Species	J	F	M	A	M	J	J	A	S	O	N	D
Coho Salmon									✦	✦	✦	
Chinook Salmon									✦	✦	✦	

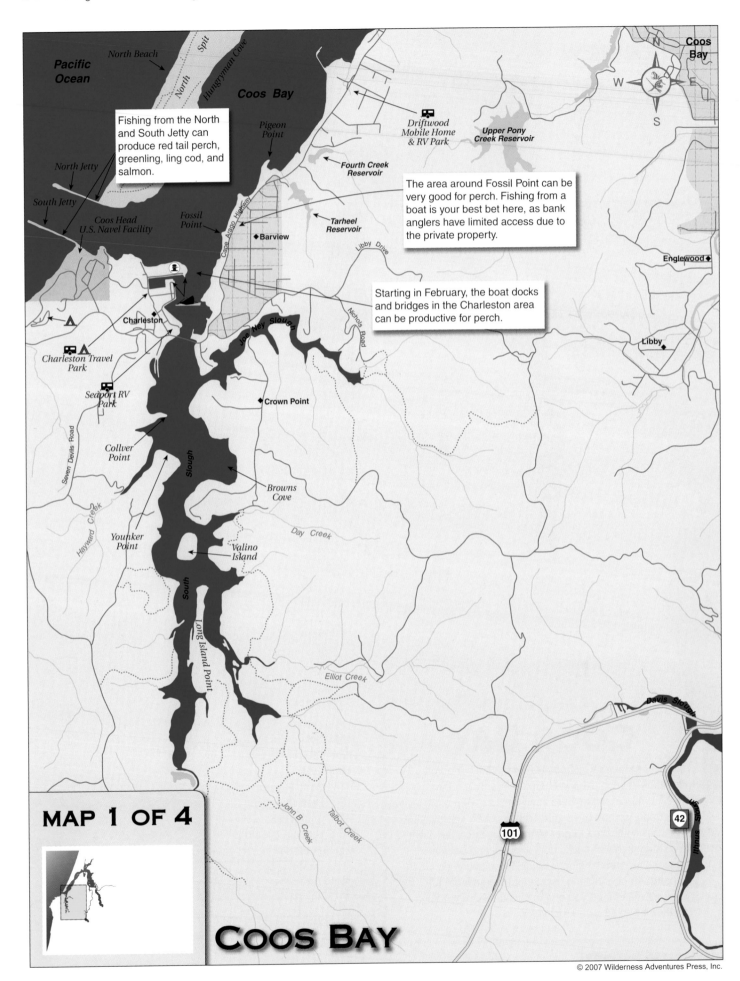

Fishing from the North and South Jetty can produce red tail perch, greenling, ling cod, and salmon.

The area around Fossil Point can be very good for perch. Fishing from a boat is your best bet here, as bank anglers have limited access due to the private property.

Starting in February, the boat docks and bridges in the Charleston area can be productive for perch.

Pacific Ocean

North Beach

Coos Bay

Hungryman Cove

North Spit

Pigeon Point

Driftwood Mobile Home & RV Park

Upper Pony Creek Reservoir

Coos Bay

North Jetty

South Jetty

Coos Head U.S. Navel Facility

Fossil Point

Fourth Creek Reservoir

Tarheel Reservoir

Barview

Cape Arago Highway

Libby Drive

Englewood

Charleston

Nichols Road

Libby

Charleston Travel Park

Seaport RV Park

Joe Ney Slough

Seven Devils Road

Collver Point

Crown Point

Slough

Browns Cove

Day Creek

Hayward Creek

Younker Point

Valino Island

South Slough

Elliot Creek

Davis Slough

Long Island Point

John B Creek

Talbot Creek

101

42

Ithnus Slough

MAP 1 OF 4

COOS BAY

MAP 2 OF 4   COOS BAY

Snag Lake

Teal Lake

Sandpoint Lake

Oregon Dunes
National Recreation Area

Spirit Lake

Pacific Ocean

Siuslaw

National

Forest

101

Fishing the surf off of Horsefall Beach
can be good for perch or striped bass.

Horsefall Lake

Rogers

Horsefall Beach Road

From Pony Point down to Fossil Point
(Map 1) rock formations make
excellent perch habitat and can be
explored by boat or on the bank.

Bluebill Lake

Cordes

Jordan Lake

Jordan
Cove

Jordan
Point

Pony Point

Municipal
Airport

Pony Slough

Simpson
Park

Coos Bay

North
Bend

Lakeshore Drive

Empire Lakes

North
Beach

North Spit

Empire

Pony Creek

Coos
Bay

Kelly's RV Park

N
W   E
S

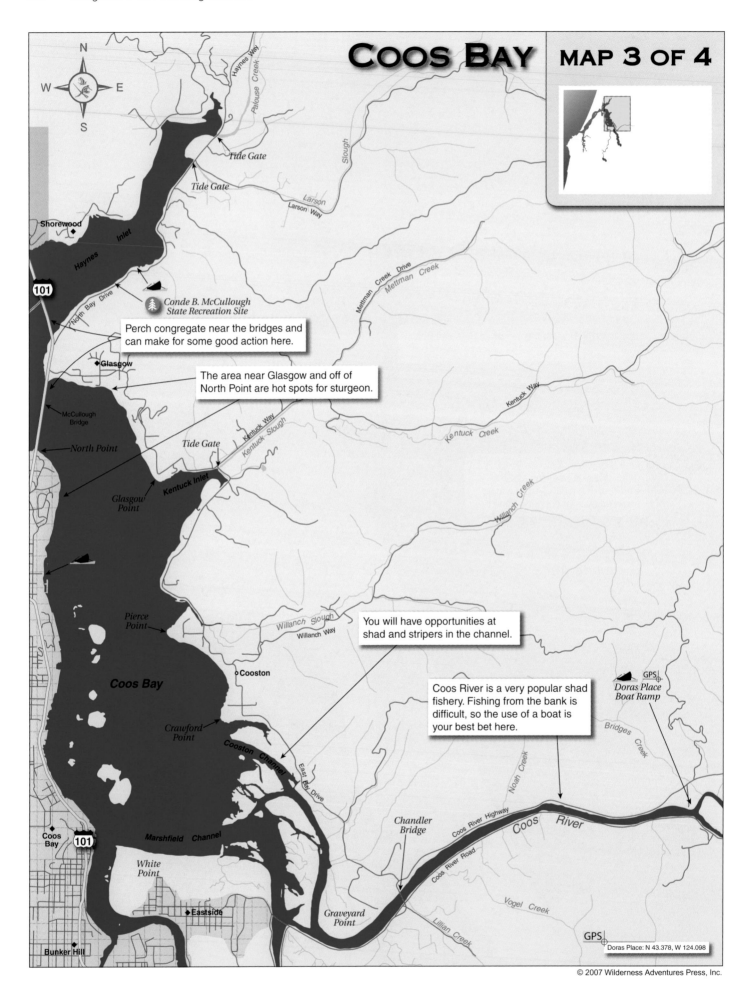

COOS BAY
MAP 3 OF 4

Tide Gate

Tide Gate

Shorewood

Conde B. McCullough State Recreation Site

Perch congregate near the bridges and can make for some good action here.

Glasgow

The area near Glasgow and off of North Point are hot spots for sturgeon.

McCullough Bridge

North Point

Tide Gate

Glasgow Point

Kentuck Inlet

Pierce Point

Coos Bay

Cooston

You will have opportunities at shad and stripers in the channel.

GPS
Doras Place Boat Ramp

Coos River is a very popular shad fishery. Fishing from the bank is difficult, so the use of a boat is your best bet here.

Crawford Point

Cooston Channel

Chandler Bridge

Coos River Highway

Coos River

Coos Bay

Marshfield Channel

White Point

Coos River Road

Eastside

Graveyard Point

Vogel Creek

Lillian Creek

Bunker Hill

GPS

Doras Place: N 43.378, W 124.098

© 2007 Wilderness Adventures Press, Inc.

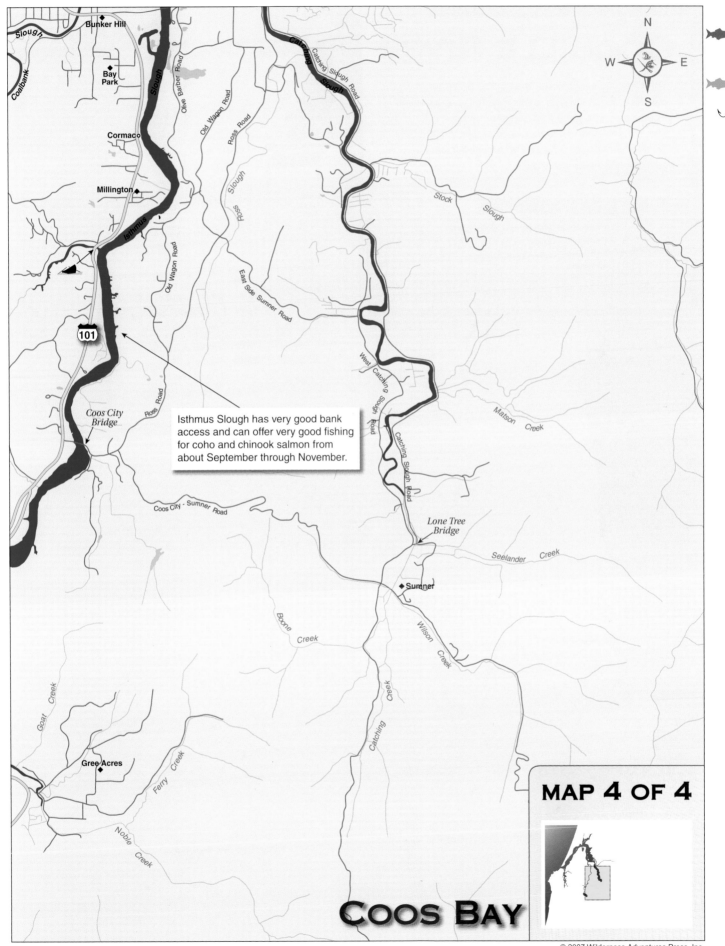

Isthmus Slough has very good bank access and can offer very good fishing for coho and chinook salmon from about September through November.

MAP 4 OF 4

COOS BAY

COQUILLE RIVER

The Coquille is located on the southern Oregon coastline. It has very good steelheading opportunities, as well as some good wild and sea-run trout action. The river is best fished by boat, but does have limited bank access. There is also a small warmwater fishery available for a change of pace.

OVERVIEW

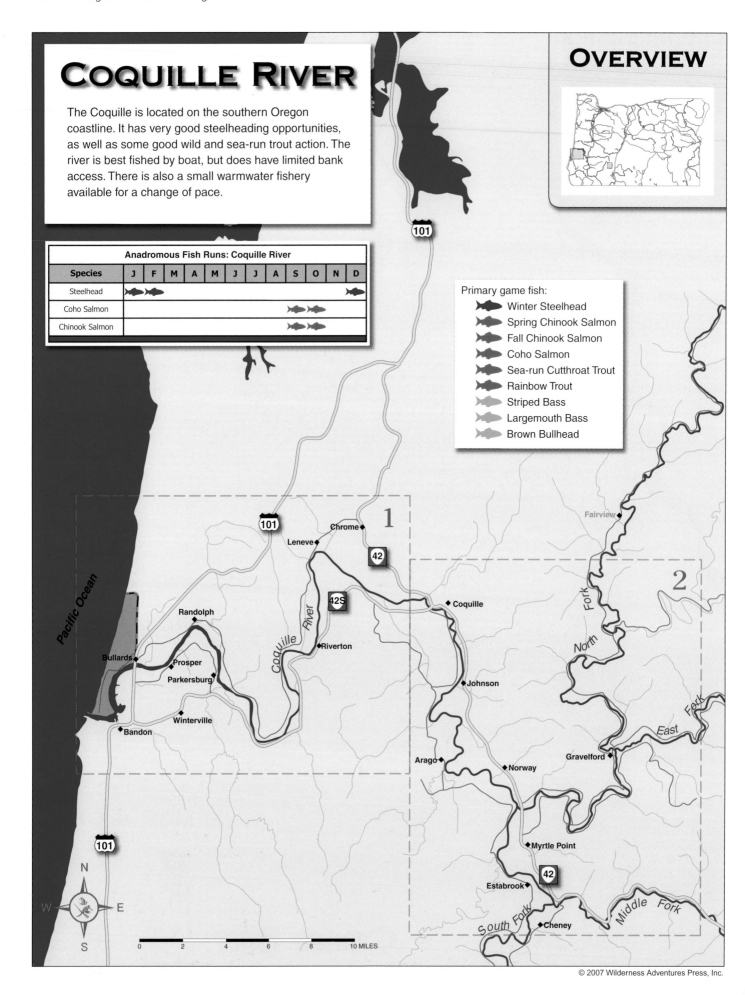

Anadromous Fish Runs: Coquille River												
Species	J	F	M	A	M	J	J	A	S	O	N	D
Steelhead	🐟🐟											🐟
Coho Salmon									🐟🐟			
Chinook Salmon									🐟🐟			

Primary game fish:
- Winter Steelhead
- Spring Chinook Salmon
- Fall Chinook Salmon
- Coho Salmon
- Sea-run Cutthroat Trout
- Rainbow Trout
- Striped Bass
- Largemouth Bass
- Brown Bullhead

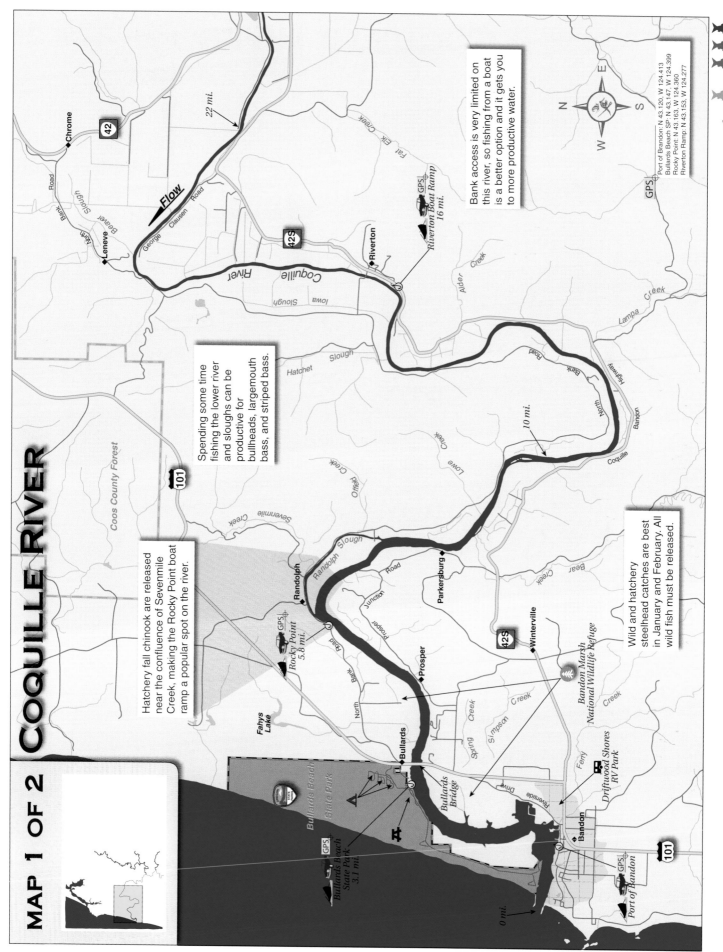

MAP 1 OF 2 COQUILLE RIVER

Flow

22 mi.

Chrome

42

North Bank Road

Beaver Slough

George Clausen Road

Leneve

Coquille River

Iowa Slough

42S

Riverton

Fat Elk Creek

GPS

Riverton Boat Ramp
16 mi.

Bank access is very limited on this river, so fishing from a boat is a better option and it gets you to more productive water.

Alder Creek

Lampa Creek

GPS
Port of Brandon: N 43.120, W 124.413
Bullards Beach SP: N 43.147, W 124.399
Rocky Point: N 43.163, W 124.360
Riverton Ramp: N 43.153, W 124.277

Spending some time fishing the lower river and sloughs can be productive for bullheads, largemouth bass, and striped bass.

Hatchet Slough

101

Coos County Forest

Sevenmile Creek

Orfield Creek

Lowe Creek

Bandon Highway

North Bank Road

Coquille

10 mi.

Hatchery fall chinook are released near the confluence of Sevenmile Creek, making the Rocky Point boat ramp a popular spot on the river.

Randolph

Randolph Slough

Prosper Junction Road

Parkersburg

Bear Creek

GPS
Rocky Point
5.8 mi.

Fahys Lake

North Bank Road

Prosper

42S

Winterville

Bandon Marsh National Wildlife Refuge

Spring Creek

Simpson Creek

Creek

Wild and hatchery steelhead catches are best in January and February. All wild fish must be released.

Bullards

Bullards Beach State Park

Ferry

Driftwood Shores RV Park

Riverside Drive

Bullards Bridge

Bandon

101

GPS
Bullards Beach State Park
3.1 mi.

GPS
Port of Bandon

0 mi.

© 2007 Wilderness Adventures Press, Inc.

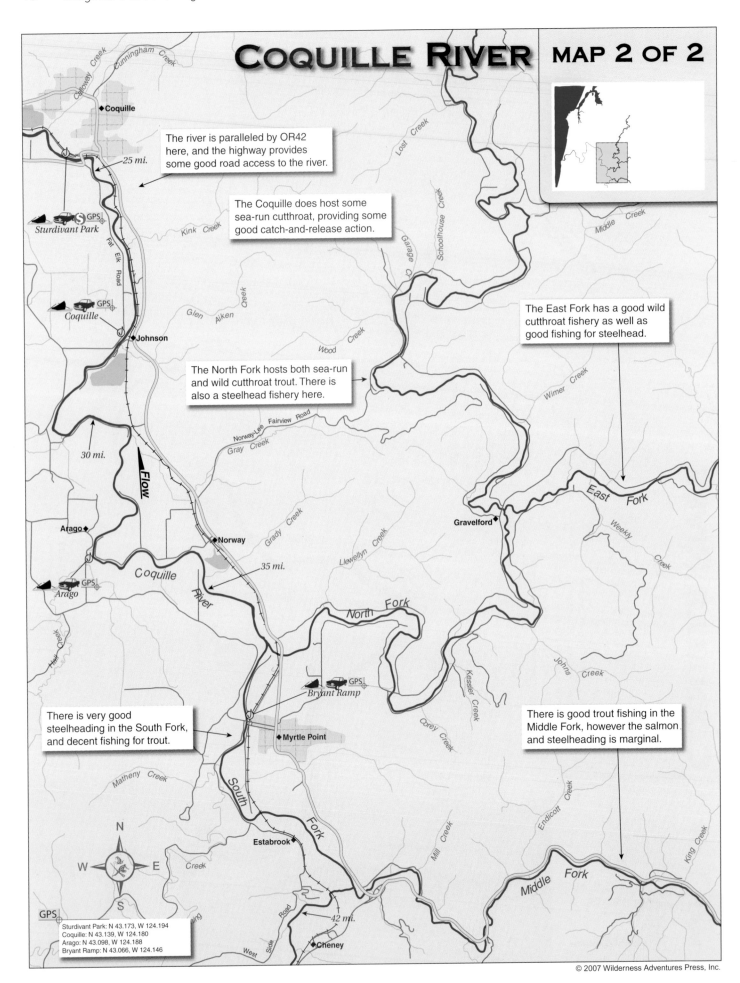

COQUILLE RIVER

MAP 2 OF 2

The river is paralleled by OR42 here, and the highway provides some good road access to the river.

The Coquille does host some sea-run cutthroat, providing some good catch-and-release action.

The North Fork hosts both sea-run and wild cutthroat trout. There is also a steelhead fishery here.

The East Fork has a good wild cutthroat fishery as well as good fishing for steelhead.

There is very good steelheading in the South Fork, and decent fishing for trout.

There is good trout fishing in the Middle Fork, however the salmon and steelheading is marginal.

Sturdivant Park: N 43.173, W 124.194
Coquille: N 43.139, W 124.180
Arago: N 43.098, W 124.188
Bryant Ramp: N 43.066, W 124.146

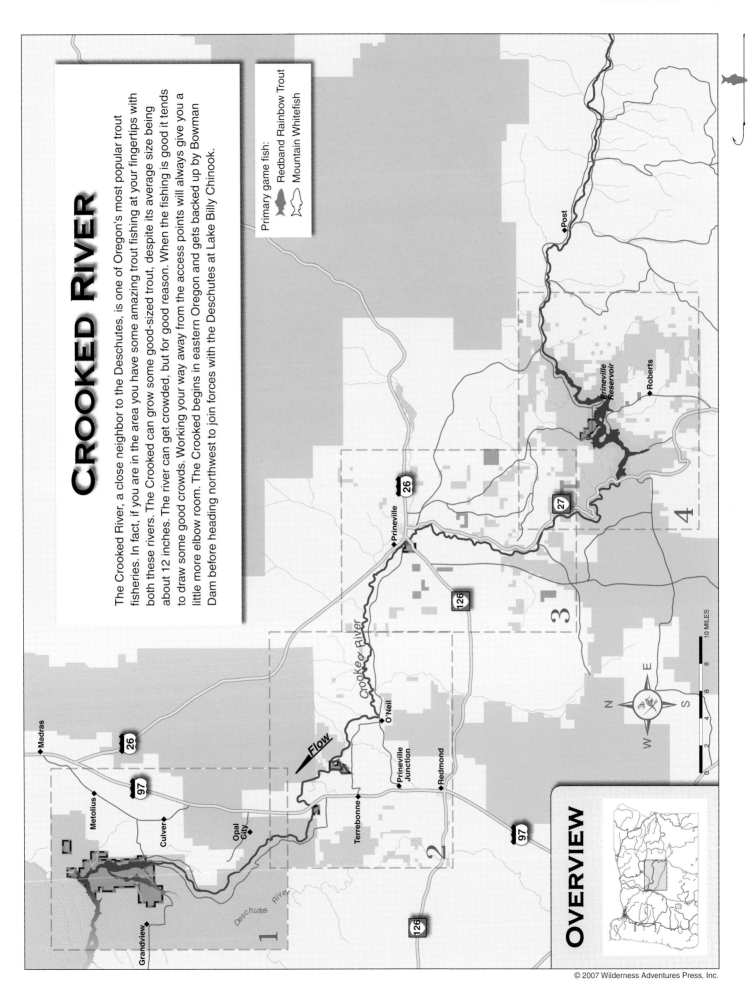

CROOKED RIVER

The Crooked River, a close neighbor to the Deschutes, is one of Oregon's most popular trout fisheries. In fact, if you are in the area you have some amazing trout fishing at your fingertips with both these rivers. The Crooked can grow some good-sized trout, despite its average size being about 12 inches. The river can get crowded, but for good reason. When the fishing is good it tends to draw some good crowds. Working your way away from the access points will always give you a little more elbow room. The Crooked begins in eastern Oregon and gets backed up by Bowman Dam before heading northwest to join forces with the Deschutes at Lake Billy Chinook.

Primary game fish:
Redband Rainbow Trout
Mountain Whitefish

OVERVIEW

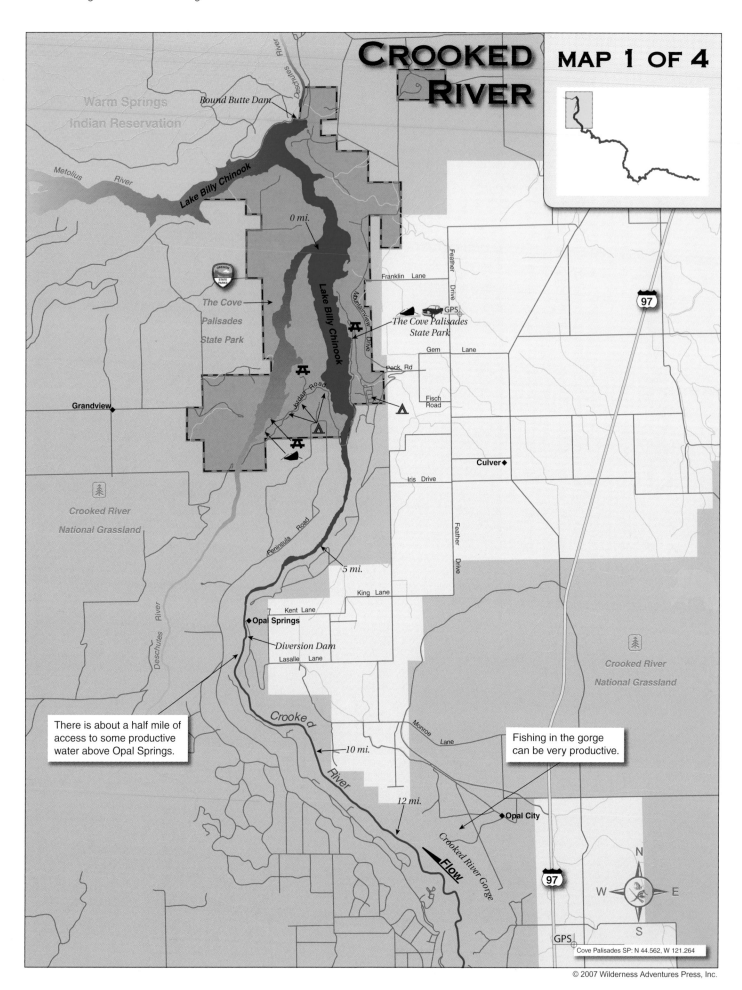

CROOKED RIVER

MAP 1 OF 4

Warm Springs
Indian Reservation

Round Butte Dam

Metolius   River

Deschutes   River

Lake Billy Chinook

0 mi.

OREGON
STATE
PARKS

The Cove
Palisades
State Park

Lake Billy Chinook

Franklin   Lane

Feather   Drive

GPS

The Cove Palisades
State Park

Mountainview   Drive

Gem   Lane

Peck   Rd

Fisch
Road

Grandview◆

Jordan   Road

Culver◆

Iris   Drive

Crooked River
National Grassland

Peninsula   Road

5 mi.

King   Lane

Kent   Lane

Opal Springs◆

Diversion Dam

Lasalle   Lane

Feather   Drive

Deschutes   River

There is about a half mile of
access to some productive
water above Opal Springs.

Crooked   River

Monroe   Lane

Fishing in the gorge
can be very productive.

10 mi.

12 mi.

Opal City◆

FLOW

Crooked River Gorge

Crooked River
National Grassland

97

97

N

W   E

S

GPS

Cove Palisades SP: N 44.562, W 121.264

© 2007 Wilderness Adventures Press, Inc.

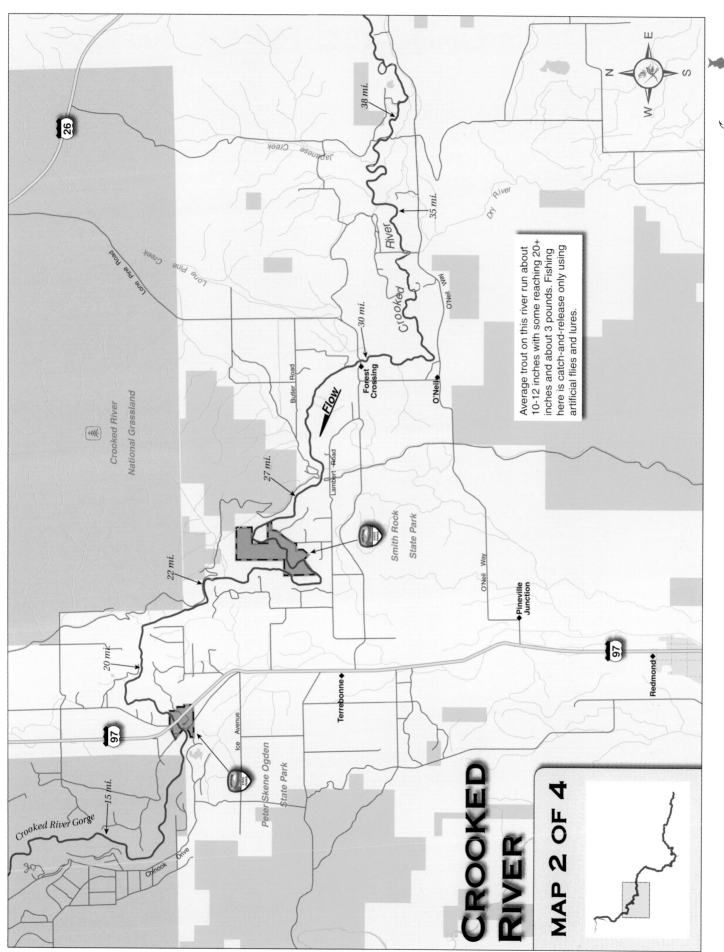

Average trout on this river run about 10-12 inches with some reaching 20+ inches and about 3 pounds. Fishing here is catch-and-release only using artificial flies and lures.

CROOKED RIVER

MAP 2 OF 4

© 2007 Wilderness Adventures Press, Inc.

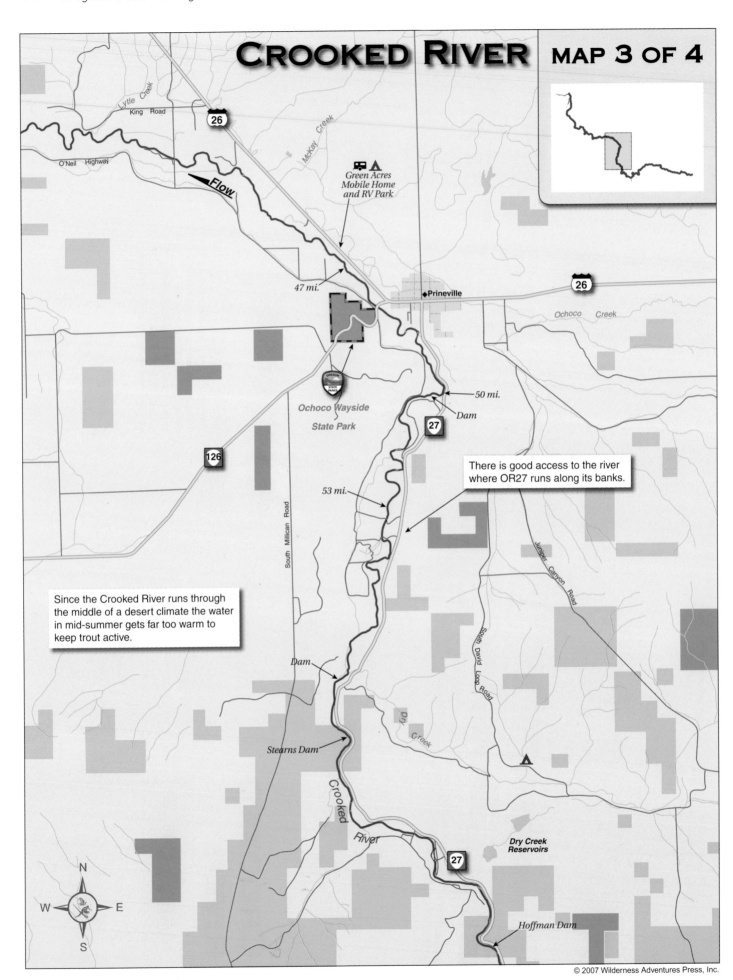

CROOKED RIVER   MAP 3 OF 4

Lytle Creek

King Road

26

O'Neil Highway

McKay Creek

Flow

Green Acres Mobile Home and RV Park

47 mi.

Prineville

26

Ochoco Creek

50 mi.

Dam

27

There is good access to the river where OR27 runs along its banks.

OREGON STATE PARKS

Ochoco Wayside State Park

126

53 mi.

Juniper Canyon Road

South Millican Road

Since the Crooked River runs through the middle of a desert climate the water in mid-summer gets far too warm to keep trout active.

Dam

South David Loop Road

Dry Creek

Stearns Dam

Crooked River

Dry Creek Reservoirs

27

N

W   E

S

Hoffman Dam

© 2007 Wilderness Adventures Press, Inc.

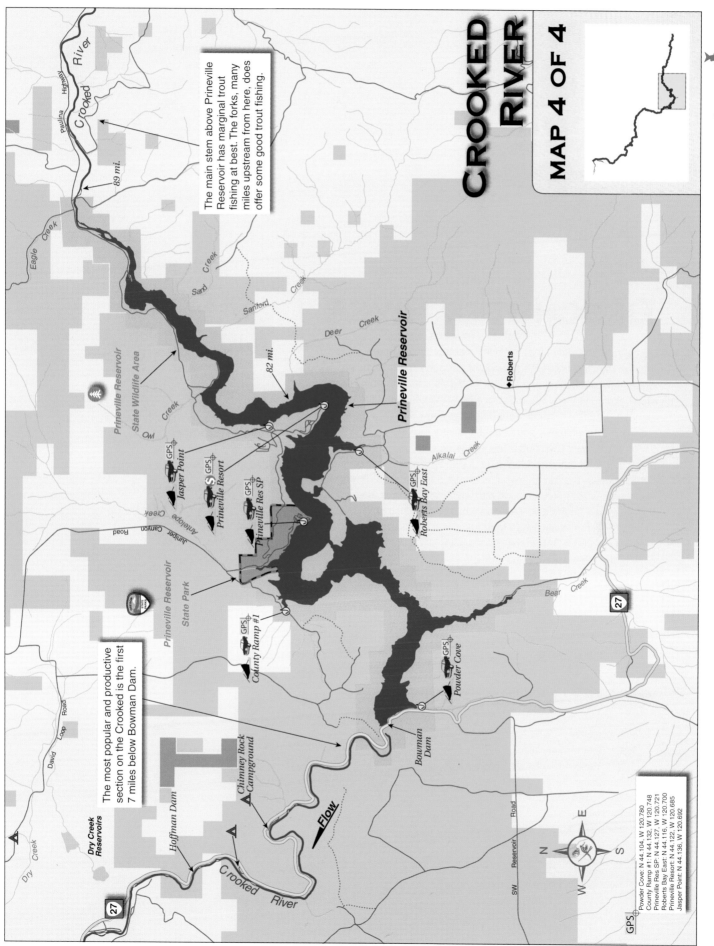

CROOKED RIVER

MAP 4 OF 4

The main stem above Prineville Reservoir has marginal trout fishing at best. The forks, many miles upstream from here, does offer some good trout fishing.

89 mi.

Crooked River

Paulina Highway

Eagle Creek

Sand Creek

Sanford Creek

Deer Creek

82 mi.

Prineville Reservoir

Prineville Reservoir State Wildlife Area

Owl Creek

Antelope Creek

GPS
Jasper Point

GPS
$ Prineville Resort

GPS
Prineville Res SP

Roberts

Alkalai Creek

GPS
Roberts Bay East

Juniper Canyon Road

Prineville Reservoir State Park

OFFICIAL STATE PARK

GPS
County Ramp #1

Bear Creek

27

GPS
Powder Cove

The most popular and productive section on the Crooked is the first 7 miles below Bowman Dam.

Bowman Dam

David Loop Road

Dry Creek Reservoirs

Dry Creek

Hoffman Dam

Chimney Rock Campground

Flow

Crooked River

27

SW Reservoir Road

N
E
W
S

© 2007 Wilderness Adventures Press, Inc.

GPS
Powder Cove: N 44.104, W 120.780
County Ramp #1: N 44.132, W 120.748
Prineville Res SP: N 44.127, W 120.721
Roberts Bay East: N 44.116, W 120.700
Prineville Resort: N 44.122, W 120.685
Jasper Point: N 44.136, W 120.692

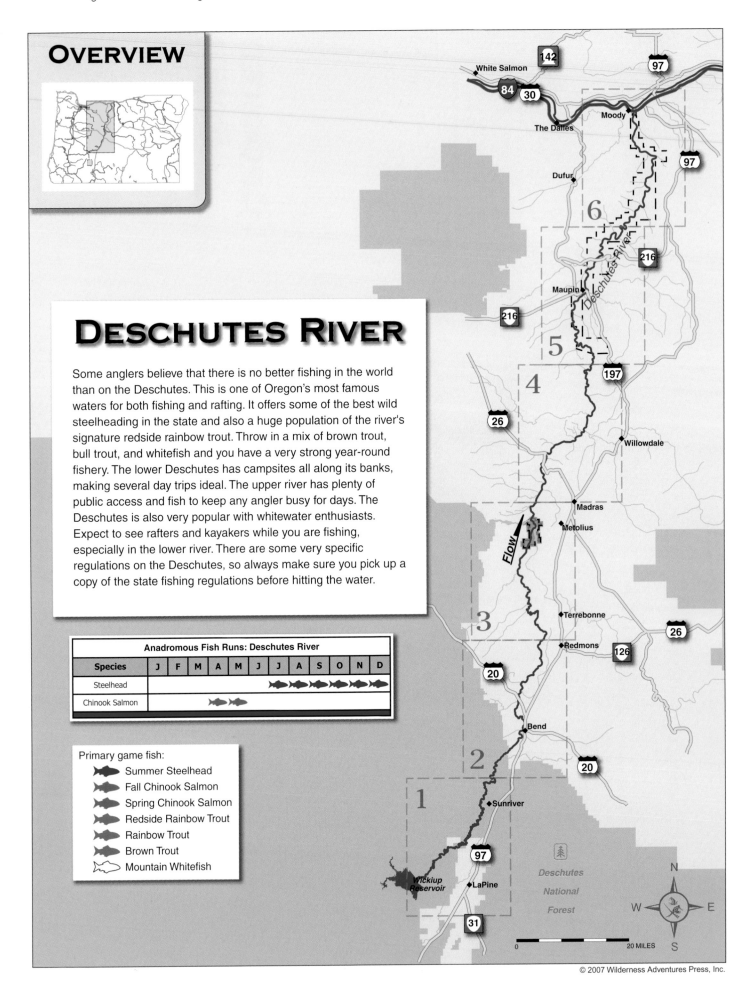

OVERVIEW

DESCHUTES RIVER

Some anglers believe that there is no better fishing in the world than on the Deschutes. This is one of Oregon's most famous waters for both fishing and rafting. It offers some of the best wild steelheading in the state and also a huge population of the river's signature redside rainbow trout. Throw in a mix of brown trout, bull trout, and whitefish and you have a very strong year-round fishery. The lower Deschutes has campsites all along its banks, making several day trips ideal. The upper river has plenty of public access and fish to keep any angler busy for days. The Deschutes is also very popular with whitewater enthusiasts. Expect to see rafters and kayakers while you are fishing, especially in the lower river. There are some very specific regulations on the Deschutes, so always make sure you pick up a copy of the state fishing regulations before hitting the water.

Anadromous Fish Runs: Deschutes River												
Species	J	F	M	A	M	J	J	A	S	O	N	D
Steelhead												
Chinook Salmon												

Primary game fish:
- Summer Steelhead
- Fall Chinook Salmon
- Spring Chinook Salmon
- Redside Rainbow Trout
- Rainbow Trout
- Brown Trout
- Mountain Whitefish

MAP 1 OF 6

DESCHUTES RIVER

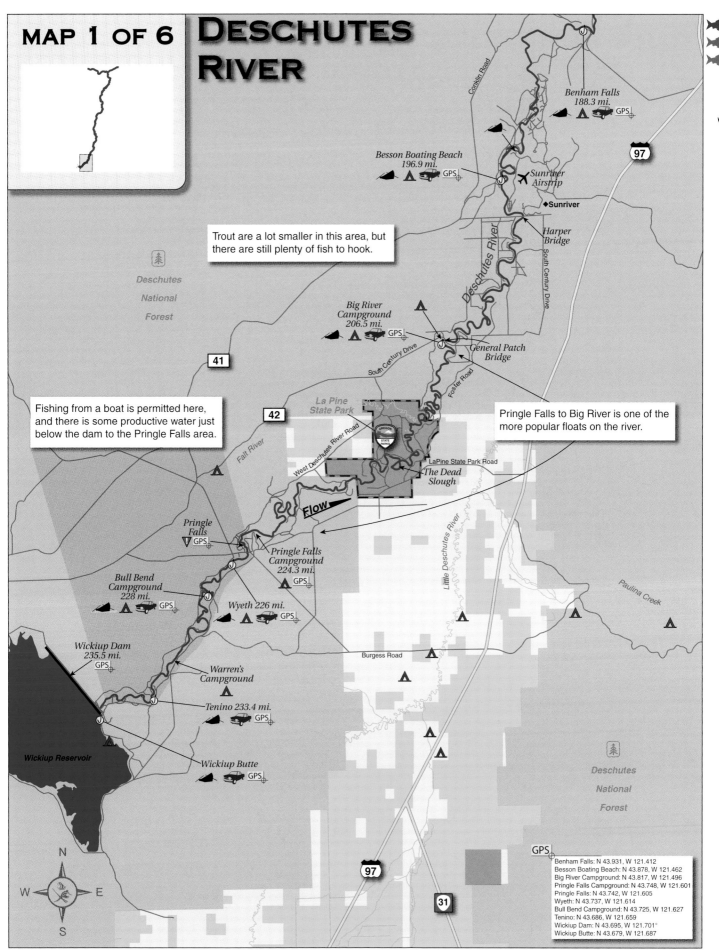

Trout are a lot smaller in this area, but there are still plenty of fish to hook.

Benham Falls
188.3 mi. GPS

Besson Boating Beach
196.9 mi. GPS

Sunriver Airstrip

◆Sunriver

Deschutes River

Harper Bridge

South Century Drive

Conklin Road

Deschutes National Forest

41

Big River Campground
206.5 mi. GPS

South Century Drive

General Patch Bridge

Foster Road

Fishing from a boat is permitted here, and there is some productive water just below the dam to the Pringle Falls area.

42

La Pine State Park

West Deschutes River Road

Falt River

OREGON STATE PARKS

LaPine State Park Road

The Dead Slough

Pringle Falls to Big River is one of the more popular floats on the river.

Flow

Little Deschutes River

Paulina Creek

Pringle Falls GPS

Pringle Falls Campground
224.3 mi. GPS

Bull Bend Campground
228 mi. GPS

Wyeth 226 mi. GPS

Burgess Road

Wickiup Dam
235.5 mi. GPS

Warren's Campground

Tenino 233.4 mi. GPS

Wickiup Reservoir

Wickiup Butte GPS

Deschutes National Forest

97

31

N
W   E
S

GPS
Benham Falls: N 43.931, W 121.412
Besson Boating Beach: N 43.878, W 121.462
Big River Campground: N 43.817, W 121.496
Pringle Falls Campground: N 43.748, W 121.601
Pringle Falls: N 43.742, W 121.605
Wyeth: N 43.737, W 121.614
Bull Bend Campground: N 43.725, W 121.627
Tenino: N 43.686, W 121.659
Wickiup Dam: N 43.695, W 121.701°
Wickiup Butte: N 43.679, W 121.687

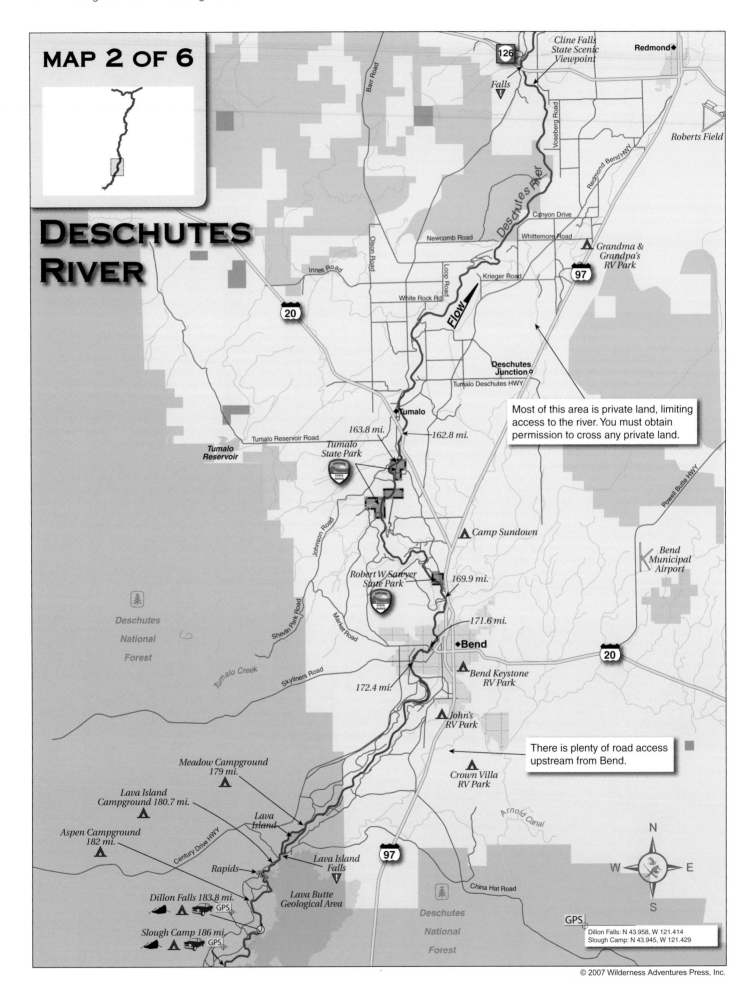

MAP 2 OF 6

DESCHUTES RIVER

Most of this area is private land, limiting access to the river. You must obtain permission to cross any private land.

There is plenty of road access upstream from Bend.

Cline Falls State Scenic Viewpoint

Redmond

Falls

Roberts Field

Barr Road

Voseberg Road

Redmond Bend HWY

Deschutes River

Canyon Drive

Newcomb Road

Whittemore Road

Olson Road

Innes Road

Loop Road

Krieger Road

White Rock Rd

Flow

Grandma & Grandpa's RV Park

97

20

Deschutes Junction

Tumalo Deschutes HWY

Tumalo

163.8 mi.

162.8 mi.

Tumalo Reservoir Road

Tumalo Reservoir

Tumalo State Park

Powell Butte HWY

Camp Sundown

Bend Municipal Airport

Deschutes National Forest

Robert W Sawyer State Park

169.9 mi.

171.6 mi.

Johnson Road

Shevlin Park Road

Market Road

Bend

20

Tumalo Creek

Skyliners Road

172.4 mi.

Bend Keystone RV Park

John's RV Park

Meadow Campground 179 mi.

Crown Villa RV Park

Lava Island Campground 180.7 mi.

Lava Island

Arnold Canal

Aspen Campground 182 mi.

Century Drive HWY

Rapids

Lava Island Falls

97

Dillon Falls 183.8 mi.

GPS

Lava Butte Geological Area

China Hat Road

Slough Camp 186 mi.

GPS

Deschutes National Forest

N W E S

GPS

Dillon Falls: N 43.958, W 121.414
Slough Camp: N 43.945, W 121.429

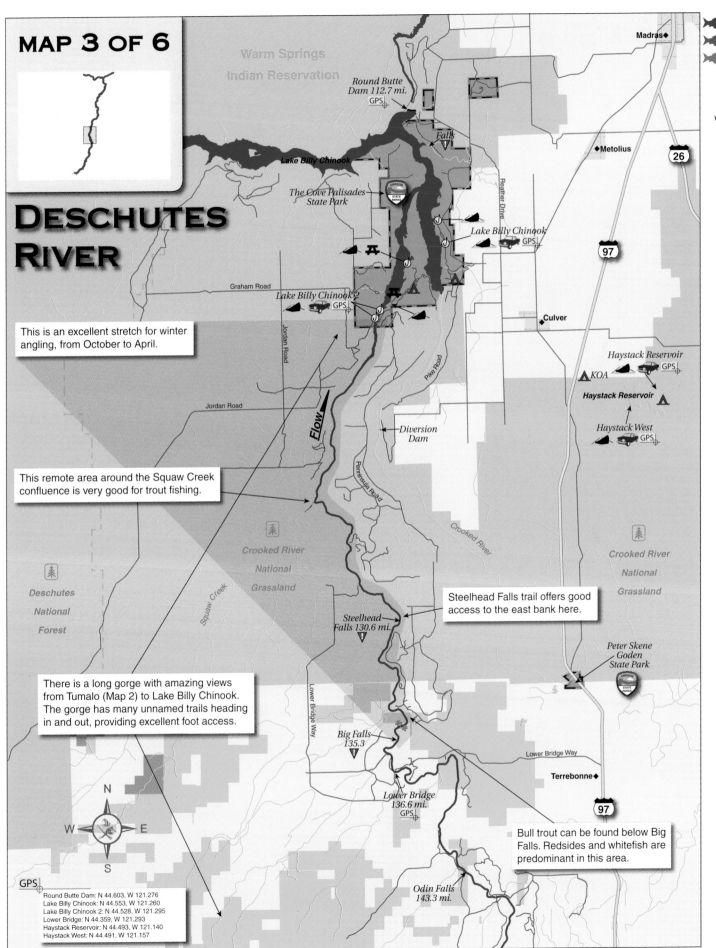

MAP 3 OF 6

DESCHUTES RIVER

Warm Springs
Indian Reservation

Round Butte
Dam 112.7 mi.
GPS

Falls

Lake Billy Chinook

The Cove Palisades
State Park

OREGON STATE PARKS

Lake Billy Chinook
GPS

Reather Drive

Metolius

26

97

Graham Road

Lake Billy Chinook 2
GPS

Culver

This is an excellent stretch for winter angling, from October to April.

Jordan Road

Haystack Reservoir
GPS

KOA

Haystack Reservoir

Jordan Road

Flow

Diversion
Dam

Haystack West
GPS

This remote area around the Squaw Creek confluence is very good for trout fishing.

Peninsula Road

Crooked River

Crooked River

National

Grassland

Crooked River

National

Grassland

Deschutes

National

Forest

Squaw Creek

Crooked River

National

Grassland

Steelhead Falls trail offers good access to the east bank here.

Steelhead
Falls 130.6 mi.

Peter Skene
Goden
State Park

OREGON STATE PARKS

There is a long gorge with amazing views from Tumalo (Map 2) to Lake Billy Chinook. The gorge has many unnamed trails heading in and out, providing excellent foot access.

Lower Bridge Way

Big Falls
135.3

Lower Bridge Way

Terrebonne

Lower Bridge
136.6 mi.
GPS

Bull trout can be found below Big Falls. Redsides and whitefish are predominant in this area.

97

N
W   E
S

Odin Falls
143.3 mi.

GPS

Round Butte Dam: N 44.603, W 121.276
Lake Billy Chinook: N 44.553, W 121.260
Lake Billy Chinook 2: N 44.528, W 121.295
Lower Bridge: N 44.359, W 121.293
Haystack Reservoir: N 44.493, W 121.140
Haystack West: N 44.491, W 121.157

© 2007 Wilderness Adventures Press, Inc.

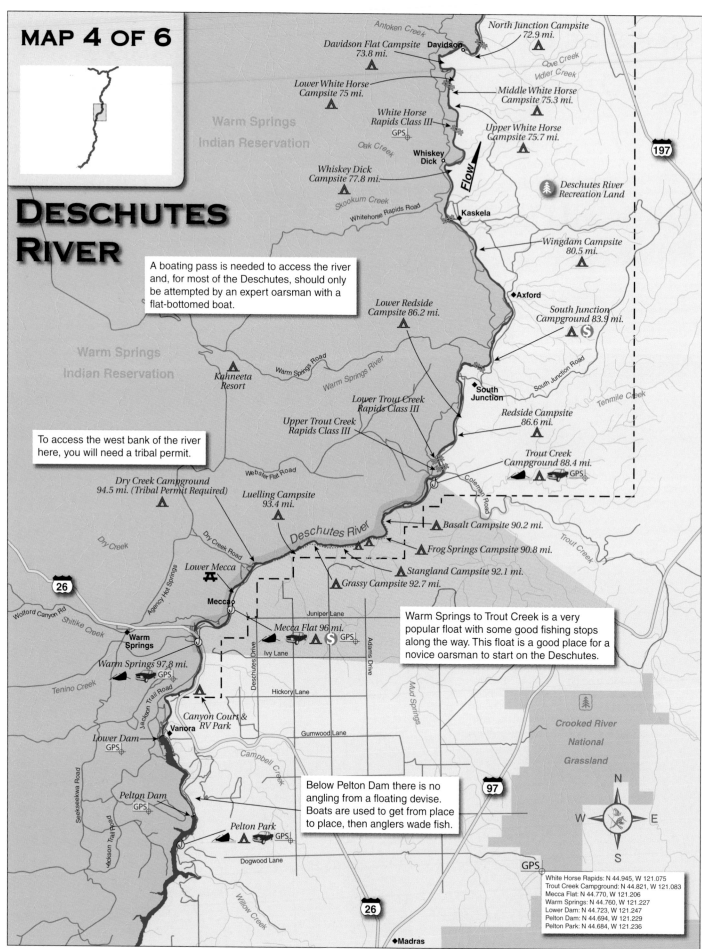

MAP 4 OF 6

DESCHUTES RIVER

Antoken Creek

North Junction Campsite
72.9 mi.

Davidson Flat Campsite
73.8 mi.   Davidson

Cove Creek
Idler Creek

Lower White Horse
Campsite 75 mi.

Middle White Horse
Campsite 75.3 mi.

White Horse
Rapids Class III
GPS

Upper White Horse
Campsite 75.7 mi.

197

Warm Springs
Indian Reservation

Oak Creek

Whiskey
Dick

Flow

Deschutes River
Recreation Land

Whiskey Dick
Campsite 77.8 mi.

Skookum Creek

Whitehorse Rapids Road

Kaskela

Wingdam Campsite
80.5 mi.

A boating pass is needed to access the river
and, for most of the Deschutes, should only
be attempted by an expert oarsman with a
flat-bottomed boat.

Lower Redside
Campsite 86.2 mi.

Axford

South Junction
Campground 83.9 mi.

Warm Springs
Indian Reservation

Kahneeta
Resort

Warm Springs Road

Warm Springs River

South
Junction

South Junction Road

Tenmile Creek

Lower Trout Creek
Rapids Class III

Redside Campsite
86.6 mi.

Upper Trout Creek
Rapids Class III

To access the west bank of the river
here, you will need a tribal permit.

Webster Flat Road

Trout Creek
Campground 88.4 mi.
GPS

Coleman Road

Dry Creek Campground
94.5 mi. (Tribal Permit Required)

Luelling Campsite
93.4 mi.

Deschutes River

Basalt Campsite 90.2 mi.

Frog Springs Campsite 90.8 mi.

Trout Creek

Dry Creek

Dry Creek Road

Stangland Campsite 92.1 mi.

Lower Mecca

Grassy Campsite 92.7 mi.

26

Mecca

Juniper Lane

Warm Springs to Trout Creek is a very
popular float with some good fishing stops
along the way. This float is a good place for a
novice oarsman to start on the Deschutes.

Wolford Canyon Rd

Shitike Creek

Warm
Springs

Agency Hot Springs

Mecca Flat 96 mi.
GPS

Ivy Lane

Adams Drive

Warm Springs 97.8 mi.
GPS

Tenino Creek

Jackson Trail Road

Hickory Lane

Mud Springs

Crooked River

Canyon Court &
RV Park

Vanora

Gumwood Lane

National

Grassland

Lower Dam
GPS

Campbell Creek

97

N

Pelton Dam
GPS

Seekseekwa Road

Below Pelton Dam there is no
angling from a floating devise.
Boats are used to get from place
to place, then anglers wade fish.

W   E

Pelton Park

Jackson Trail Road

Pelton Park
GPS

Dogwood Lane

S

GPS

Willow Creek

26

White Horse Rapids: N 44.945, W 121.075
Trout Creek Campground: N 44.821, W 121.083
Mecca Flat: N 44.770, W 121.206
Warm Springs: N 44.760, W 121.227
Lower Dam: N 44.723, W 121.247
Pelton Dam: N 44.694, W 121.229
Pelton Park: N 44.684, W 121.236

Madras

© 2007 Wilderness Adventures Press, Inc.

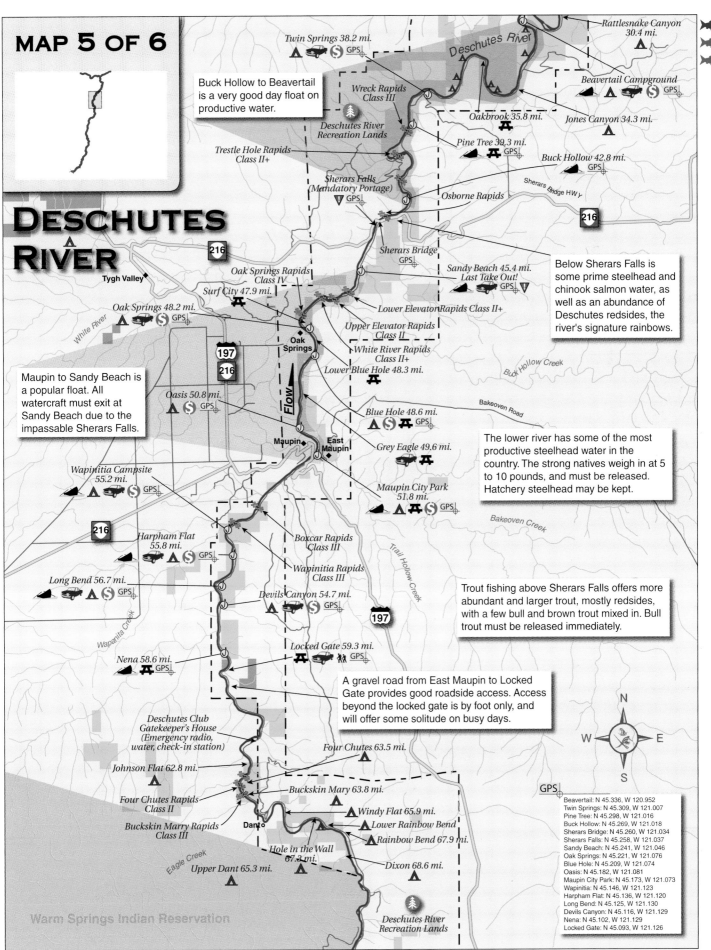

MAP 5 OF 6

DESCHUTES RIVER

Tygh Valley ♦

Twin Springs 38.2 mi.

Buck Hollow to Beavertail is a very good day float on productive water.

Wreck Rapids Class III

Deschutes River Recreation Lands

Trestle Hole Rapids Class II+

Sherars Falls (Mandatory Portage)

Osborne Rapids

Oakbrook 35.8 mi.

Pine Tree 39.3 mi.

Rattlesnake Canyon 30.4 mi.

Beavertail Campground

Jones Canyon 34.3 mi.

Buck Hollow 42.8 mi.

Sherars Bridge HWY

216

Below Sherars Falls is some prime steelhead and chinook salmon water, as well as an abundance of Deschutes redsides, the river's signature rainbows.

Sherars Bridge GPS

Sandy Beach 45.4 mi. Last Take Out!

Oak Springs Rapids Class IV

Surf City 47.9 mi.

Oak Springs 48.2 mi.

White River

197

216

Oak Springs ♦

Maupin to Sandy Beach is a popular float. All watercraft must exit at Sandy Beach due to the impassable Sherars Falls.

Lower Elevator Rapids Class II+

Upper Elevator Rapids Class II

White River Rapids Class II+

Lower Blue Hole 48.3 mi.

Blue Hole 48.6 mi.

Buck Hollow Creek

Bakeoven Road

Oasis 50.8 mi.

Maupin ♦

East Maupin ♦

Flow

Grey Eagle 49.6 mi.

Maupin City Park 51.8 mi.

The lower river has some of the most productive steelhead water in the country. The strong natives weigh in at 5 to 10 pounds, and must be released. Hatchery steelhead may be kept.

Bakeoven Creek

Wapinitia Campsite 55.2 mi.

216

Harpham Flat 55.8 mi.

Long Bend 56.7 mi.

Boxcar Rapids Class III

Wapinitia Rapids Class III

Devils Canyon 54.7 mi.

Trail Hollow Creek

197

Trout fishing above Sherars Falls offers more abundant and larger trout, mostly redsides, with a few bull and brown trout mixed in. Bull trout must be released immediately.

Nena 58.6 mi.

Wapanitia Creek

Locked Gate 59.3 mi.

A gravel road from East Maupin to Locked Gate provides good roadside access. Access beyond the locked gate is by foot only, and will offer some solitude on busy days.

Deschutes Club Gatekeeper's House (Emergency radio, water, check-in station)

Johnson Flat 62.8 mi.

Four Chutes 63.5 mi.

Four Chutes Rapids Class II

Buckskin Mary 63.8 mi.

Buckskin Marry Rapids Class III

Dant ♦

Windy Flat 65.9 mi.

Lower Rainbow Bend

Rainbow Bend 67.9 mi.

Hole in the Wall 67.3 mi.

Dixon 68.6 mi.

Eagle Creek

Upper Dant 65.3 mi.

GPS

Warm Springs Indian Reservation

Deschutes River Recreation Lands

Beavertail: N 45.336, W 120.952
Twin Springs: N 45.309, W 121.007
Pine Tree: N 45.298, W 121.016
Buck Hollow: N 45.269, W 121.018
Sherars Bridge: N 45.260, W 121.034
Sherars Falls: N 45.258, W 121.037
Sandy Beach: N 45.241, W 121.046
Oak Springs: N 45.221, W 121.076
Blue Hole: N 45.209, W 121.074
Oasis: N 45.182, W 121.081
Maupin City Park: N 45.173, W 121.073
Wapinitia: N 45.146, W 121.123
Harpham Flat: N 45.136, W 121.120
Long Bend: N 45.125, W 121.130
Devils Canyon: N 45.116, W 121.129
Nena: N 45.102, W 121.129
Locked Gate: N 45.093, W 121.126

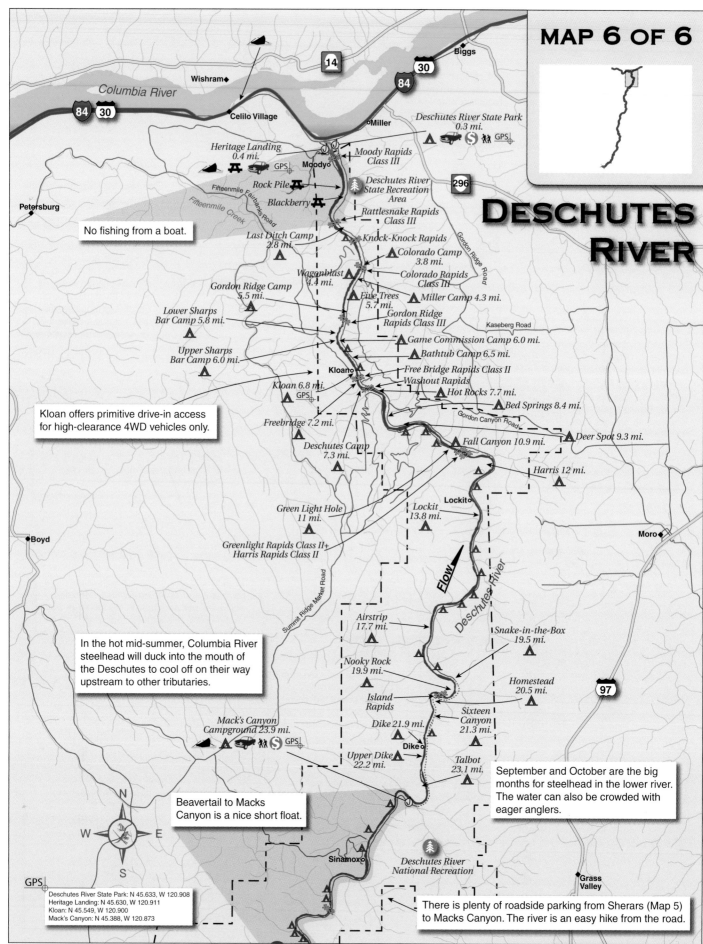

MAP 6 OF 6

Columbia River

Wishram♦

Biggs

14

30

84

84 30

Celilo Village

◦Miller

Deschutes River State Park
0.3 mi.

296

DESCHUTES RIVER

Heritage Landing
0.4 mi.

GPS

Moody◦

Moody Rapids
Class III

Rock Pile

Deschutes River
State Recreation
Area

Blackberry

Rattlesnake Rapids
Class III

Petersburg
♦

Fifteenmile   Fairbanks Road

Fifteenmile Creek

No fishing from a boat.

Last Ditch Camp
2.8 mi.

Knock-Knock Rapids

Colorado Camp
3.8 mi.

Wagonblast
4.4 mi.

Colorado Rapids
Class III

Gordon Ridge Camp
5.5 mi.

Five Trees
5.7 mi.

Miller Camp 4.3 mi.

Gordon Ridge Road

Lower Sharps
Bar Camp 5.8 mi.

Gordon Ridge
Rapids Class III

Kaseberg Road

Upper Sharps
Bar Camp 6.0 mi.

Game Commission Camp 6.0 mi.

Bathtub Camp 6.5 mi.

Kloan◦

Free Bridge Rapids Class II

Washout Rapids

Kloan 6.8 mi.

GPS

Hot Rocks 7.7 mi.

Bed Springs 8.4 mi.

Kloan offers primitive drive-in access
for high-clearance 4WD vehicles only.

Freebridge 7.2 mi.

Gordon Canyon Road

Deer Spot 9.3 mi.

Deschutes Camp
7.3 mi.

Fall Canyon 10.9 mi.

Harris 12 mi.

Green Light Hole
11 mi.

Lockit◦

Lockit
13.8 mi.

Moro♦

Greenlight Rapids Class II+
Harris Rapids Class II

Flow

Deschutes River

Boyd
♦

Airstrip
17.7 mi.

Snake-in-the-Box
19.5 mi.

97

In the hot mid-summer, Columbia River
steelhead will duck into the mouth of
the Deschutes to cool off on their way
upstream to other tributaries.

Summit Ridge Market Road

Nooky Rock
19.9 mi.

Homestead
20.5 mi.

Island
Rapids

Sixteen
Canyon
21.3 mi.

Mack's Canyon
Campground 23.9 mi.

Dike 21.9 mi.

Dike◦

GPS

Upper Dike
22.2 mi.

Talbot
23.1 mi.

September and October are the big
months for steelhead in the lower river.
The water can also be crowded with
eager anglers.

N

W   E

S

Beavertail to Macks
Canyon is a nice short float.

Sinamox◦

Deschutes River
National Recreation

Grass
Valley

GPS

Deschutes River State Park: N 45.633, W 120.908
Heritage Landing: N 45.630, W 120.911
Kloan: N 45.549, W 120.900
Mack's Canyon: N 45.388, W 120.873

There is plenty of roadside parking from Sherars (Map 5)
to Macks Canyon. The river is an easy hike from the road.

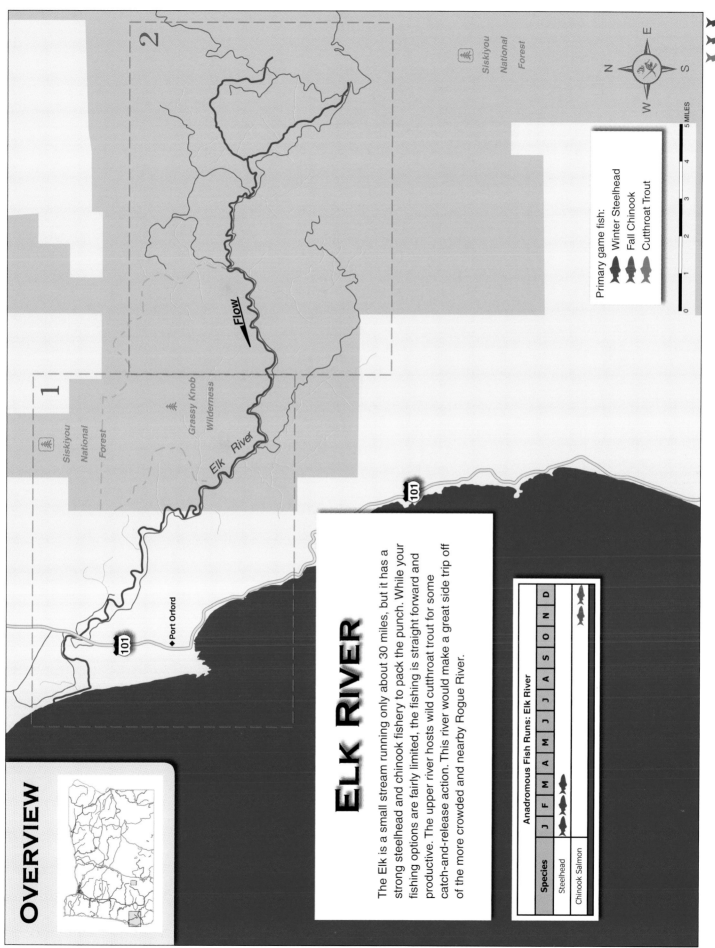

OVERVIEW

ELK RIVER

The Elk is a small stream running only about 30 miles, but it has a strong steelhead and chinook fishery to pack the punch. While your fishing options are fairly limited, the fishing is straight forward and productive. The upper river hosts wild cutthroat trout for some catch-and-release action. This river would make a great side trip off of the more crowded and nearby Rogue River.

Anadromous Fish Runs: Elk River

Species	J	F	M	A	M	J	J	A	S	O	N	D
Steelhead												
Chinook Salmon												

Primary game fish:

Winter Steelhead
Fall Chinook
Cutthroat Trout

Siskiyou National Forest

Grassy Knob Wilderness

Elk River

Port Orford

Flow

0   1   2   3   4   5 MILES

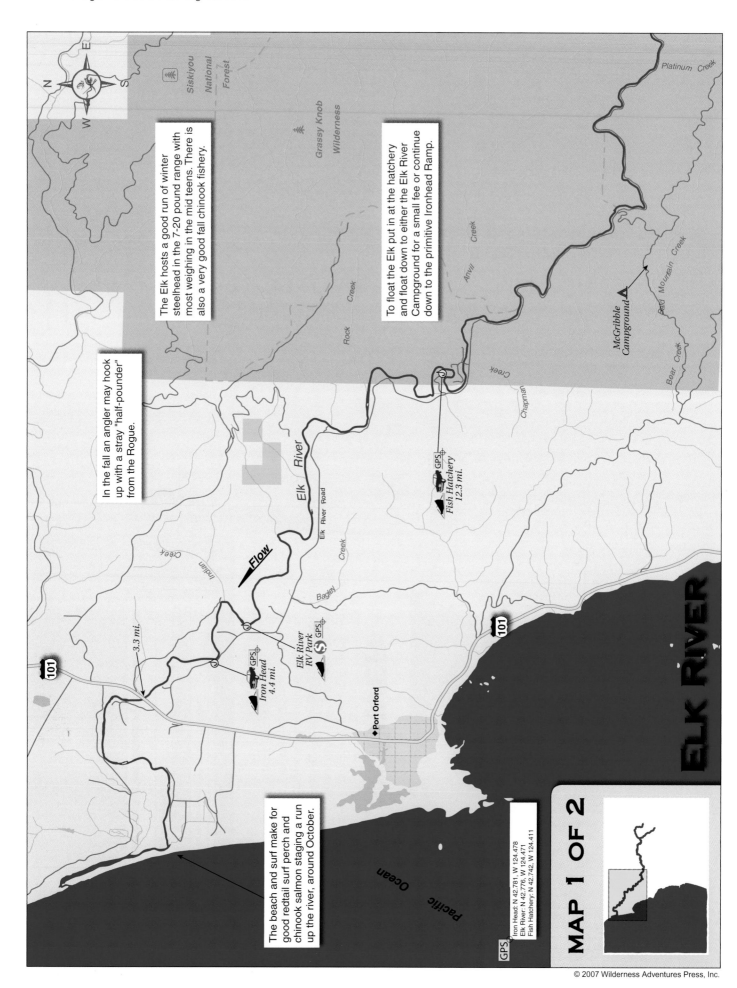

The Elk hosts a good run of winter steelhead in the 7-20 pound range with most weighing in the mid teens. There is also a very good fall chinook fishery.

To float the Elk put in at the hatchery and float down to either the Elk River Campground for a small fee or continue down to the primitive Ironhead Ramp.

In the fall an angler may hook up with a stray "half-pounder" from the Rogue.

The beach and surf make for good redtail surf perch and chinook salmon staging a run up the river, around October.

Siskiyou National Forest

Grassy Knob Wilderness

Platinum Creek

Bald Mountain Creek

McGribble Campground

Bear Creek

Anvil Creek

Chapman Creek

Rock Creek

Elk River

Elk River Road

Creek

Bagley Creek

Indian Creek

3.3 mi.

Flow

GPS
Iron Head
4.4 mi.

GPS
Fish Hatchery
12.3 mi.

Elk River
RV Park

Port Orford

101

101

Pacific Ocean

ELK RIVER

MAP 1 OF 2

GPS
Iron Head: N 42.781, W 124.478
Elk River: N 42.776, W 124.471
Fish Hatchery: N 42.742, W 124.411

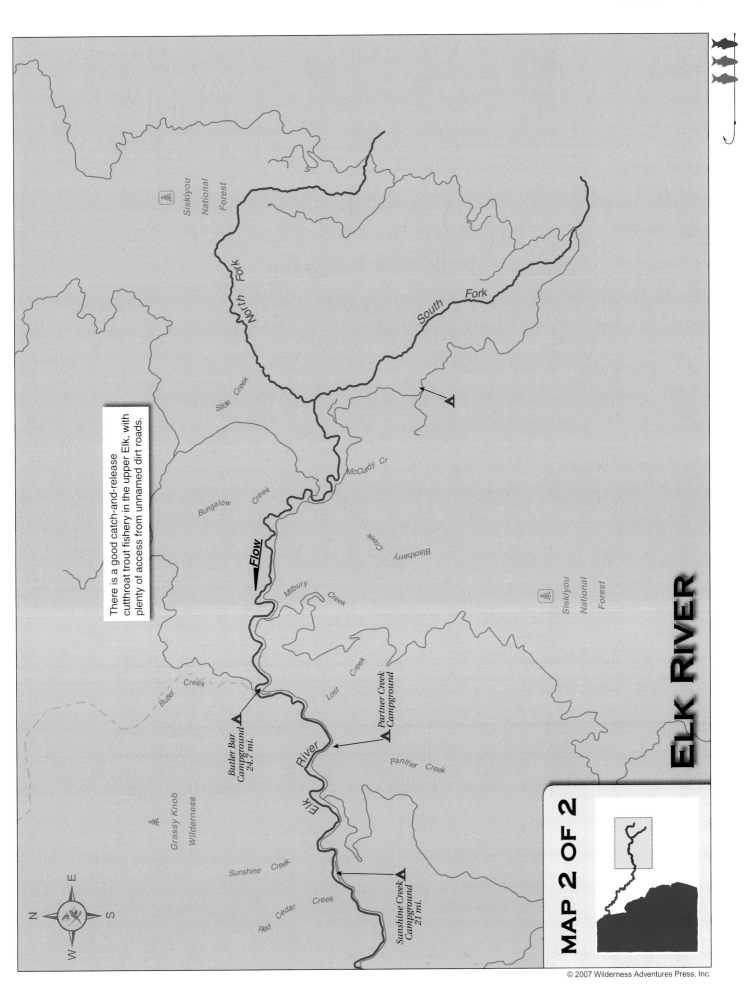

There is a good catch-and-release cutthroat trout fishery in the upper Elk, with plenty of access from unnamed dirt roads.

Siskiyou National Forest

North Fork

South Fork

Slide Creek

McCurdy Cr

Bungalow Creek

Flow

Blackberry Creek

Milbury Creek

Lost Creek

Butler Creek

Butler Bar Campground 24.7 mi.

River

Partner Creek Campground

Panther Creek

Grassy Knob Wilderness

Elk

Sunshine Creek

Sunshine Creek Campground 21 mi.

Red Cedar Creek

Siskiyou National Forest

ELK RIVER

MAP 2 OF 2

N E W S

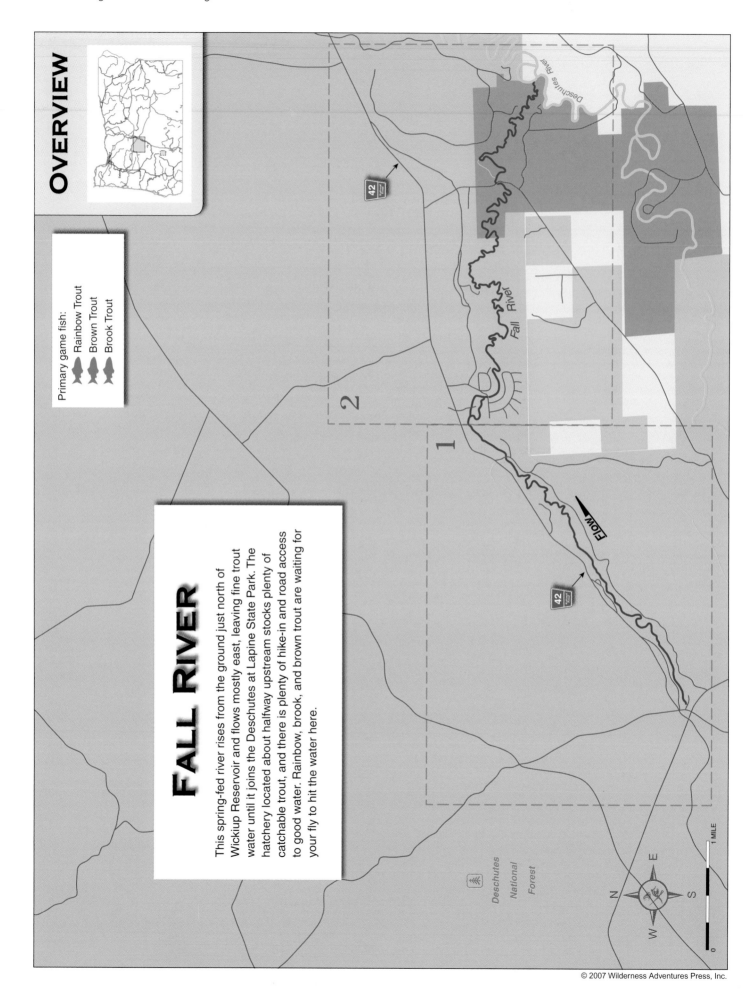

OVERVIEW

Primary game fish:
- Rainbow Trout
- Brown Trout
- Brook Trout

Deschutes River

Fall River

2

1

FLOW

42

42

Deschutes
National
Forest

N
E
S
W

0   1 MILE

FALL RIVER

This spring-fed river rises from the ground just north of Wickiup Reservoir and flows mostly east, leaving fine trout water until it joins the Deschutes at Lapine State Park. The hatchery located about halfway upstream stocks plenty of catchable trout, and there is plenty of hike-in and road access to good water. Rainbow, brook, and brown trout are waiting for your fly to hit the water here.

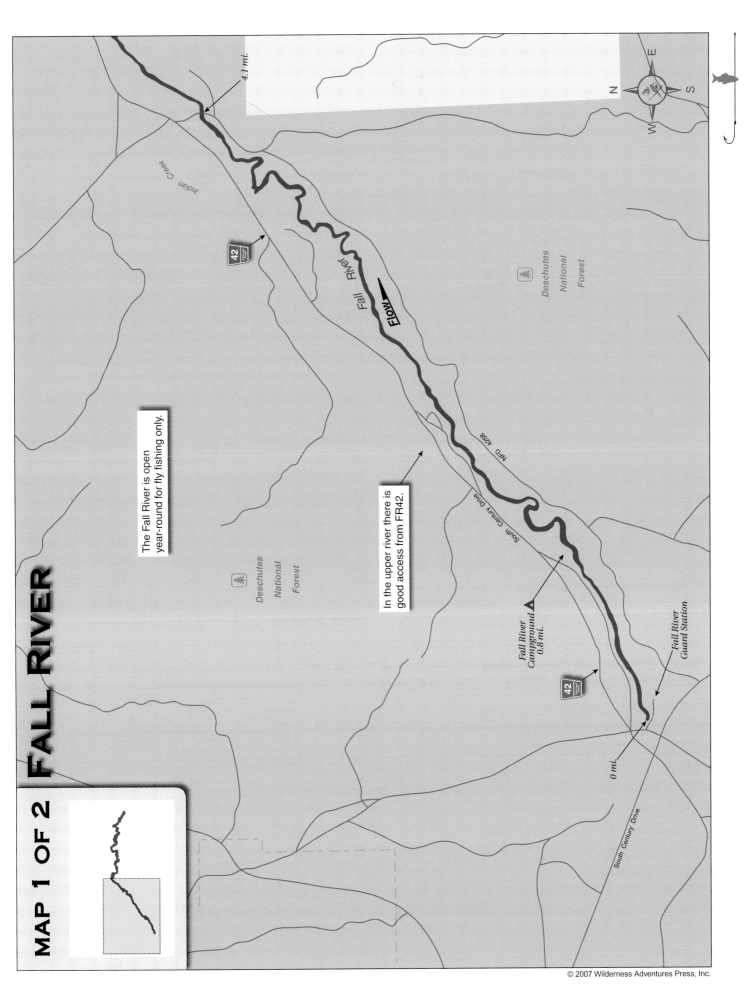

MAP 1 OF 2   FALL RIVER

4.1 mi.

Indian Creek

42

The Fall River is open year-round for fly fishing only.

Fall River

FLOW

Deschutes National Forest

Deschutes National Forest

NFD 4258

South Century Drive

In the upper river there is good access from FR42.

Fall River Campground 0.8 mi.

42

Fall River Guard Station

0 mi.

South Century Drive

N E
W S

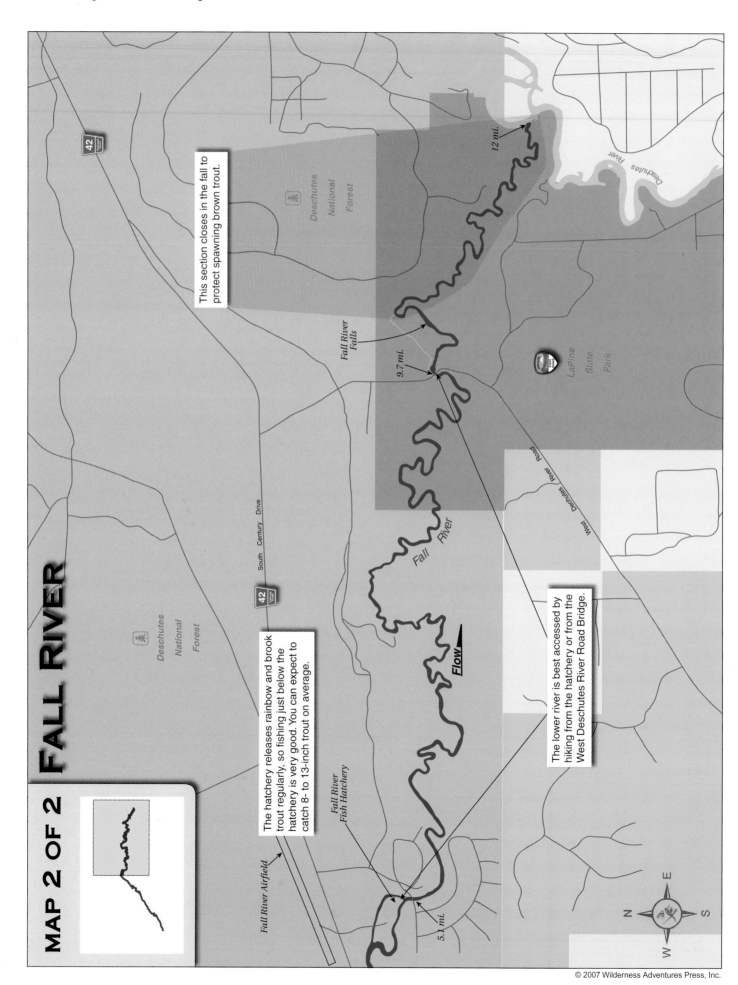

MAP 2 OF 2 FALL RIVER

This section closes in the fall to protect spawning brown trout.

The hatchery releases rainbow and brook trout regularly, so fishing just below the hatchery is very good. You can expect to catch 8- to 13-inch trout on average.

The lower river is best accessed by hiking from the hatchery or from the West Deschutes River Road Bridge.

Fall River Falls

Deschutes National Forest

Deschutes River

LaPine State Park

West Deschutes River Road

South Century Drive

Fall River

Flow

Fall River Airfield

Fall River Fish Hatchery

12 mi.

9.7 mi.

5.1 mi.

N E S W

© 2007 Wilderness Adventures Press, Inc.

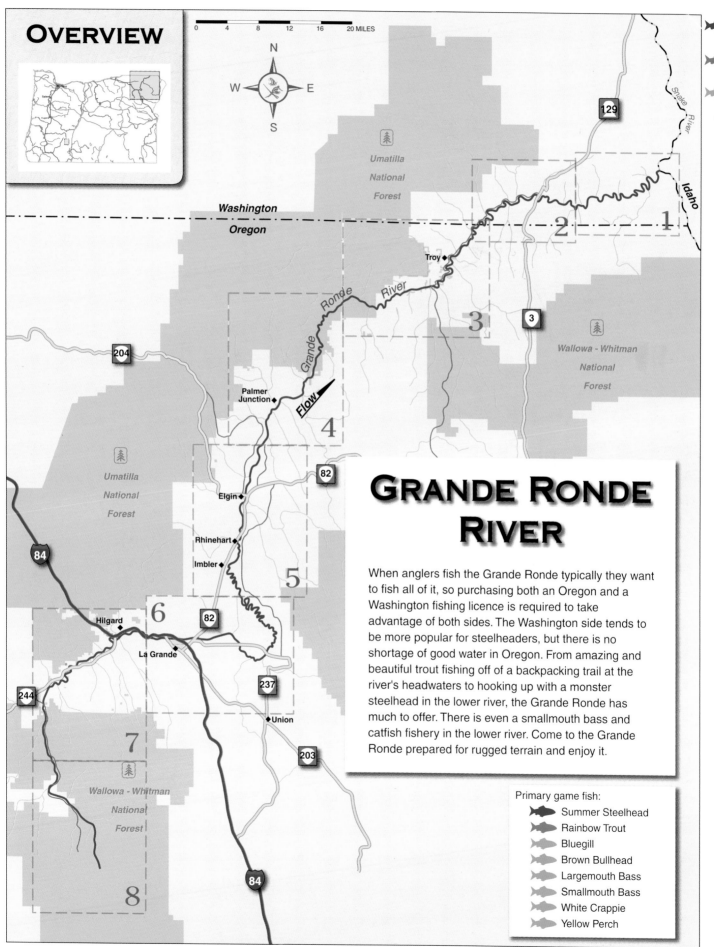

GRANDE RONDE RIVER

When anglers fish the Grande Ronde typically they want to fish all of it, so purchasing both an Oregon and a Washington fishing licence is required to take advantage of both sides. The Washington side tends to be more popular for steelheaders, but there is no shortage of good water in Oregon. From amazing and beautiful trout fishing off of a backpacking trail at the river's headwaters to hooking up with a monster steelhead in the lower river, the Grande Ronde has much to offer. There is even a smallmouth bass and catfish fishery in the lower river. Come to the Grande Ronde prepared for rugged terrain and enjoy it.

Primary game fish:
- Summer Steelhead
- Rainbow Trout
- Bluegill
- Brown Bullhead
- Largemouth Bass
- Smallmouth Bass
- White Crappie
- Yellow Perch

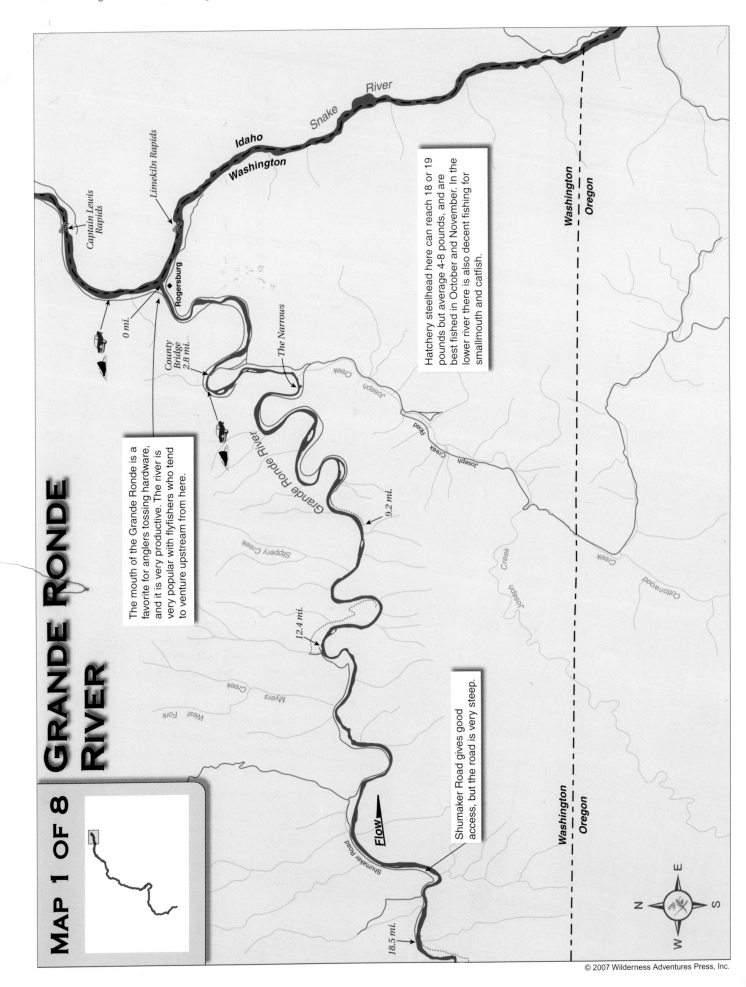

MAP 1 OF 8

GRANDE RONDE RIVER

Captain Lewis Rapids

Limekiln Rapids

Idaho

Washington

Snake River

Rogersburg

0 mi.

County Bridge 2.8 mi.

The Narrows

Grande Ronde River

Joseph Creek

Joseph Creek Road

The mouth of the Grande Ronde is a favorite for anglers tossing hardware, and it is very productive. The river is very popular with flyfishers who tend to venture upstream from here.

Hatchery steelhead here can reach 18 or 19 pounds but average 4-8 pounds, and are best fished in October and November. In the lower river there is also decent fishing for smallmouth and catfish.

Washington
Oregon

9.2 mi.

Slippery Creek

12.4 mi.

Myers Creek

West Fork

Joseph Creek

Cottonwood Creek

Shumaker Road gives good access, but the road is very steep.

FLOW

Shumaker Road

Washington
Oregon

18.5 mi.

N E S W

© 2007 Wilderness Adventures Press, Inc.

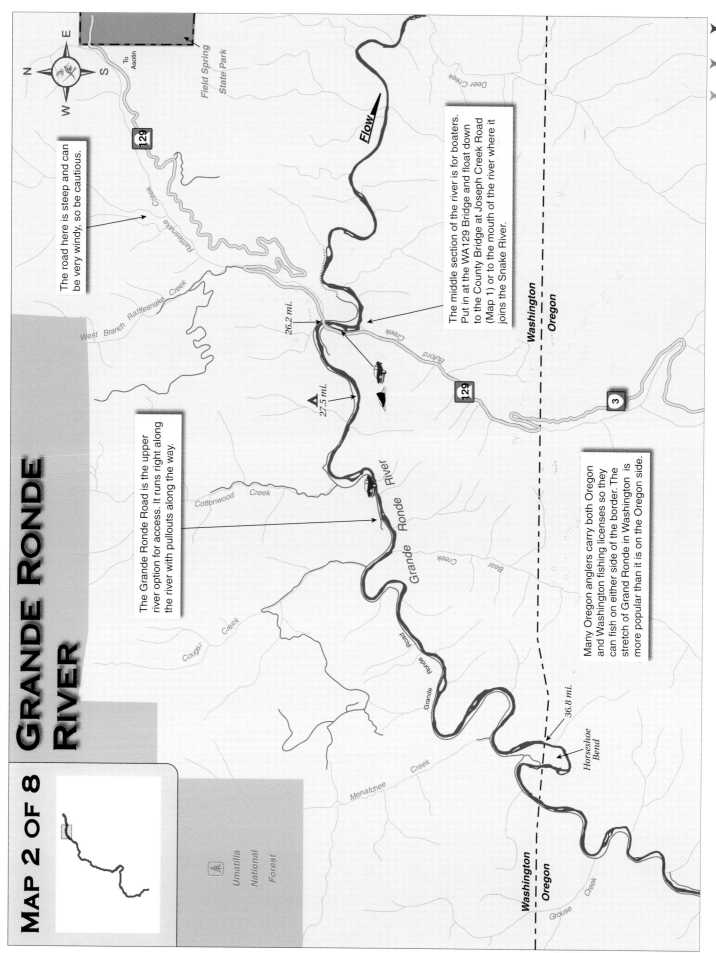

MAP 2 OF 8

GRANDE RONDE RIVER

The road here is steep and can be very windy, so be cautious.

The middle section of the river is for boaters. Put in at the WA129 Bridge and float down to the County Bridge at Joseph Creek Road (Map 1) or to the mouth of the river where it joins the Snake River.

The Grande Ronde Road is the upper river option for access. It runs right along the river with pullouts along the way.

Many Oregon anglers carry both Oregon and Washington fishing licenses so they can fish on either side of the border. The stretch of Grand Ronde in Washington is more popular than it is on the Oregon side.

To Asotin

Field Spring State Park

Rattlesnake Creek

West Branch Rattlesnake Creek

129

Flow

Deer Creek

Washington

Oregon

26.2 mi.

27.5 mi.

Buford Creek

129

3

Cottonwood Creek

Grande Ronde River

Cougar Creek

Grande Ronde Road

Bear Creek

36.8 mi.

Horseshoe Bend

Menatchee Creek

Washington

Oregon

Grouse Creek

Umatilla National Forest

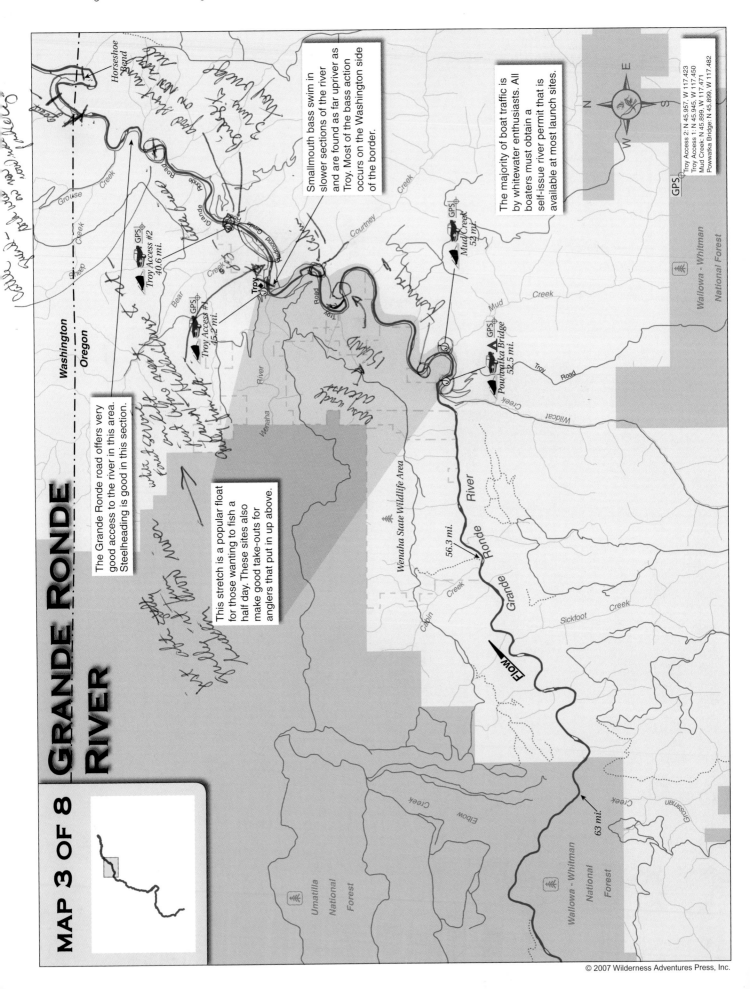

MAP 3 OF 8

GRANDE RONDE RIVER

The Grande Ronde road offers very good access to the river in this area. Steelheading is good in this section.

This stretch is a popular float for those wanting to fish a half day. These sites also make good take-outs for anglers that put in up above.

Smallmouth bass swim in slower sections of the river and are found as far upriver as Troy. Most of the bass action occurs on the Washington side of the border.

The majority of boat traffic is by whitewater enthusiasts. All boaters must obtain a self-issue river permit that is available at most launch sites.

Troy Access #2
40.6 mi.

Troy Access #1
45.2 mi.

Mud Creek
52 mi.

Powtrotka Bridge
52.5 mi.

56.3 mi.

63 mi.

Washington
Oregon

Troy

Horseshoe Bend

Grouse Creek

Sheep Creek

Bear Creek

Courtney Creek

Creek

Mud Creek

Troy Road

Wildcat Creek

Wenaha River

Wenaha State Wildlife Area

Cabin Creek

Elbow Creek

Grossman Creek

Sickfoot Creek

Grande Ronde River

FLOW

Umatilla National Forest

Wallowa - Whitman National Forest

Wallowa - Whitman National Forest

GPS:
Troy Access 2: N 45.957, W 117.423
Troy Access 1: N 45.945, W 117.450
Mud Creek: N 45.899, W 117.471
Powtatka Bridge: N 45.899, W 117.482

© 2007 Wilderness Adventures Press, Inc.

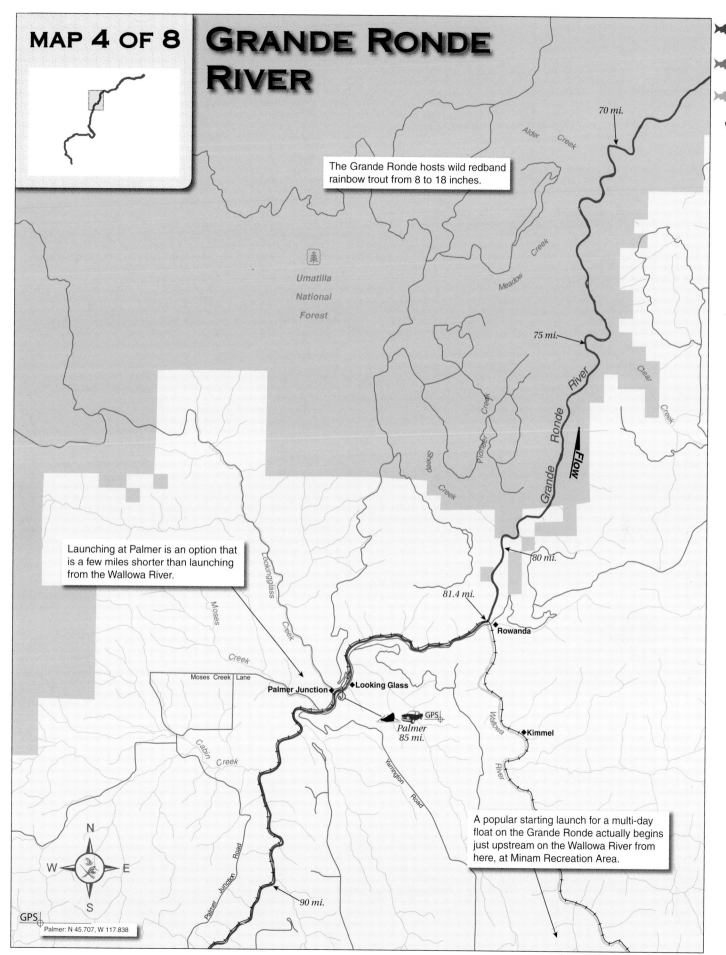

MAP 4 OF 8

GRANDE RONDE RIVER

The Grande Ronde hosts wild redband rainbow trout from 8 to 18 inches.

Umatilla National Forest

70 mi.

75 mi.

Launching at Palmer is an option that is a few miles shorter than launching from the Wallowa River.

80 mi.

81.4 mi.

Rowanda

Palmer Junction ◆ Looking Glass

Kimmel

Palmer
85 mi.

A popular starting launch for a multi-day float on the Grande Ronde actually begins just upstream on the Wallowa River from here, at Minam Recreation Area.

90 mi.

N W E S

Palmer: N 45.707, W 117.838

© 2007 Wilderness Adventures Press, Inc.

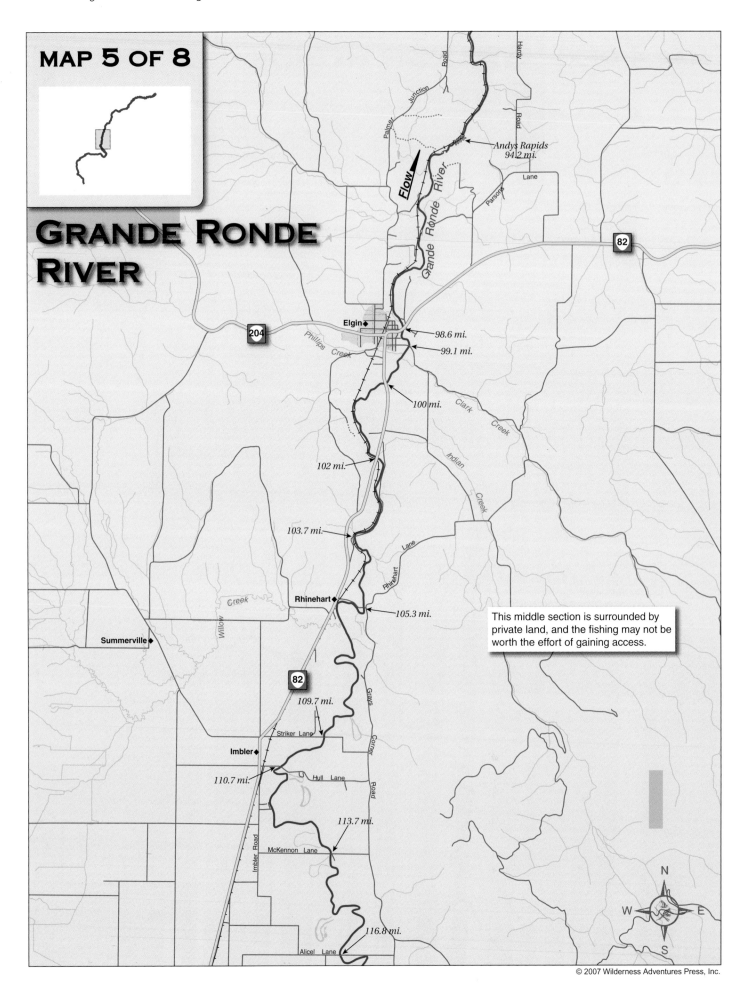

MAP 5 OF 8

GRANDE RONDE RIVER

Andys Rapids
94.2 mi.

Flow

Grande Ronde River

82

204

Elgin

98.6 mi.

99.1 mi.

100 mi.

102 mi.

103.7 mi.

Rhinehart

105.3 mi.

This middle section is surrounded by private land, and the fishing may not be worth the effort of gaining access.

82

109.7 mi.

Striker Lane

Imbler

110.7 mi.

Hull Lane

113.7 mi.

McKennon Lane

116.8 mi.

Alicel Lane

Summerville

Willow Creek

Phillips Creek

Clark Creek

Indian Creek

Rhinehart Lane

Grays Corner Road

Imbler Road

Junction Road

Hardy Road

Palmer

Parsons Lane

N
W E
S

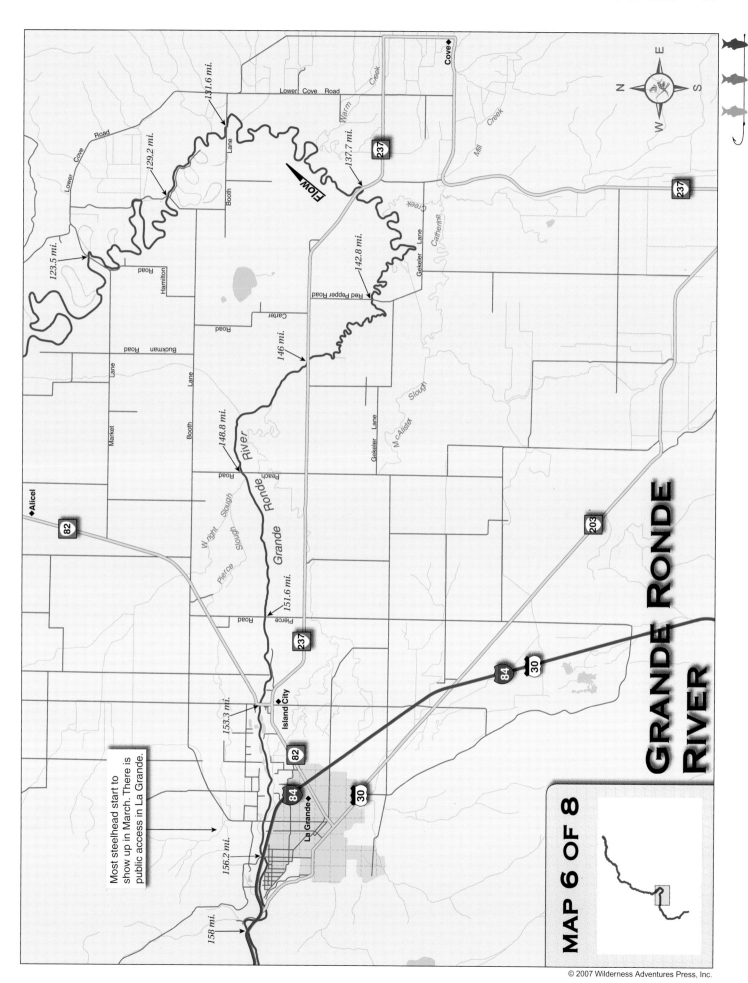

131.6 mi.

Lower Cove Road

Cove◆

129.2 mi.

137.7 mi.

237

237

Flow

123.5 mi.

142.8 mi.

Most steelhead start to show up in March. There is public access in La Grande.

146 mi.

148.8 mi.

151.6 mi.

153.3 mi.

Island City

156.2 mi.

158 mi.

La Grande◆

◆Alicel

82

82

84

30

203

84

30

237

MAP 6 OF 8

GRANDE RONDE RIVER

© 2007 Wilderness Adventures Press, Inc.

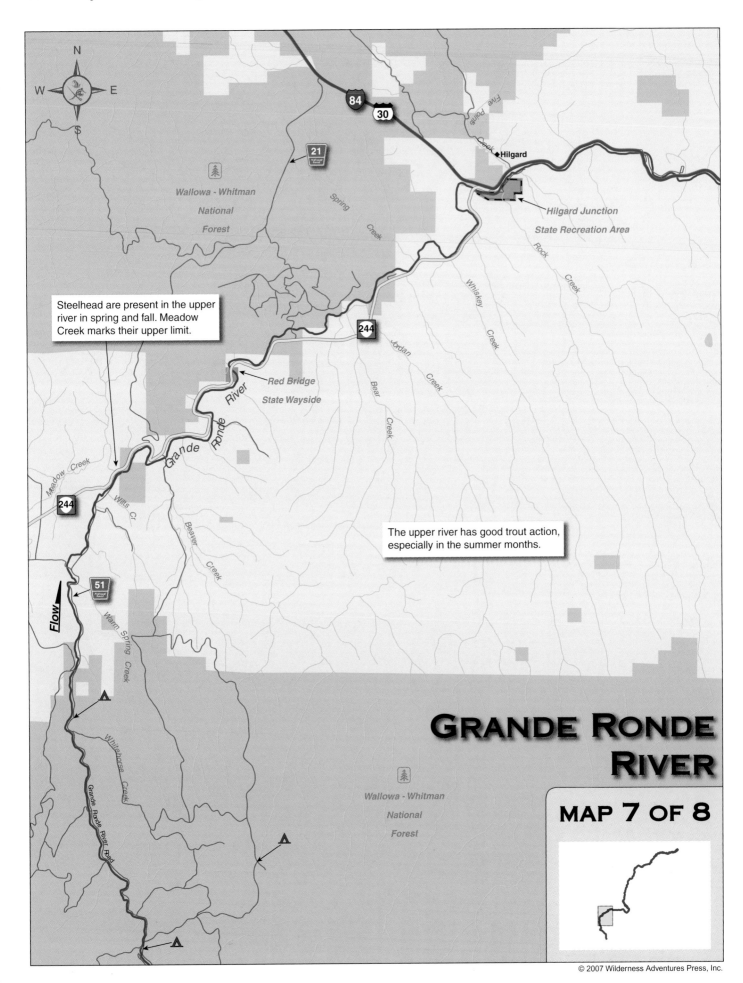

Steelhead are present in the upper river in spring and fall. Meadow Creek marks their upper limit.

The upper river has good trout action, especially in the summer months.

Hilgard

Hilgard Junction
State Recreation Area

Wallowa - Whitman
National
Forest

Red Bridge
State Wayside

Wallowa - Whitman
National
Forest

GRANDE RONDE
RIVER

MAP 7 OF 8

© 2007 Wilderness Adventures Press, Inc.

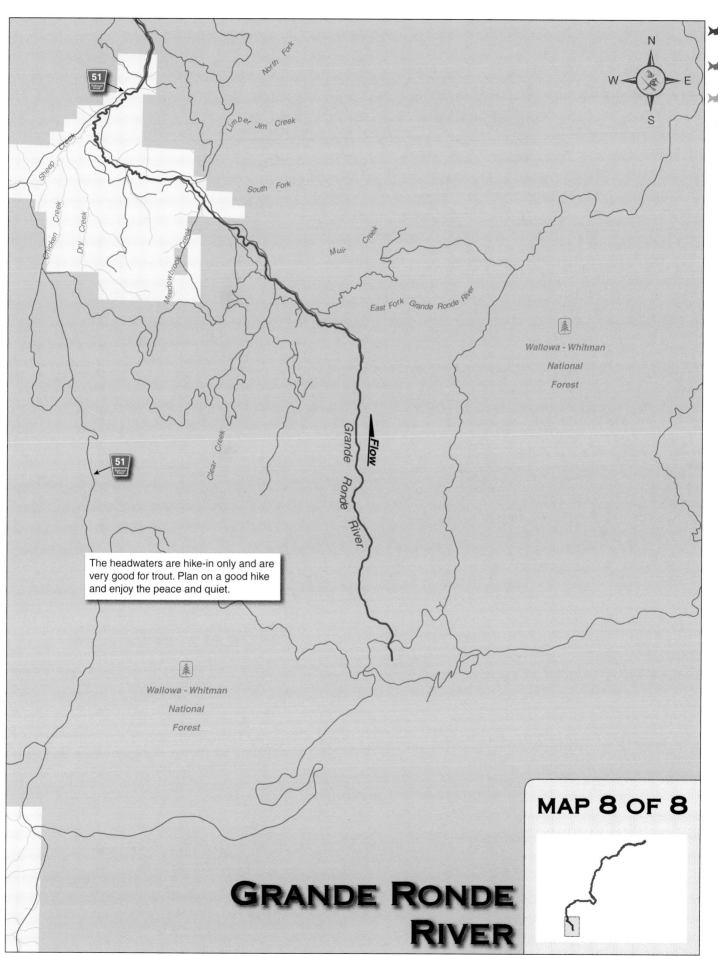

The headwaters are hike-in only and are very good for trout. Plan on a good hike and enjoy the peace and quiet.

MAP 8 OF 8

GRANDE RONDE RIVER

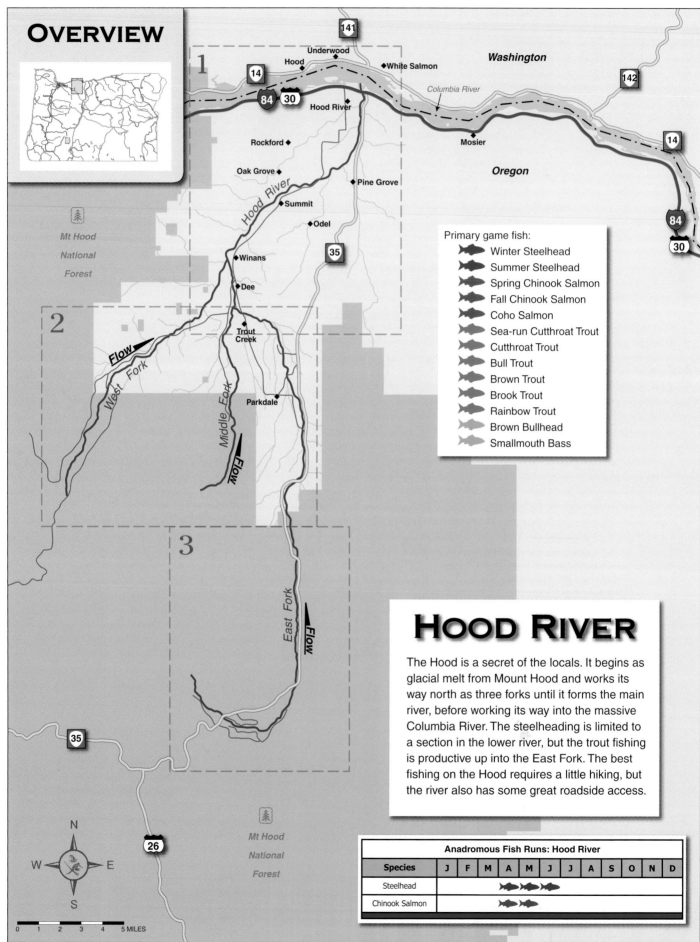

OVERVIEW

Washington

Columbia River

Oregon

Underwood
Hood
White Salmon
Hood River
Mosier
Rockford ◆
Oak Grove ◆
Pine Grove ◆
Summit
Odel ◆
Winans ◆
Dee ◆
Trout Creek
Parkdale

Mt Hood National Forest

Flow
West Fork
Middle Fork
East Fork
Flow
Flow

Primary game fish:

- Winter Steelhead
- Summer Steelhead
- Spring Chinook Salmon
- Fall Chinook Salmon
- Coho Salmon
- Sea-run Cutthroat Trout
- Cutthroat Trout
- Bull Trout
- Brown Trout
- Brook Trout
- Rainbow Trout
- Brown Bullhead
- Smallmouth Bass

HOOD RIVER

The Hood is a secret of the locals. It begins as glacial melt from Mount Hood and works its way north as three forks until it forms the main river, before working its way into the massive Columbia River. The steelheading is limited to a section in the lower river, but the trout fishing is productive up into the East Fork. The best fishing on the Hood requires a little hiking, but the river also has some great roadside access.

Mt Hood National Forest

N
W E
S

0 1 2 3 4 5 MILES

Anadromous Fish Runs: Hood River												
Species	J	F	M	A	M	J	J	A	S	O	N	D
Steelhead												
Chinook Salmon												

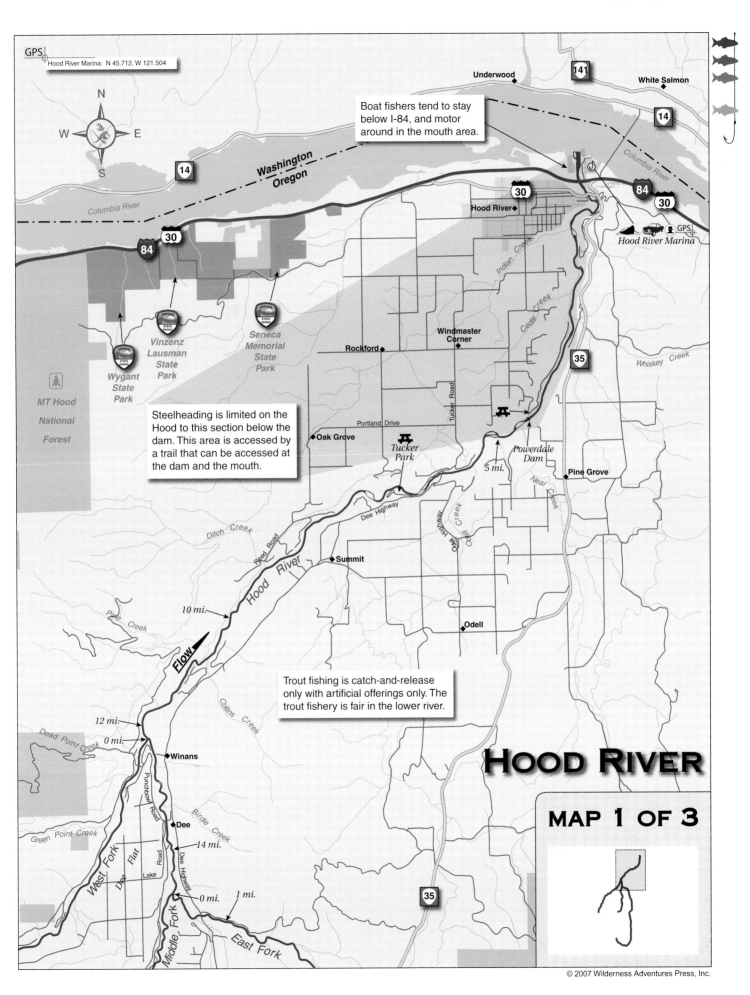

GPS
Hood River Marina: N 45.712, W 121.504

Boat fishers tend to stay below I-84, and motor around in the mouth area.

Washington
Oregon

Columbia River

Underwood

141

White Salmon

14

Columbia River

14

30

84   30

Hood River

30

84   30

GPS

Hood River Marina

Indian Creek

Cedar Creek

Whiskey Creek

Wygant State Park

Vinzenz Lausman State Park

Seneca Memorial State Park

Windmaster Corner

Rockford

35

MT Hood National Forest

Steelheading is limited on the Hood to this section below the dam. This area is accessed by a trail that can be accessed at the dam and the mouth.

Portland Drive

Oak Grove

Tucker Park

Powerdale Dam

5 mi.

Pine Grove

Neal Creek

Tucker Road

Odell Creek

Odell Highway

Ditch Creek

Reed Road

Dee Highway

Hood River

Summit

10 mi.

Pine Creek

Flow

Collins Creek

Trout fishing is catch-and-release only with artificial offerings only. The trout fishery is fair in the lower river.

Odell

12 mi.

Dead Point Creek

0 mi.

Winans

Green Point Creek

West Fork

Dee Flat Road

Punchbowl Road

Dee

Birdie Creek

Dee Highway

14 mi.

Lake

Middle Fork

0 mi.   1 mi.

East Fork

35

HOOD RIVER

MAP 1 OF 3

© 2007 Wilderness Adventures Press, Inc.

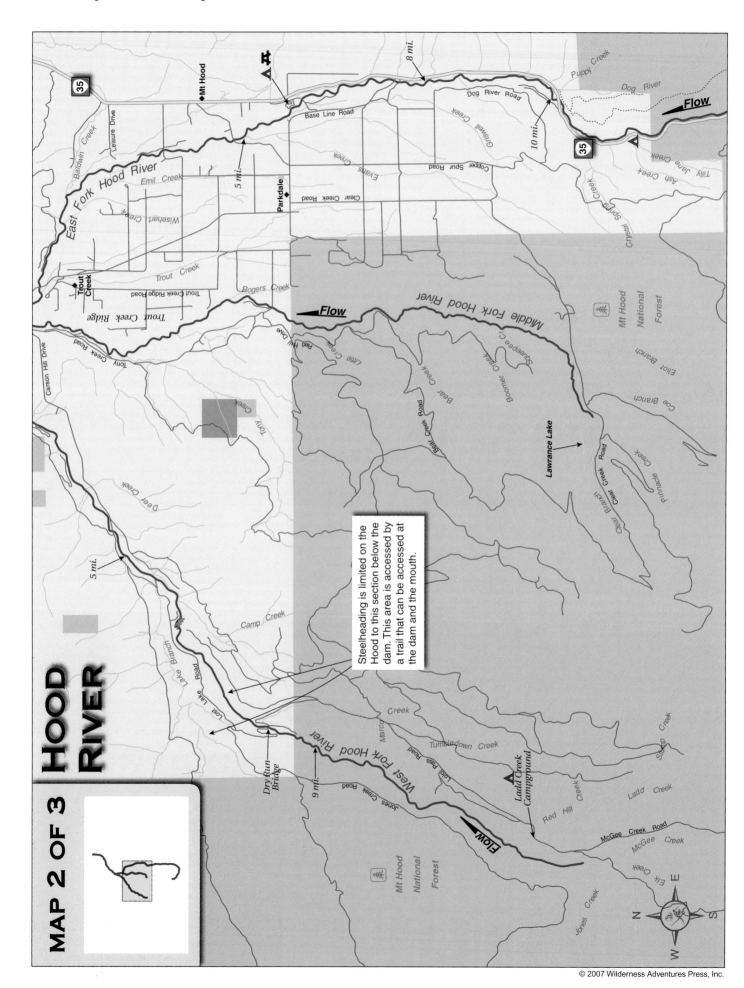

35

Flow

Mt Hood

Base Line Road

Dog River Road

8 mi.

10 mi.

Dog River

Puppy Creek

35

Tilly Jane Creek

Ash Creek

Crystal Spring

Griswell Creek

Evans Creek

Copper Spur Road

Leisure Drive

Baldwin Creek

East Fork Hood River

Emil Creek

Wishart Creek

Parkdale

Clear Creek Road

5 mi.

Trout Creek

Trout Creek

Trout Creek Ridge Road

Rogers Creek

Trout Creek Ridge

Flow

Middle Fork Hood River

Bear Creek Road

Coe Branch

Eliot Branch

Mt Hood National Forest

Bear Creek

Shreepee Creek

Boomer Creek

Lawrance Lake

Clear Branch Creek Road

Pinnacle Creek

Carson Hill Drive

Tony Creek Road

Red Hill Drive

Little Creek

Deer Creek

Tony Creek

Camp Creek

5 mi.

Lake Branch

Lost Lake Road

Steelheading is limited on the Hood to this section below the dam. This area is accessed by a trail that can be accessed at the dam and the mouth.

Marcos Creek

Tumbledown Creek

Lolo Pass Road

West Fork Hood River

Jones Creek Road

Dry Run Bridge

9 mi.

Ladd Creek Campground

Red Hill

Ladd Creek

Sheep Creek

McGee Creek Road

McGee Creek

Elk Creek

Jones Creek

Flow

Mt Hood National Forest

MAP 2 OF 3

HOOD RIVER

N
W   E
S

© 2007 WILDERNESS ADVENTURES PRESS, Inc.

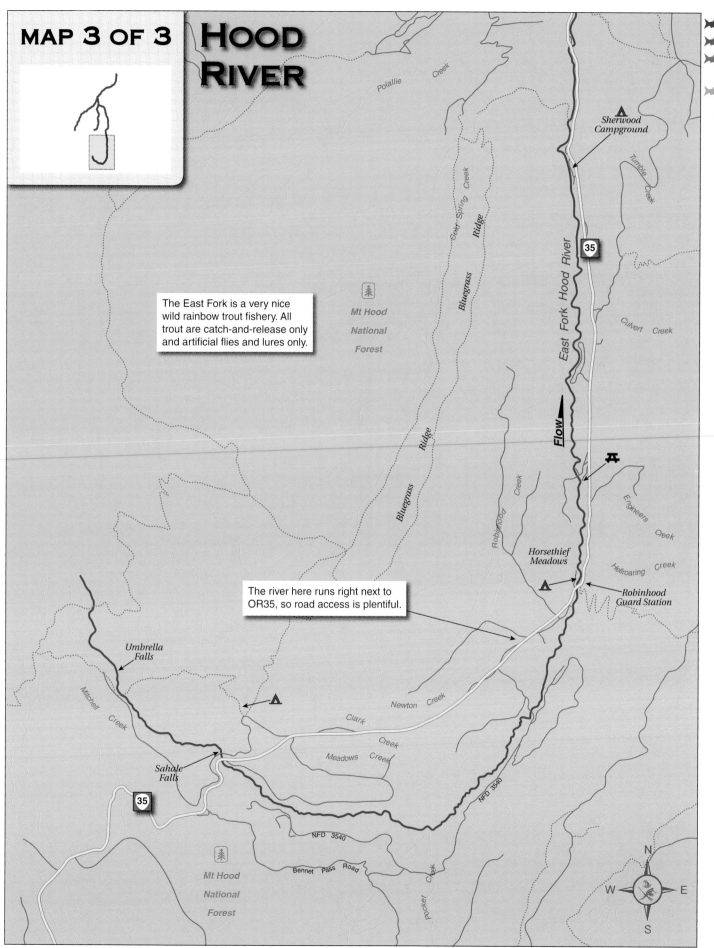

MAP **3** OF **3** HOOD RIVER

The East Fork is a very nice wild rainbow trout fishery. All trout are catch-and-release only and artificial flies and lures only.

The river here runs right next to OR35, so road access is plentiful.

Polallie Creek

Sherwood Campground

Tumble Creek

35

East Fork Hood River

Gooo Spring Creek

Bluegrass Ridge

Culvert Creek

Mt Hood National Forest

Bluegrass Ridge

Flow

Robinhood Creek

Engineers Creek

Horsethief Meadows

Hellroaring Creek

Robinhood Guard Station

Umbrella Falls

Mitchell Creek

Newton Creek

Clark Creek

Meadows Creek

Sahale Falls

NFD 3540

35

NFD 3540

Bennet Pass Road

pocket Creek

Mt Hood National Forest

N
W   E
S

JOHN DAY RIVER

The John Day River is one of the Columbia's major tributaries. Its origin is in the Malheur National Forest, and it works its way west and then north to add its flow to the massive Columbia River. As a fishery it is very popular, especially for steelhead. They inhabit the river for most of the year and offer some challenging fishing for anglers. The upper John Day is a very good trout fishery as well as offering spawning grounds for the river's wild steelhead population. There is even a section of river that has a decent smallmouth fishery. The river is touted as being one of the nation's largest undammed rivers and provides some amazing scenery, fishing, and even a little fun for whitewater enthusiasts.

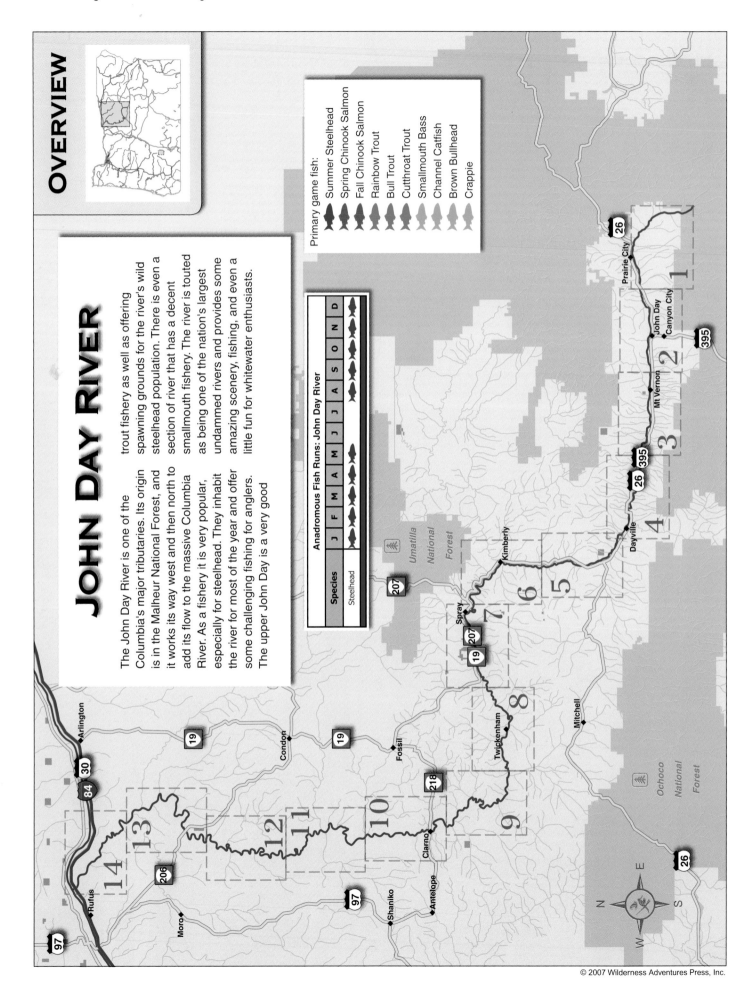

OVERVIEW

Primary game fish:

Summer Steelhead
Spring Chinook Salmon
Fall Chinook Salmon
Rainbow Trout
Bull Trout
Cutthroat Trout
Smallmouth Bass
Channel Catfish
Brown Bullhead
Crappie

Anadromous Fish Runs: John Day River

Species	J	F	M	A	M	J	J	A	S	O	N	D
Steelhead												

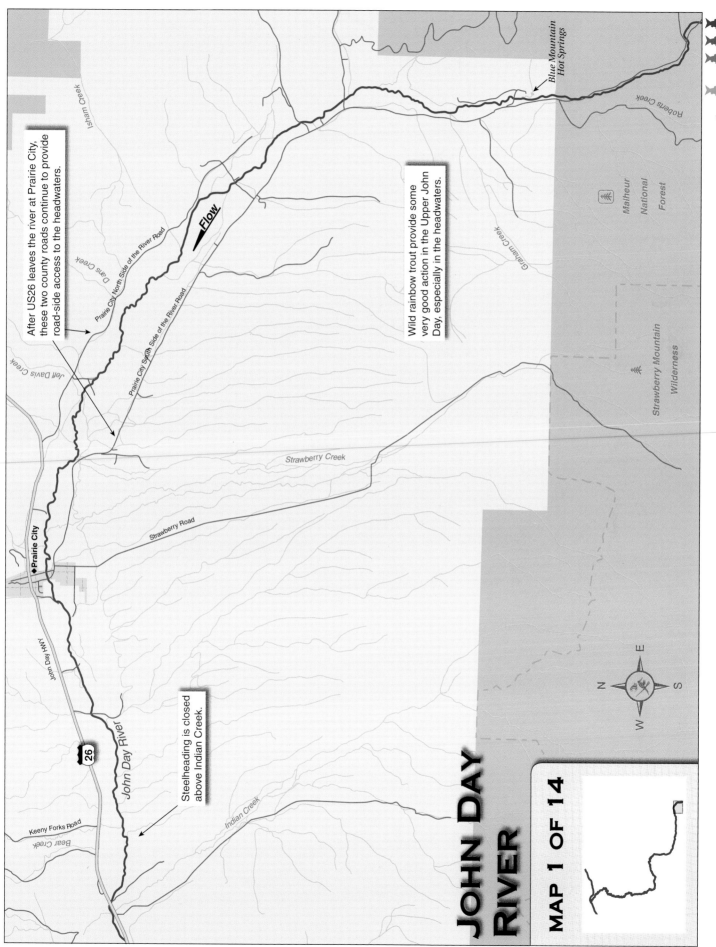

After US26 leaves the river at Prairie City, these two county roads continue to provide road-side access to the headwaters.

Wild rainbow trout provide some very good action in the Upper John Day, especially in the headwaters.

Steelheading is closed above Indian Creek.

Blue Mountain Hot Springs

Roberts Creek

Isham Creek

D' als Creek

Jeff Davis Creek

Prairie City North Side of the River Road

Prairie City South Side of the River Road

Flow

Malheur National Forest

Graham Creek

Strawberry Mountain Wilderness

Strawberry Creek

Strawberry Road

◆Prairie City

John Day HWY

John Day River

26

Keeny Forks Road

Bear Creek

Indian Creek

N E S W

JOHN DAY RIVER

MAP 1 OF 14

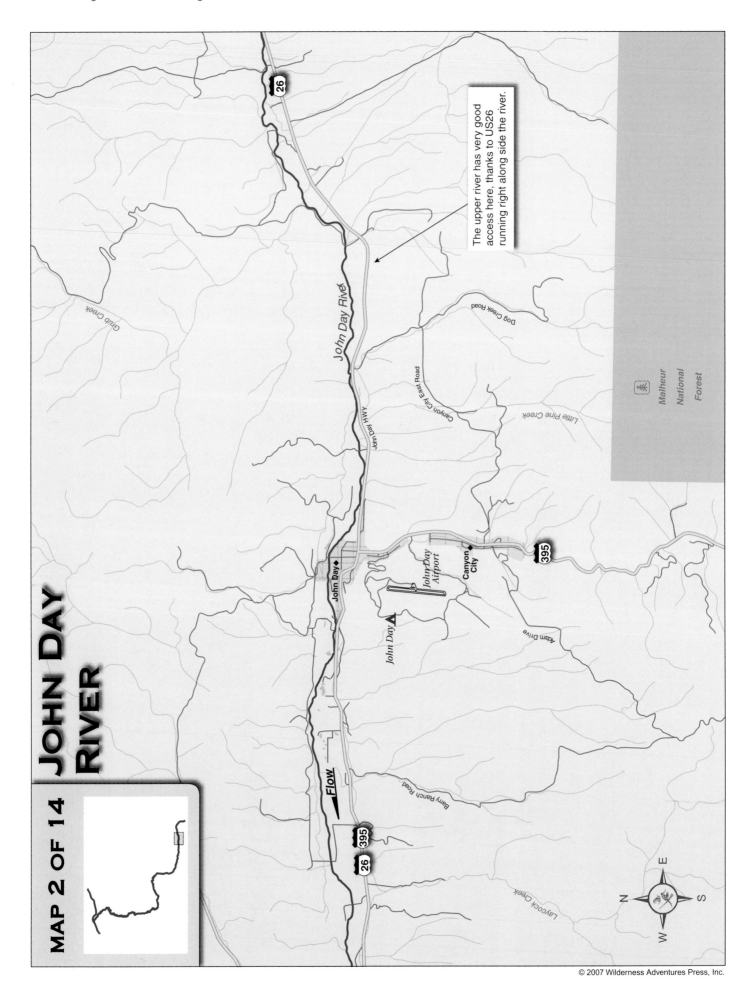

MAP 2 OF 14

JOHN DAY RIVER

26

John Day River

John Day HWY

Grub Creek

Dog Creek Road

Canyon City East Road

Little Pine Creek

Malheur National Forest

The upper river has very good access here, thanks to US26 running right along side the river.

John Day

John Day Airport

Canyon City

395

Adam Drive

Barry Ranch Road

Flow

395

26

Laycock Creek

N E W S

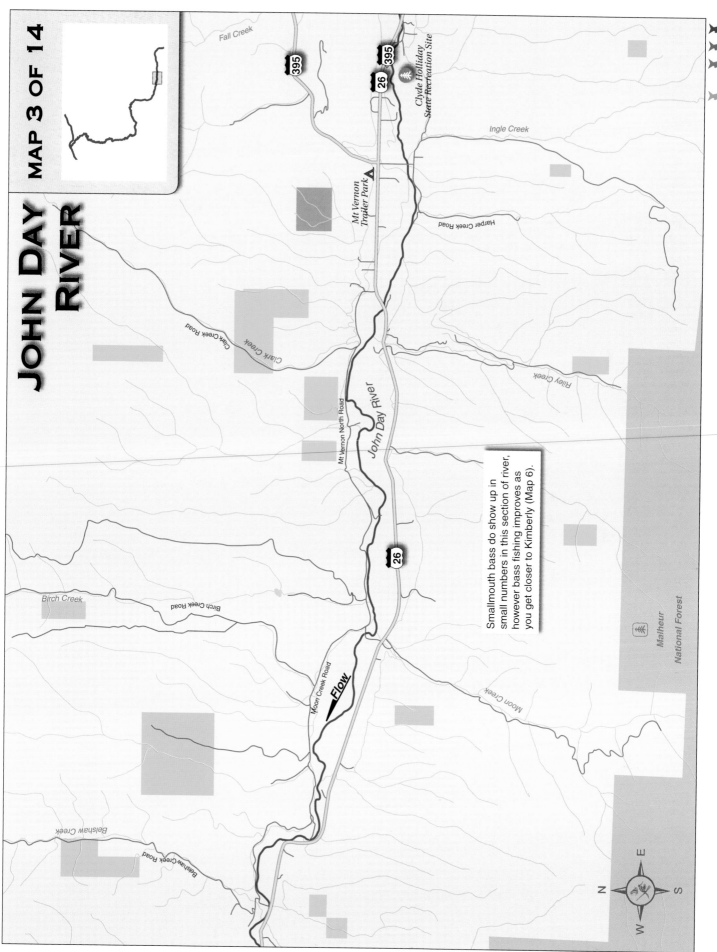

Smallmouth bass do show up in small numbers in this section of river, however bass fishing improves as you get closer to Kimberly (Map 6).

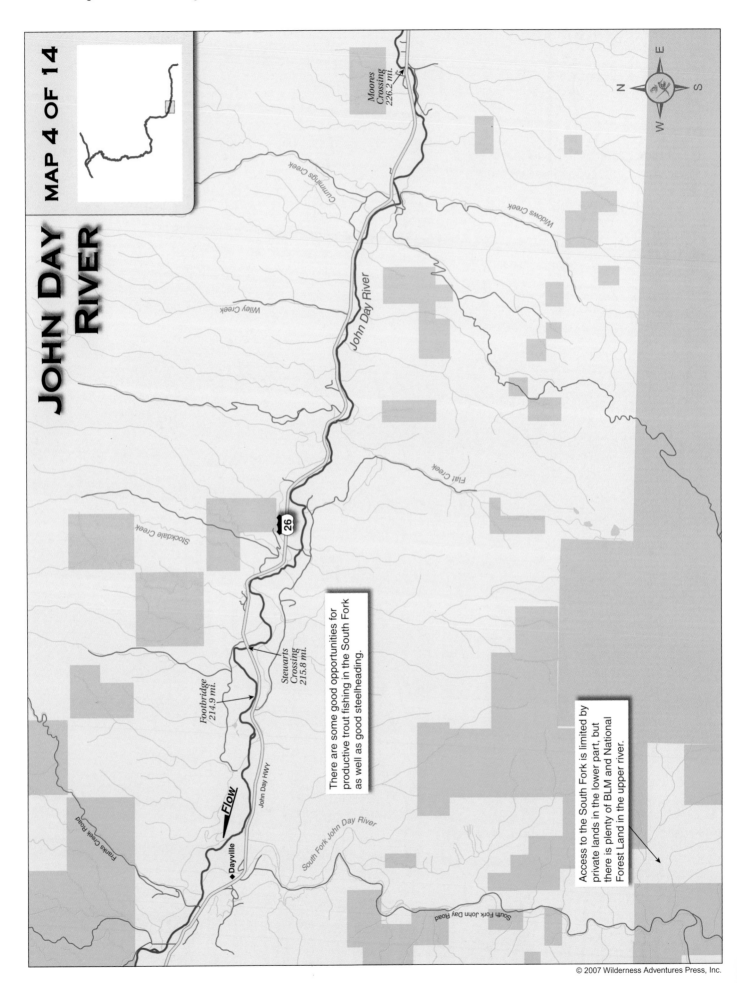

MAP 4 OF 14

JOHN DAY RIVER

Moores Crossing 226.2 mi.

Cummings Creek

Widows Creek

John Day River

Wiley Creek

Flat Creek

Stockdale Creek

26

There are some good opportunities for productive trout fishing in the South Fork as well as good steelheading.

Footbridge 214.9 mi.

Stewarts Crossing 215.8 mi.

John Day Hwy

Flow

Franks Creek Road

Dayville

South Fork John Day River

South Fork John Day Road

Access to the South Fork is limited by private lands in the lower part, but there is plenty of BLM and National Forest Land in the upper river.

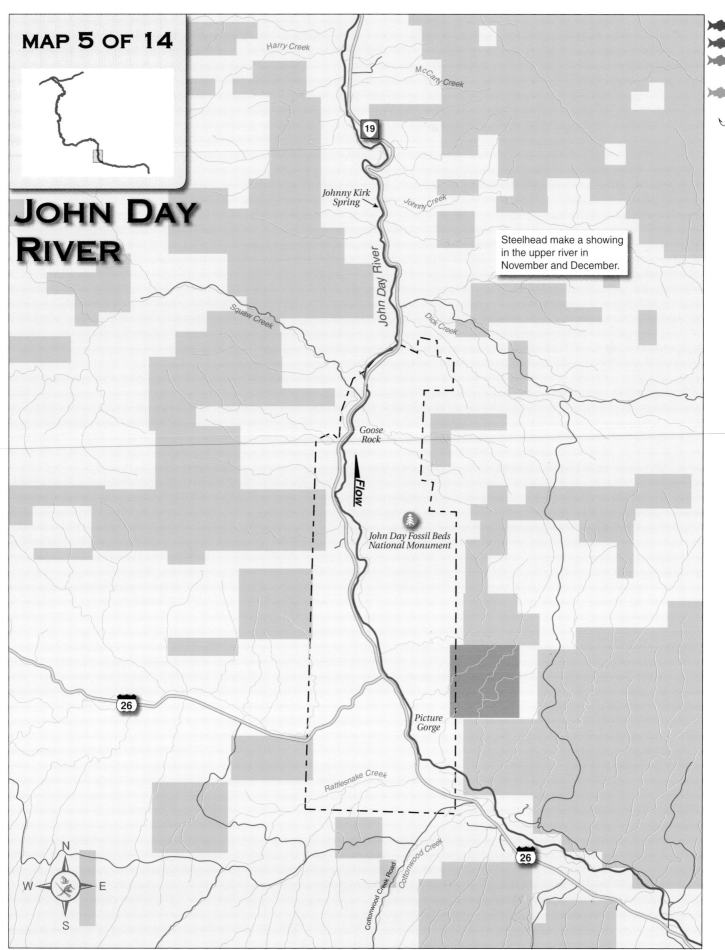

MAP 5 OF 14

JOHN DAY RIVER

Harry Creek

McCarty Creek

19

Johnny Kirk Spring

Johnny Creek

John Day River

Steelhead make a showing in the upper river in November and December.

Squaw Creek

Dick Creek

Goose Rock

Flow

John Day Fossil Beds National Monument

26

Picture Gorge

Rattlesnake Creek

N
W   E
S

Cottonwood Creek Road

Cottonwood Creek

26

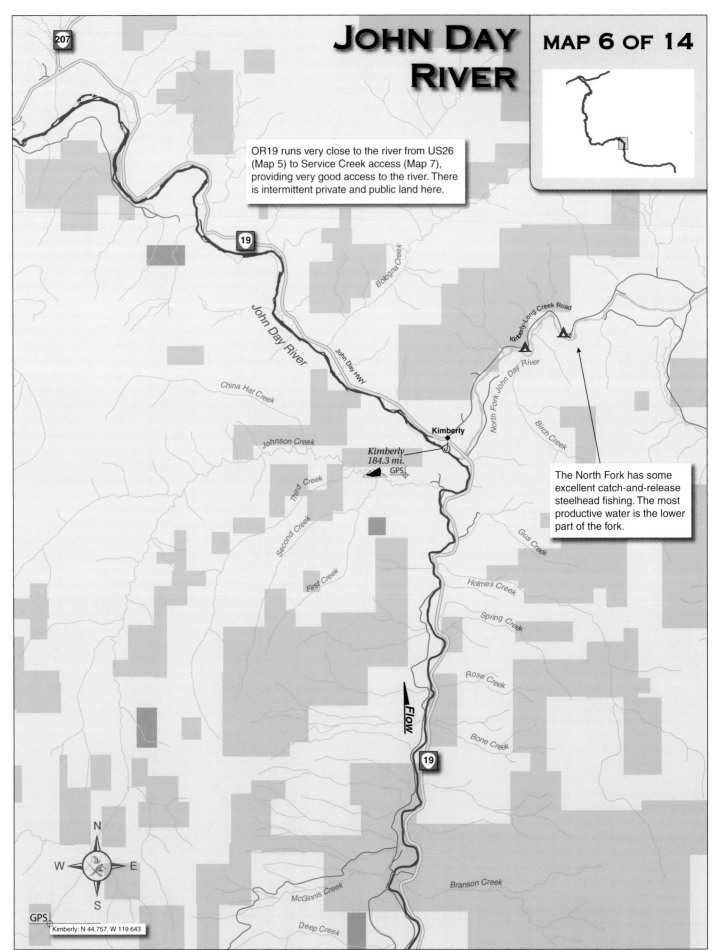

JOHN DAY RIVER

MAP 6 OF 14

OR19 runs very close to the river from US26 (Map 5) to Service Creek access (Map 7), providing very good access to the river. There is intermittent private and public land here.

The North Fork has some excellent catch-and-release steelhead fishing. The most productive water is the lower part of the fork.

Kimberly
184.3 mi.
GPS

Kimberly

Kimberly-Long Creek Road

North Fork John Day River

John Day River

John Day HWY

China Hat Creek

Johnson Creek

Third Creek

Second Creek

First Creek

McGinnis Creek

Deep Creek

Branson Creek

Bone Creek

Rose Creek

Spring Creek

Holmes Creek

Gus Creek

Birch Creek

Bologna Creek

Flow

N
W   E
S

GPS
Kimberly: N 44.757, W 119.643

© 2007 Wilderness Adventures Press, Inc.

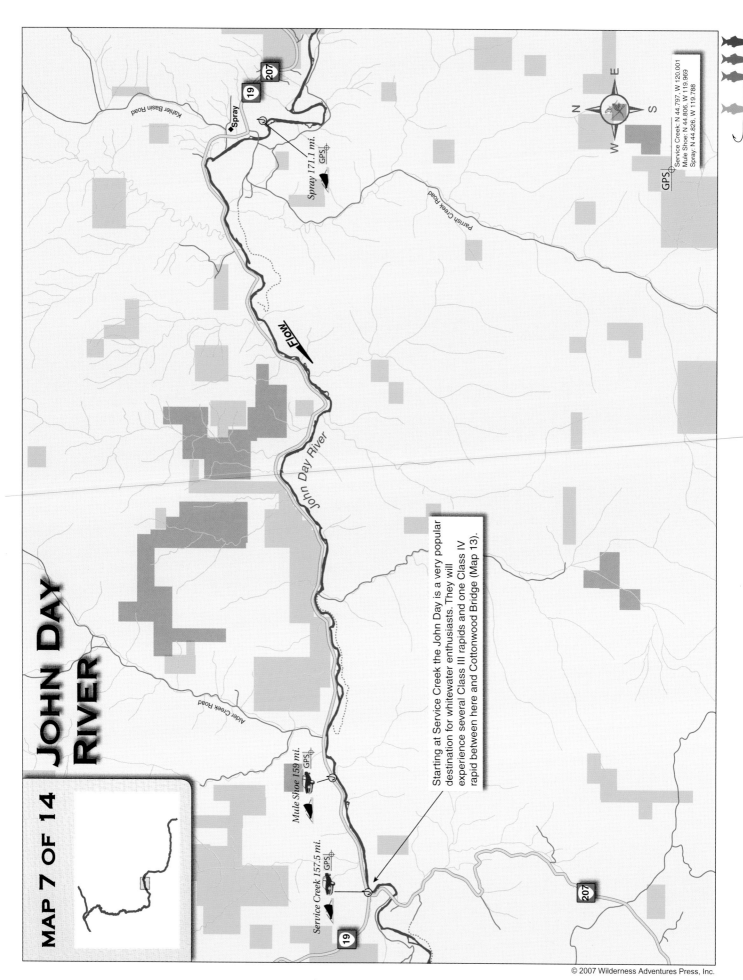

MAP 7 OF 14

JOHN DAY
RIVER

John Day River

Kahler Basin Road

Spray

19
207

Spray 171.1 mi. GPS

Parrish Creek Road

FLOW

Alder Creek Road

Mule Shoe 159 mi. GPS

Service Creek 157.5 mi. GPS

Starting at Service Creek the John Day is a very popular destination for whitewater enthusiasts. They will experience several Class III rapids and one Class IV rapid between here and Cottonwood Bridge (Map 13).

19

207

Service Creek: N 44.797, W 120.001
Mule Shoe: N 44.806, W 119.969
Spray: N 44.826, W 119.788

GPS

N E S W

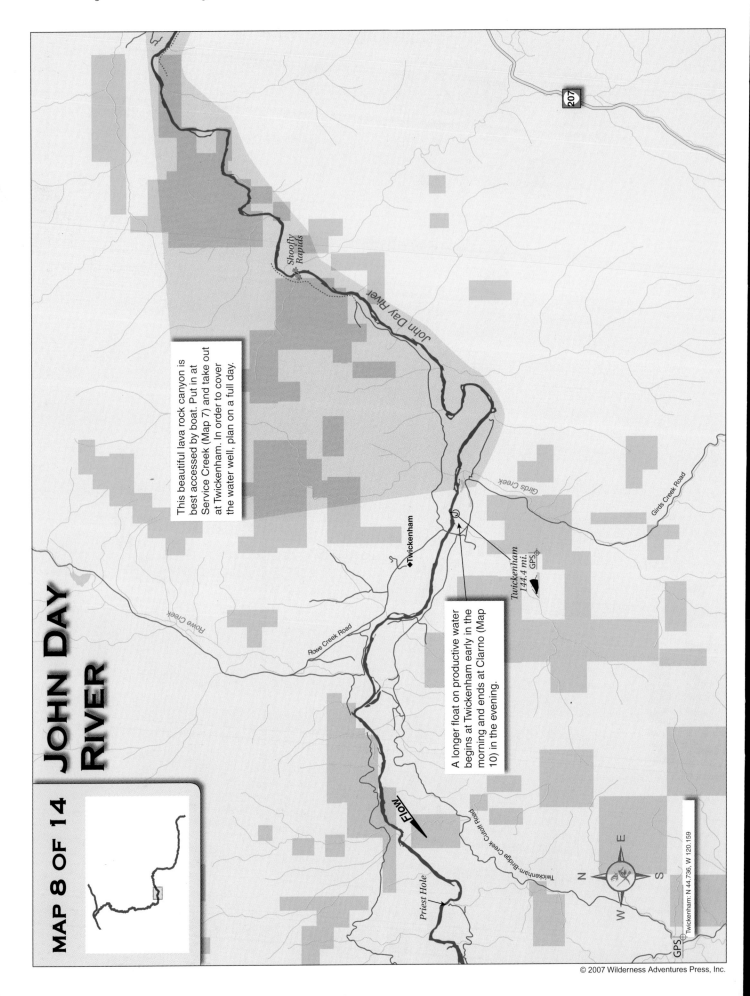

MAP 8 OF 14

JOHN DAY RIVER

This beautiful lava rock canyon is best accessed by boat. Put in at Service Creek (Map 7) and take out at Twickenham. In order to cover the water well, plan on a full day.

A longer float on productive water begins at Twickenham early in the morning and ends at Clarno (Map 10) in the evening.

Shoofly Rapids

John Day River

Twickenham

Rowe Creek

Rowe Creek Road

Girds Creek

Girds Creek Road

Twickenham 144.4 mi. GPS

FLOW

Priest Hole

Twickenham-Bridge Creek Cutoff Road

N
E
W
S

GPS Twickenham: N 44.736, W 120.159

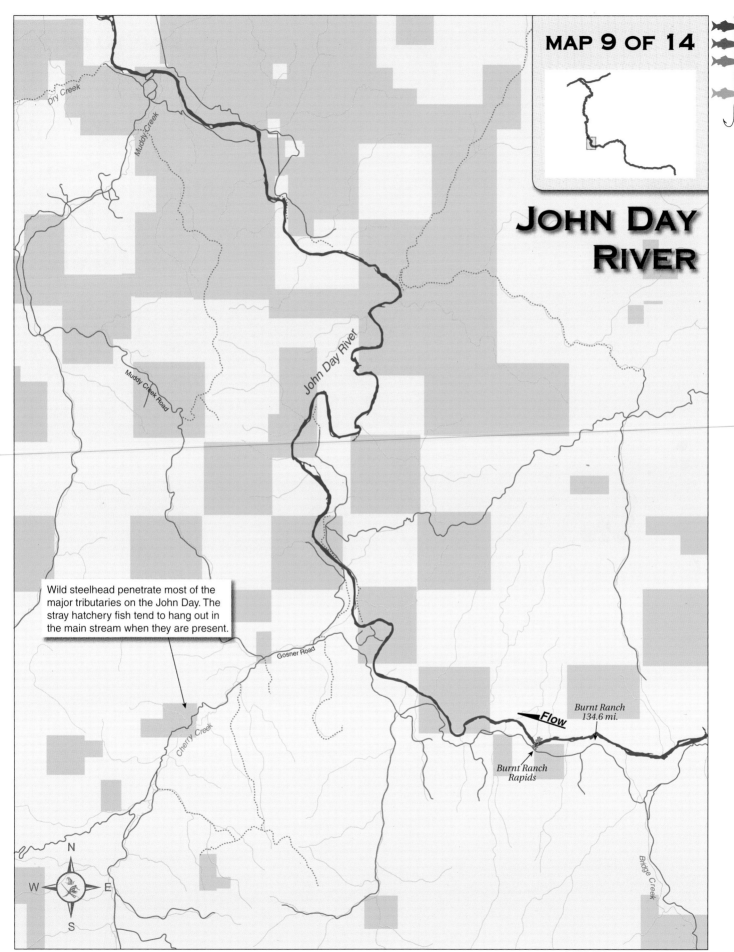

MAP **9** OF **14**

JOHN DAY RIVER

John Day River

Dry Creek

Muddy Creek

Muddy Creek Road

Wild steelhead penetrate most of the major tributaries on the John Day. The stray hatchery fish tend to hang out in the main stream when they are present.

Cherry Creek

Gosner Road

Flow

Burnt Ranch 134.6 mi.

Burnt Ranch Rapids

Bridge Creek

N
W   E
S

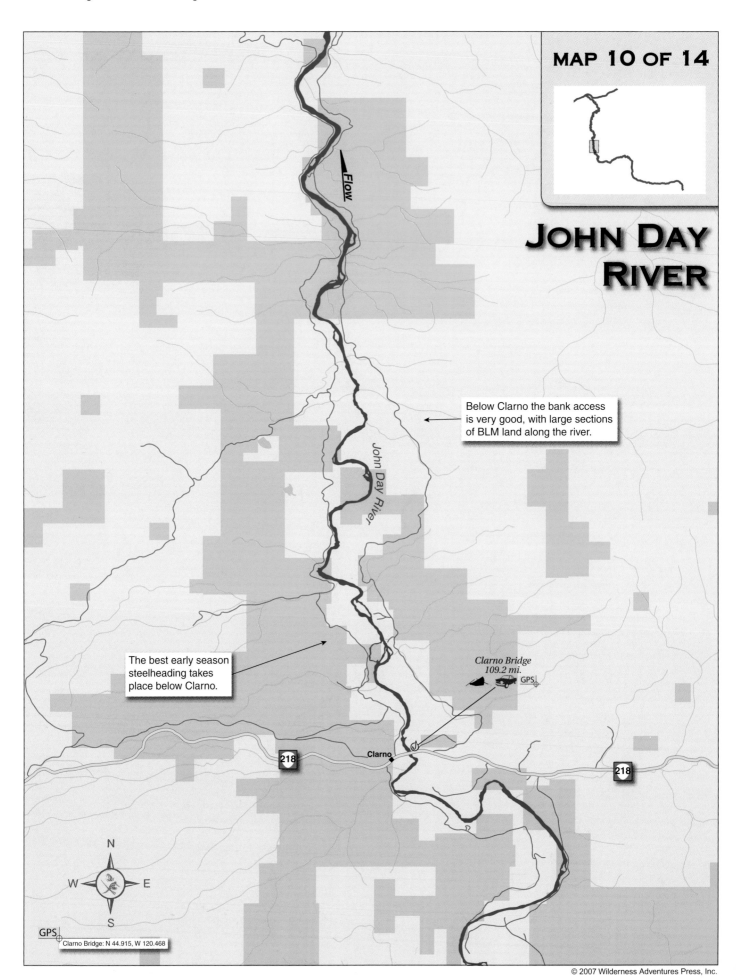

MAP 10 OF 14

JOHN DAY RIVER

Flow

Below Clarno the bank access is very good, with large sections of BLM land along the river.

John Day River

The best early season steelheading takes place below Clarno.

Clarno Bridge 109.2 mi.
GPS

218

Clarno

218

N
W   E
S

GPS
Clarno Bridge: N 44.915, W 120.468

© 2007 Wilderness Adventures Press, Inc.

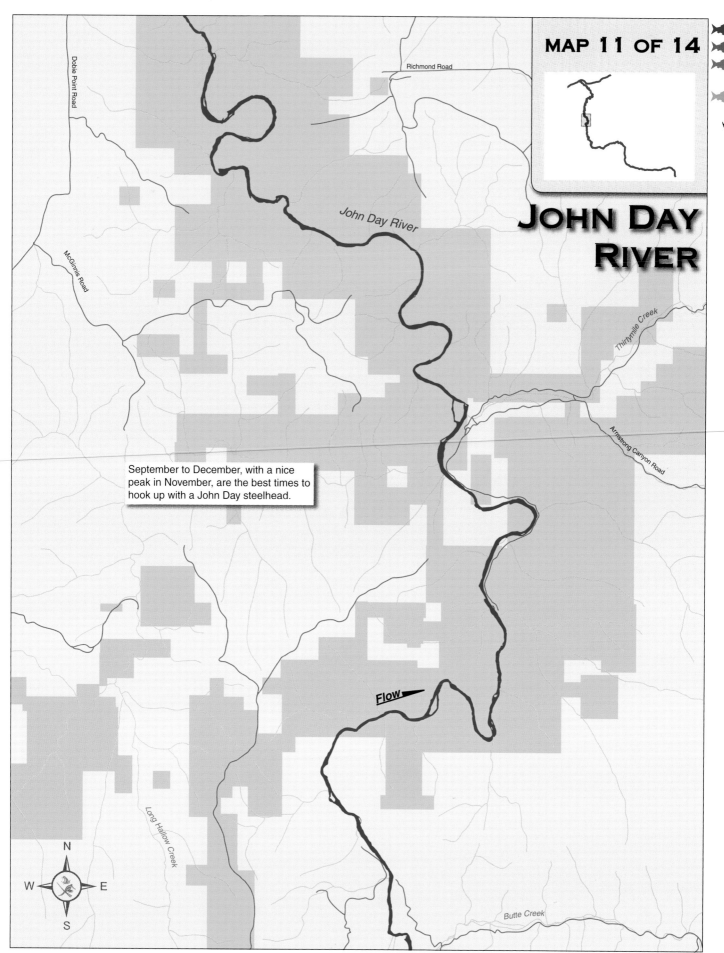

MAP **11** OF **14**

JOHN DAY RIVER

Richmond Road

John Day River

Thirtymile Creek

Armstrong Canyon Road

Dobie Point Road

McGinnis Road

September to December, with a nice peak in November, are the best times to hook up with a John Day steelhead.

Flow

Long Hallow Creek

Butte Creek

N
W E
S

© 2007 Wilderness Adventures Press, Inc.

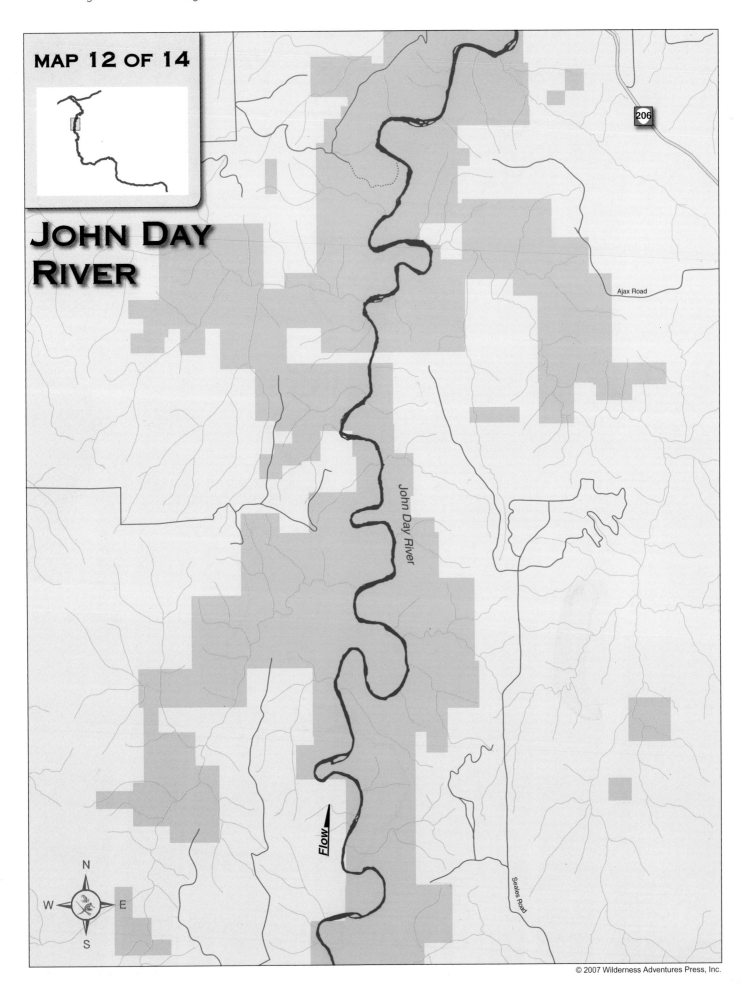

MAP 12 OF 14

JOHN DAY RIVER

206

Ajax Road

John Day River

Flow

Seales Road

N
W E
S

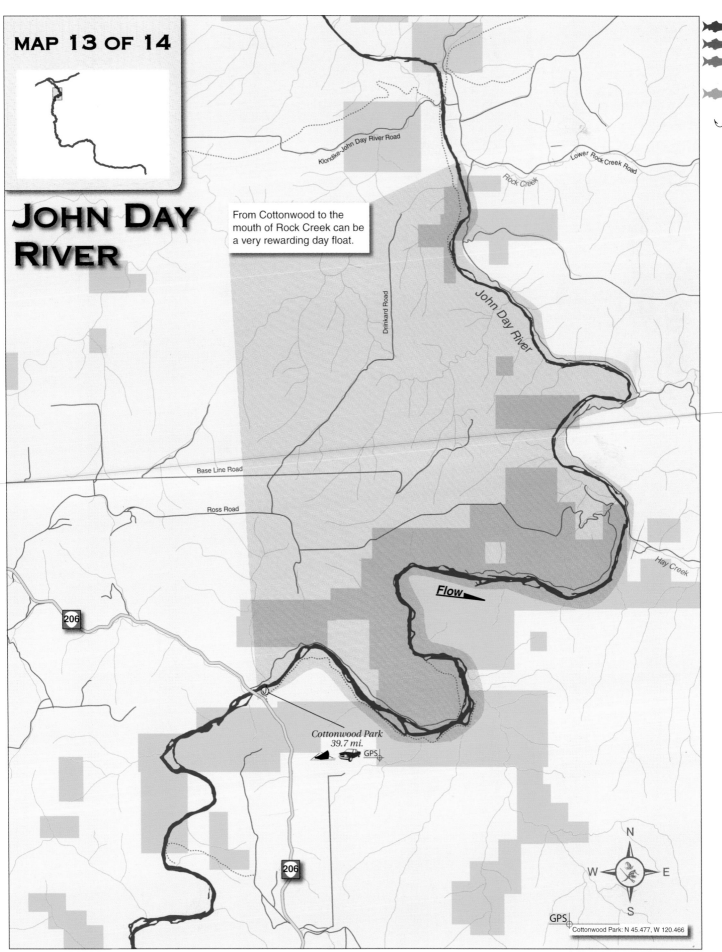

MAP 13 OF 14

JOHN DAY RIVER

Klondike-John Day River Road

Lower Rock Creek Road

Rock Creek

From Cottonwood to the
mouth of Rock Creek can be
a very rewarding day float.

Drinkard Road

John Day River

Base Line Road

Ross Road

Hay Creek

Flow

206

Cottonwood Park
39.7 mi.
GPS

206

N
W   E
S

GPS
Cottonwood Park: N 45.477, W 120.466

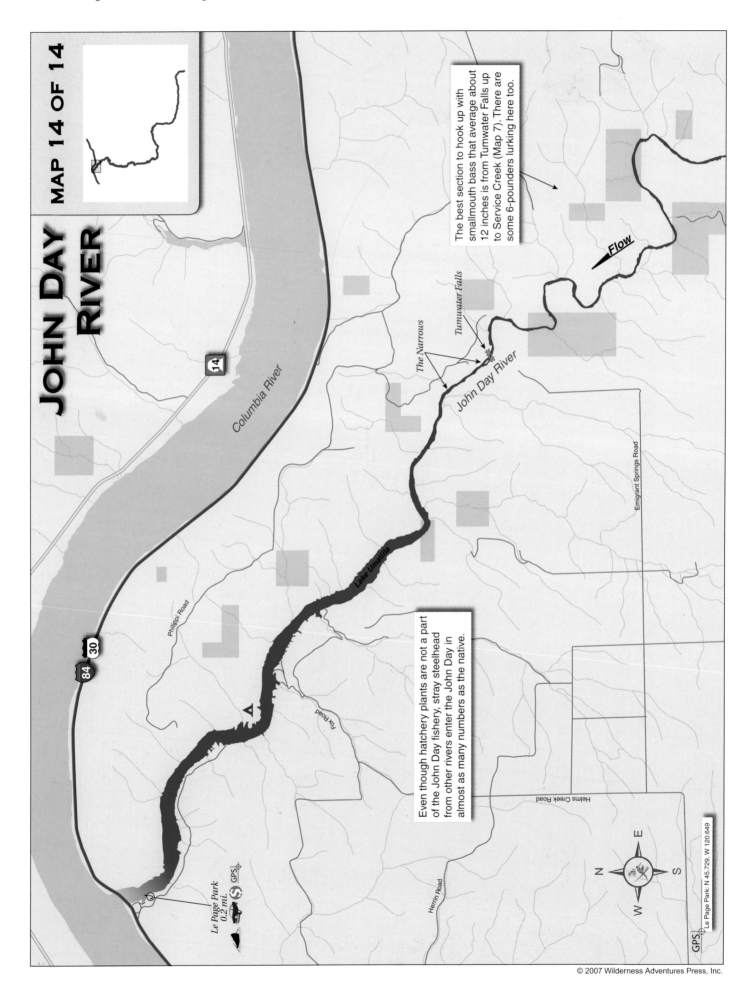

MAP 14 OF 14

JOHN DAY RIVER

The best section to hook up with smallmouth bass that average about 12 inches is from Tumwater Falls up to Service Creek (Map 7). There are some 6-pounders lurking here too.

Flow

Tumwater Falls

The Narrows

John Day River

Columbia River

14

Emigrant Springs Road

30

84

Phillippi Road

Lake Umatilla

Fox Road

Even though hatchery plants are not a part of the John Day fishery, stray steelhead from other rivers enter the John Day in almost as many numbers as the native.

Helms Creek Road

Herrin Road

Le Page Park
0.2 mi.

GPS

N
W   E
S

GPS | Le Page Park: N 45.729, W 120.649

© 2007 Wilderness Adventures Press, Inc.

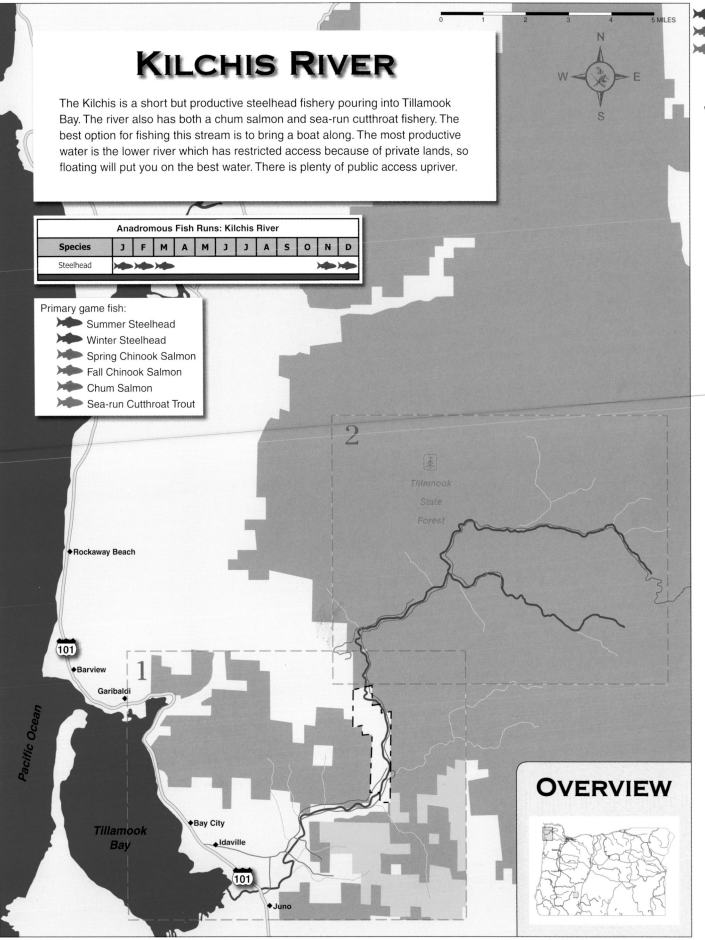

KILCHIS RIVER

The Kilchis is a short but productive steelhead fishery pouring into Tillamook Bay. The river also has both a chum salmon and sea-run cutthroat fishery. The best option for fishing this stream is to bring a boat along. The most productive water is the lower river which has restricted access because of private lands, so floating will put you on the best water. There is plenty of public access upriver.

Anadromous Fish Runs: Kilchis River												
Species	J	F	M	A	M	J	J	A	S	O	N	D
Steelhead	🐟	🐟	🐟	🐟							🐟	🐟

Primary game fish:
- Summer Steelhead
- Winter Steelhead
- Spring Chinook Salmon
- Fall Chinook Salmon
- Chum Salmon
- Sea-run Cutthroat Trout

2

Tillamook State Forest

♦Rockaway Beach

1

♦Barview

Garibaldi

Pacific Ocean

Tillamook Bay

♦Bay City

♦Idaville

101

♦Juno

OVERVIEW

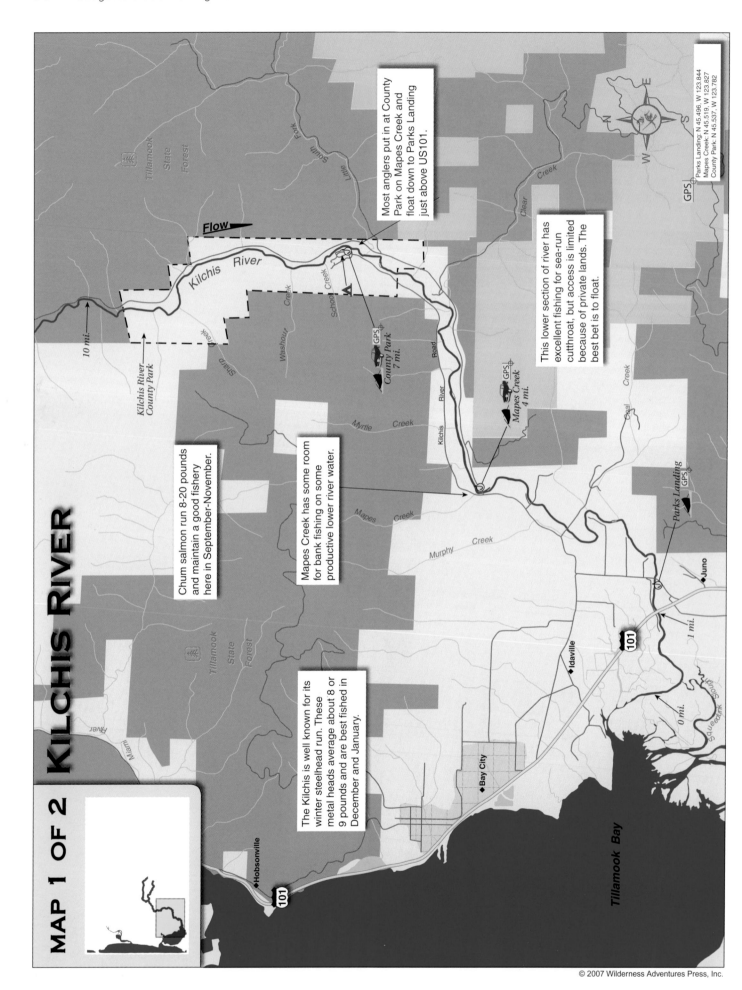

MAP 1 OF 2   KILCHIS RIVER

Most anglers put in at County Park on Mapes Creek and float down to Parks Landing just above US101.

This lower section of river has excellent fishing for sea-run cutthroat, but access is limited because of private lands. The best bet is to float.

Chum salmon run 8-20 pounds and maintain a good fishery here in September-November.

Mapes Creek has some room for bank fishing on some productive lower river water.

The Kilchis is well known for its winter steelhead run. These metal heads average about 8 or 9 pounds and are best fished in December and January.

Flow

Kilchis River

Tillamook State Forest

Kilchis River County Park

10 mi.

Sharp Creek

Washout Creek

South Fork

Little Creek

Clear Creek

School Creek

GPS County Park 7 mi.

Myrtle Creek

Kilchis River Road

GPS Mapes Creek 4 mi.

Mapes Creek

Murphy Creek

Coal Creek

Parks Landing GPS

Juno

1 mi.

0 mi.

Squeedunk Slough

Idaville

101

Bay City

Tillamook State Forest

Miami River

Hobsonville

101

Tillamook Bay

GPS
Parks Landing: N 45.496, W 123.844
Mapes Creek: N 45.519, W 123.827
County Park: N 45.537, W 123.782

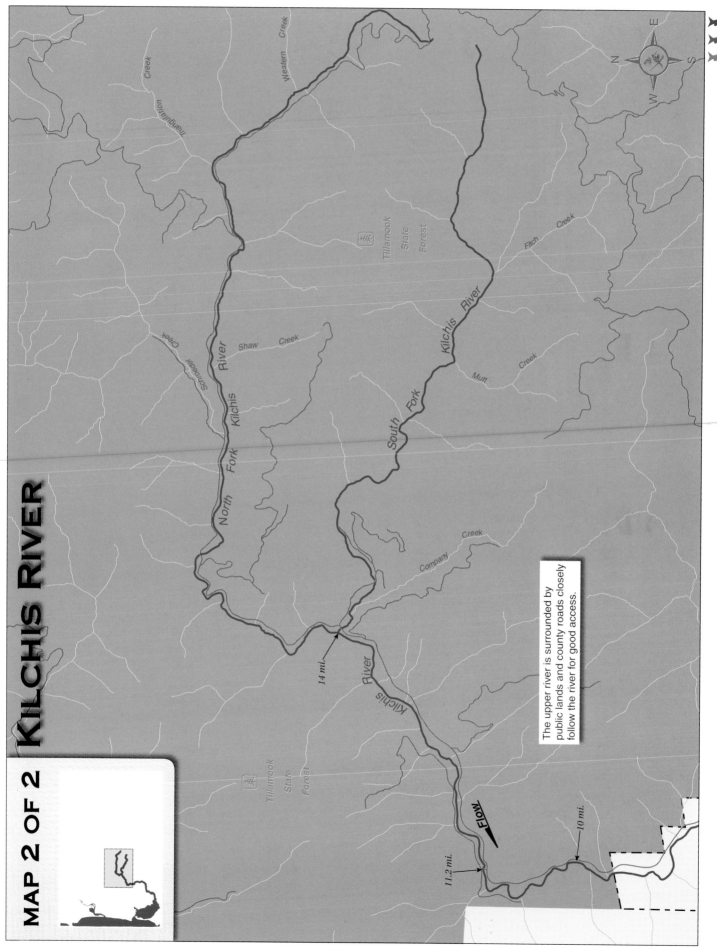

KILCHIS RIVER

MAP 2 OF 2

The upper river is surrounded by
public lands and county roads closely
follow the river for good access.

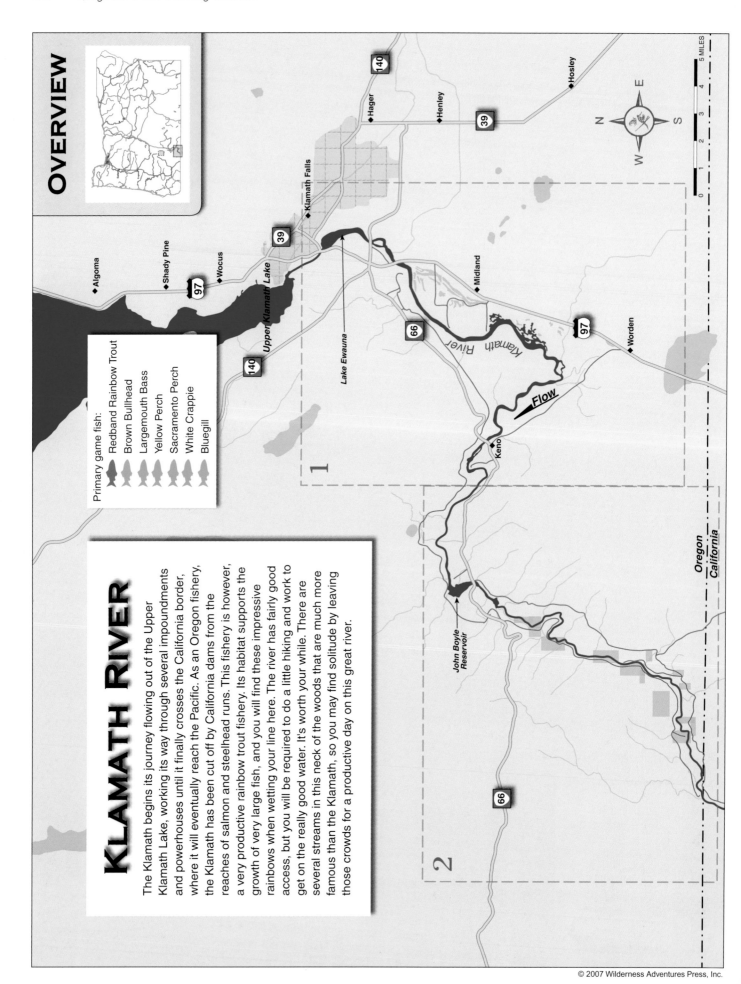

OVERVIEW

KLAMATH RIVER

The Klamath begins its journey flowing out of the Upper Klamath Lake, working its way through several impoundments and powerhouses until it finally crosses the California border, where it will eventually reach the Pacific. As an Oregon fishery, the Klamath has been cut off by California dams from the reaches of salmon and steelhead runs. This fishery is however, a very productive rainbow trout fishery. Its habitat supports the growth of very large fish, and you will find these impressive rainbows when wetting your line here. The river has fairly good access, but you will be required to do a little hiking and work to get on the really good water. It's worth your while. There are several streams in this neck of the woods that are much more famous than the Klamath, so you may find solitude by leaving those crowds for a productive day on this great river.

Primary game fish:
Redband Rainbow Trout
Brown Bullhead
Largemouth Bass
Yellow Perch
Sacramento Perch
White Crappie
Bluegill

Algoma
Shady Pine
Wocus
Upper Klamath Lake
Klamath Falls
Hager
Henley
Hosley
Lake Ewauna
Midland
Klamath River
Worden
Flow
Keno
John Boyle Reservoir
Oregon
California

1

2

N
E
S
W

0 1 2 3 4 5 MILES

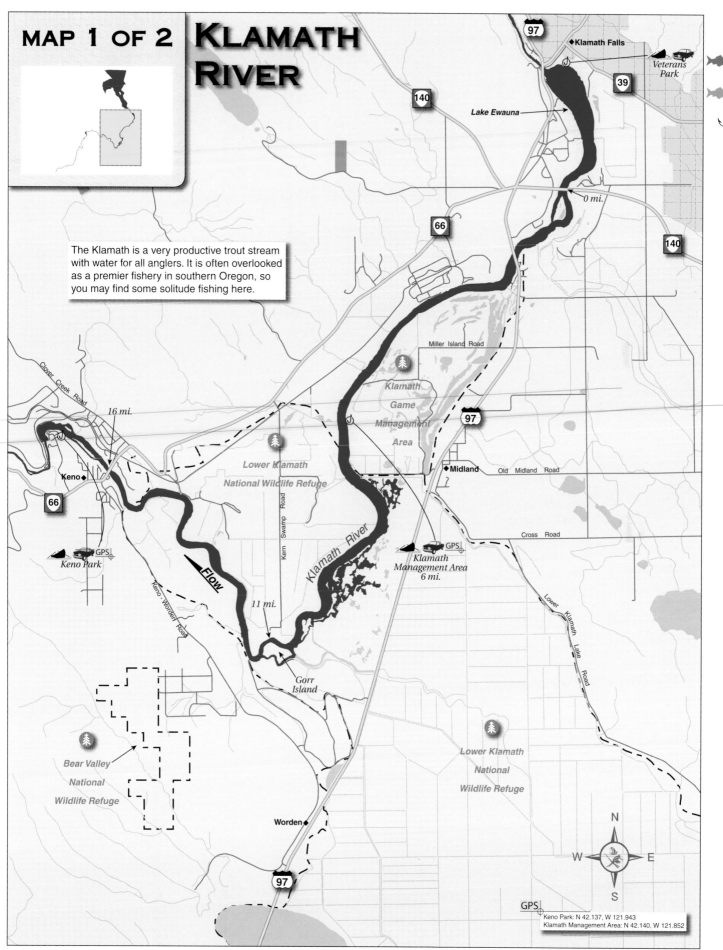

MAP 1 OF 2 KLAMATH RIVER

The Klamath is a very productive trout stream with water for all anglers. It is often overlooked as a premier fishery in southern Oregon, so you may find some solitude fishing here.

Klamath Falls

Veterans Park

Lake Ewauna

0 mi.

Miller Island Road

Klamath Game Management Area

Midland

Old Midland Road

Clover Creek Road

16 mi.

Lower Klamath National Wildlife Refuge

Kern Swamp Road

Keno

Keno Park

GPS

Keno-Worden Road

Flow

Klamath River

11 mi.

Cross Road

Klamath Management Area 6 mi.

GPS

Lower Klamath Lake Road

Gorr Island

Bear Valley National Wildlife Refuge

Lower Klamath National Wildlife Refuge

Worden

N
W   E
S

GPS

Keno Park: N 42.137, W 121.943
Klamath Management Area: N 42.140, W 121.852

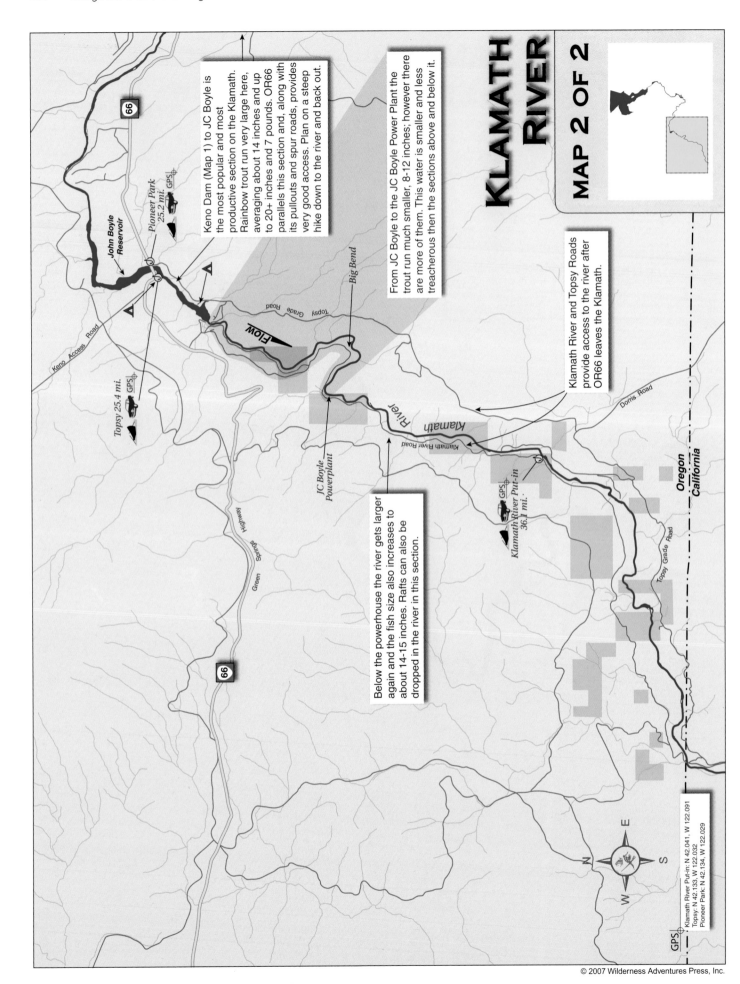

KLAMATH RIVER
MAP 2 OF 2

Keno Dam (Map 1) to JC Boyle is the most popular and most productive section on the Klamath. Rainbow trout run very large here, averaging about 14 inches and up to 20+ inches and 7 pounds. OR66 parallels this section and, along with its pullouts and spur roads, provides very good access. Plan on a steep hike down to the river and back out.

From JC Boyle to the JC Boyle Power Plant the trout run much smaller, 8-12 inches; however there are more of them. This water is smaller and less treacherous then the sections above and below it.

Klamath River and Topsy Roads provide access to the river after OR66 leaves the Klamath.

Below the powerhouse the river gets larger again and the fish size also increases to about 14-15 inches. Rafts can also be dropped in the river in this section.

John Boyle Reservoir

Pioneer Park 25.2 mi.

Topsy 25.4 mi.

Big Bend

Topsy Grade Road

Flow

JC Boyle Powerplant

Klamath River

Klamath River Road

Dorris Road

Green Springs Highway

Highway

Klamath River Put-in 36.1 mi.

Keno Access Road

Oregon
California

Topsy Grade Road

GPS
Klamath River Put-in: N 42.041, W 122.091
Topsy: N 42.133, W 122.032
Pioneer Park: N 42.134, W 122.029

66

N E W S

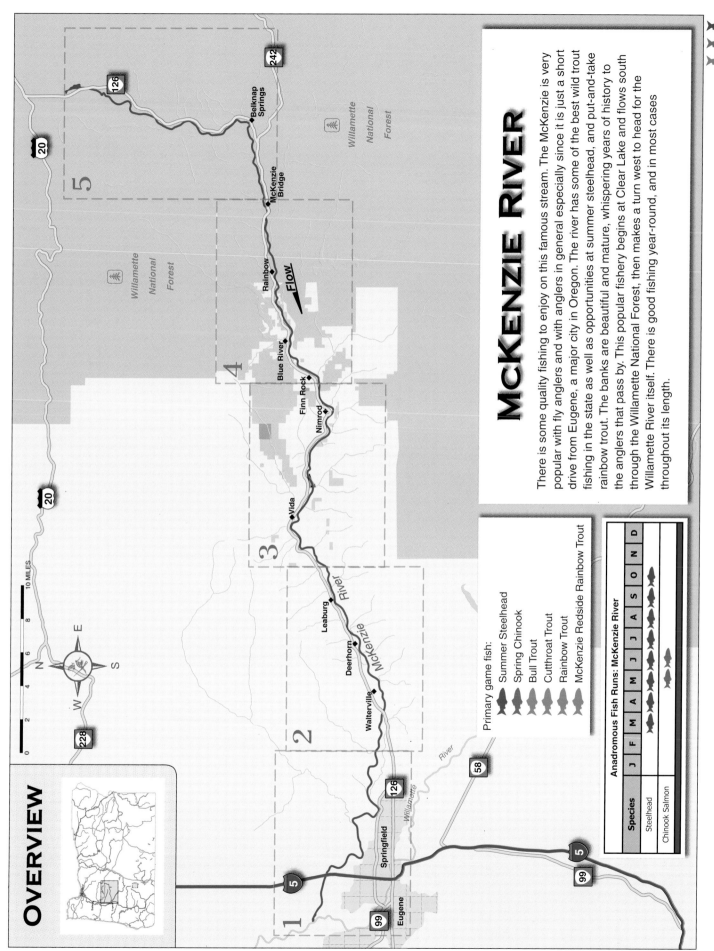

McKenzie River

There is some quality fishing to enjoy on this famous stream. The McKenzie is very popular with fly anglers and with anglers in general especially since it is just a short drive from Eugene, a major city in Oregon. The river has some of the best wild trout fishing in the state as well as opportunities at summer steelhead, and put-and-take rainbow trout. The banks are beautiful and mature, whispering years of history to the anglers that pass by. This popular fishery begins at Clear Lake and flows south through the Willamette National Forest, then makes a turn west to head for the Willamette River itself. There is good fishing year-round, and in most cases throughout its length.

Primary game fish:
Summer Steelhead
Spring Chinook
Bull Trout
Cutthroat Trout
Rainbow Trout
McKenzie Redside Rainbow Trout

Anadromous Fish Runs: McKenzie River

Species	J	F	M	A	M	J	J	A	S	O	N	D
Steelhead												
Chinook Salmon												

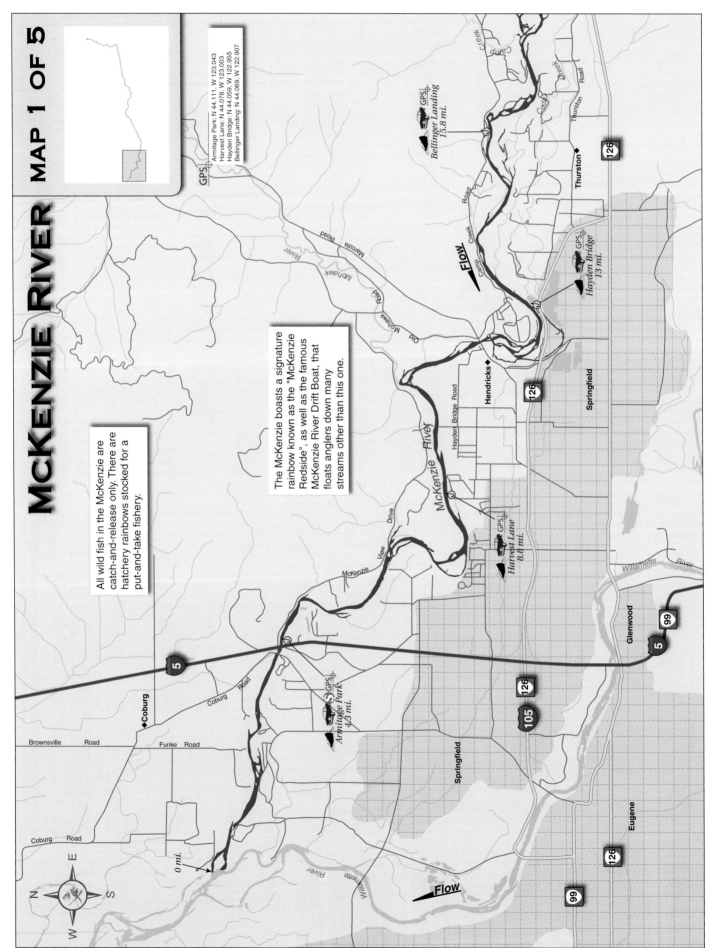

MAP 1 OF 5

McKENZIE RIVER

GPS

Armitage Park: N 44.111, W 123.043
Harvest Lane: N 44.078, W 123.003
Hayden Bridge: N 44.059, W 122.955
Bellinger Landing: N 44.069, W 122.907

All wild fish in the McKenzie are catch-and-release only. There are hatchery rainbows stocked for a put-and-take fishery.

The McKenzie boasts a signature rainbow known as the "McKenzie Redside", as well as the famous McKenzie River Drift Boat, that floats anglers down many streams other than this one.

GPS
Bellinger Landing
15.8 mi.

Thurston

126

FLOW

GPS
Hayden Bridge
13 mi.

Springfield

126

Hendricks ◆

Hayden Bridge Road

McKenzie River

GPS
Harvest Lane
8.8 mi.

Willamette River

Glenwood

5

99

126

105

Springfield

GPS
Armitage Park
4.3 mi.

S

Eugene

126

99

5

◆ Coburg

Coburg Road

Brownsville Road

Funke Road

Coburg Road

0 mi.

Willamette River

Flow

N
E
W
S

Marcola Road

Mohawk Road

Old McKenzie

Camp Creek Road

Cadit Creek

Thurston Road

McKenzie View Drive

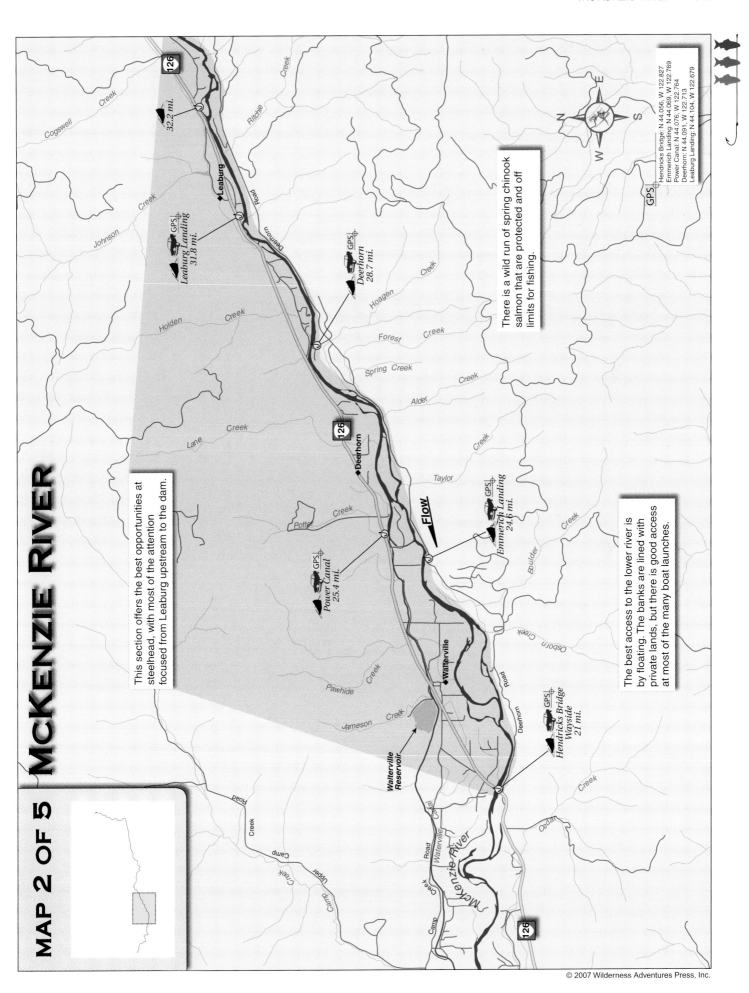

McKenzie River

MAP 2 OF 5

This section offers the best opportunities at steelhead, with most of the attention focused from Leaburg upstream to the dam.

There is a wild run of spring chinook salmon that are protected and off limits for fishing.

The best access to the lower river is by floating. The banks are lined with private lands, but there is good access at most of the many boat launches.

32.2 mi.

Leaburg Landing
31.8 mi.
GPS

Leaburg

Deerhorn
28.7 mi.
GPS

Power Canal
25.4 mi.
GPS

Deerhorn

FLOW

Emmerich Landing
24.6 mi.
GPS

Taylor

Walterville

Hendricks Bridge Wayside
21 mi.
GPS

Walterville Reservoir

McKenzie River

GPS

Hendricks Bridge: N 44.056, W 122.827
Emmerich Landing: N 44.069, W 122.769
Power Canal: N 44.076, W 122.764
Deerhorn: N 44.091, W 122.713
Leaburg Landing: N 44.104, W 122.679

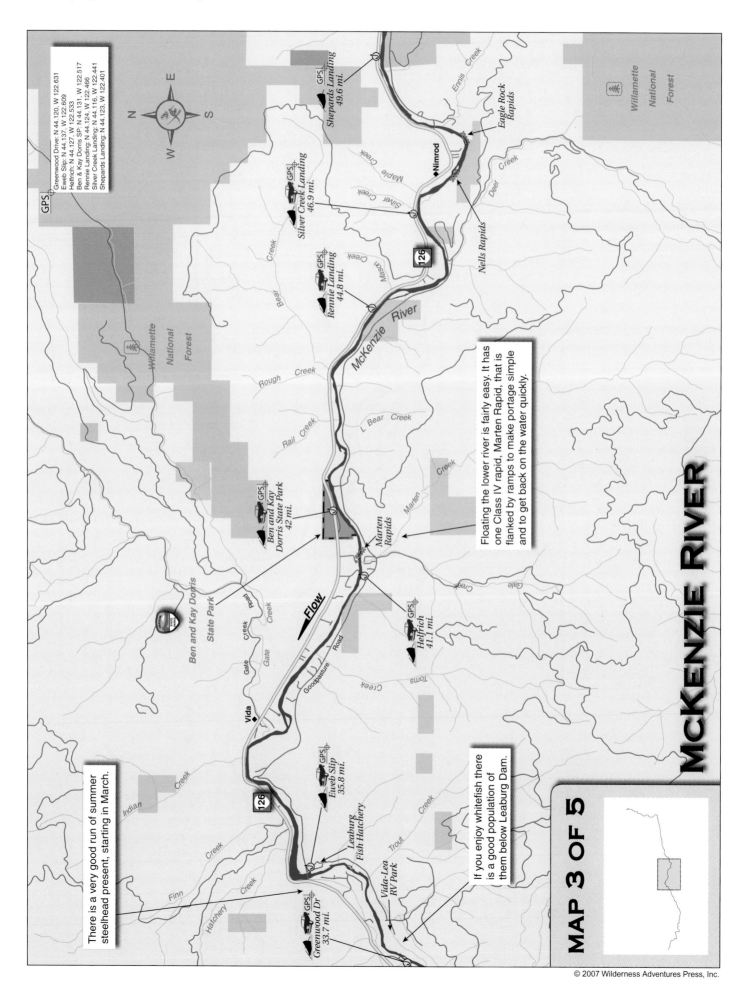

GPS
Greenwood Drive: N 44.120, W 122.631
Eweb Slip: N 44.137, W 122.609
Helfrich: N 44.127, W 122.533
Ben & Kay Dorris SP: N 44.131, W 122.517
Rennie Landing: N 44.124, W 122.466
Silver Creek Landing: N 44.116, W 122.441
Shepards Landing: N 44.123, W 122.401

Shepards Landing
49.6 mi.

Eagle Rock Rapids

◆Nimrod

Silver Creek Landing
46.9 mi.

Nells Rapids

Rennie Landing
44.8 mi.

McKenzie River

Floating the lower river is fairly easy. It has one Class IV rapid, Marten Rapid, that is flanked by ramps to make portage simple and to get back on the water quickly.

Ben and Kay Dorris State Park
42 mi.

Marten Rapids

Ben and Kay Dorris State Park

Flow

Helfrich
41.1 mi.

Vida◆

If you enjoy whitefish there is a good population of them below Leaburg Dam.

There is a very good run of summer steelhead present, starting in March.

Eweb Slip
35.8 mi.

Leaburg Fish Hatchery

Vida-Lea RV Park

Greenwood Dr
33.7 mi.

McKENZIE RIVER

MAP 3 OF 5

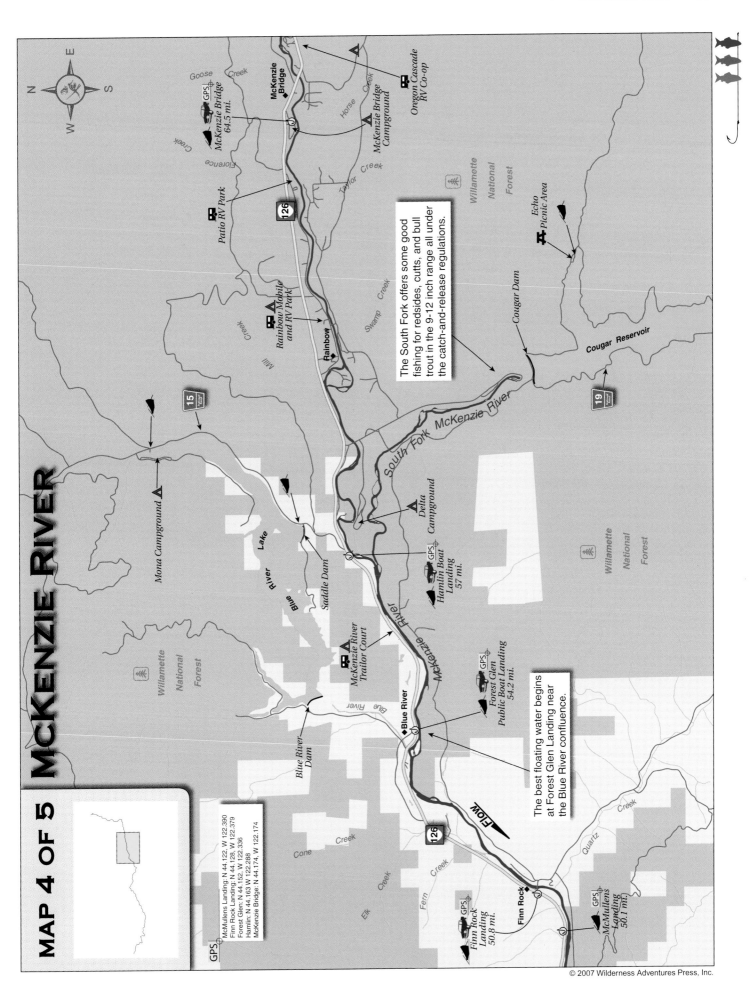

McKenzie River

MAP 4 OF 5

© 2007 Wilderness Adventures Press, Inc.

GPS

McMullens Landing: N 44.122, W 122.390
Finn Rock Landing: N 44.128, W 122.379
Forest Glen: N 44.152, W 122.336
Hamlin: N 44.163 W 122.288
McKenzie Bridge: N 44.174, W 122.174

Goose Creek

McKenzie Bridge

McKenzie Bridge
64.5 mi.

Horse Creek

Oregon Cascade
RV Co-op

McKenzie Bridge
Campground

Florence Creek

Patio RV Park

Taylor Creek

126

Willamette
National
Forest

Echo
Picnic Area

Swamp Creek

Rainbow Mobile
and RV Park

Rainbow

Cougar Dam

Cougar Reservoir

The South Fork offers some good
fishing for redsides, cutts, and bull
trout in the 9-12 inch range all under
the catch-and-release regulations.

South Fork McKenzie River

15

19

Mill Creek

Mona Campground

Lake

Blue River

Saddle Dam

Delta
Campground

Hamlin Boat
Landing
57 mi.

Willamette
National
Forest

McKenzie River
Trailor Court

McKenzie River

Blue River
Dam

Blue River

Blue River

Forest Glen
Public Boat Landing
54.2 mi.

The best floating water begins
at Forest Glen Landing near
the Blue River confluence.

FLOW

126

Cone Creek

Quartz Creek

Elk Creek

Fern Creek

Finn Rock
Landing
50.8 mi.

Finn Rock

McMullens
Landing
50.1 mi.

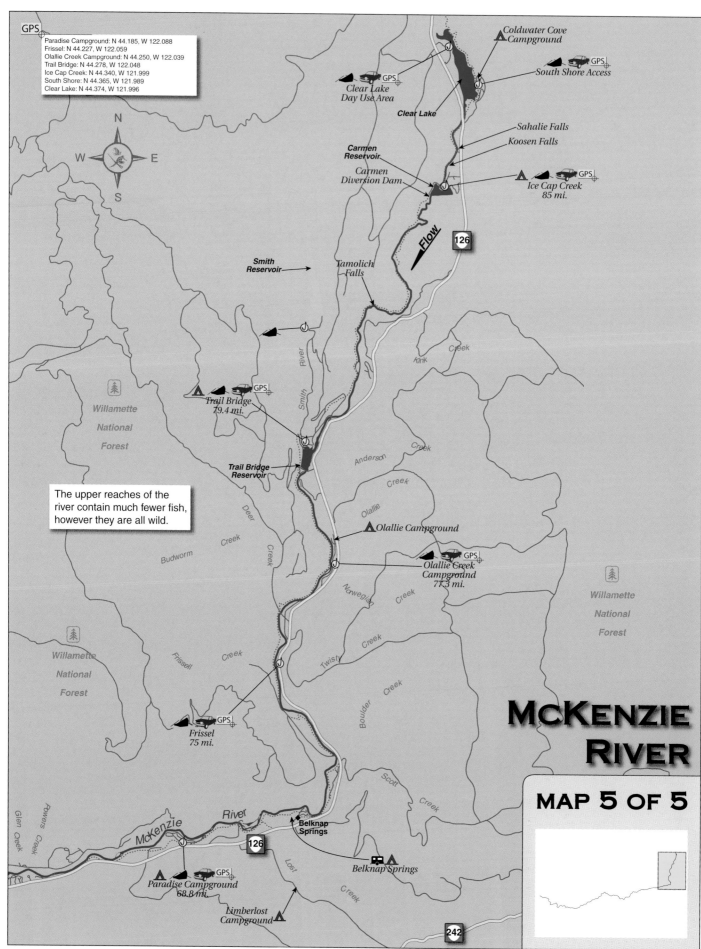

GPS

Paradise Campground: N 44.185, W 122.088
Frissel: N 44.227, W 122.059
Olallie Creek Campground: N 44.250, W 122.039
Trail Bridge: N 44.278, W 122.048
Ice Cap Creek: N 44.340, W 121.999
South Shore: N 44.365, W 121.989
Clear Lake: N 44.374, W 121.996

Coldwater Cove
Campground

GPS

South Shore Access

Clear Lake
Day Use Area

Clear Lake

Sahalie Falls

Koosen Falls

**Carmen
Reservoir**

Carmen
Diversion Dam

GPS

Ice Cap Creek
85 mi.

Flow

126

Smith
Reservoir

Tamolich
Falls

Kink   Creek

Smith   River

Trail Bridge
79.4 mi.

GPS

Willamette
National
Forest

Anderson   Creek

Trail Bridge
Reservoir

Olallie   Creek

The upper reaches of the
river contain much fewer fish,
however they are all wild.

Olallie Campground

Deer   Creek

Olallie Creek
Campground
77.3 mi.

GPS

Budworm   Creek

Willamette
National
Forest

Norwegian   Creek

Twisty   Creek

Willamette
National
Forest

Frissell   Creek

Boulder   Creek

Frissel
75 mi.

GPS

MCKENZIE
RIVER

Scott   Creek

McKenzie   River

Belknap
Springs

MAP 5 OF 5

126

Glen Creek

Powers Creek

Lost   Creek

Belknap Springs

Paradise Campground
68.8 mi.

GPS

Limberlost
Campground

242

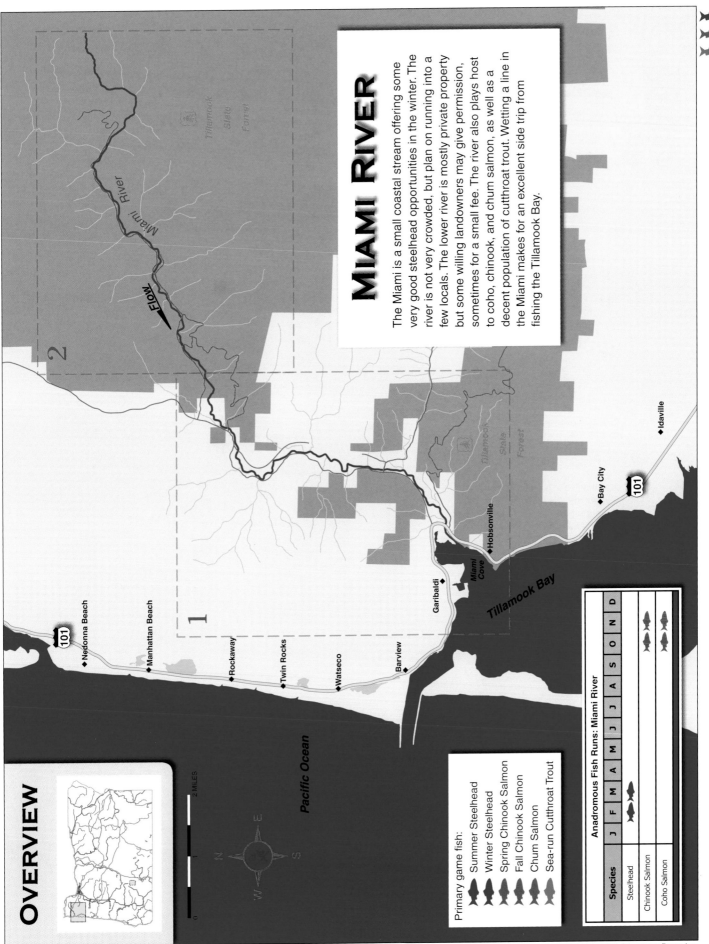

MIAMI RIVER

The Miami is a small coastal stream offering some very good steelhead opportunities in the winter. The river is not very crowded, but plan on running into a few locals. The lower river is mostly private property but some willing landowners may give permission, sometimes for a small fee. The river also plays host to coho, chinook, and chum salmon, as well as a decent population of cutthroat trout. Wetting a line in the Miami makes for an excellent side trip from fishing the Tillamook Bay.

Primary game fish:
- Summer Steelhead
- Winter Steelhead
- Spring Chinook Salmon
- Fall Chinook Salmon
- Chum Salmon
- Sea-run Cutthroat Trout

Species	J	F	M	A	M	J	J	A	S	O	N	D
Steelhead												
Chinook Salmon												
Coho Salmon												

Anadromous Fish Runs: Miami River

OVERVIEW

MAP 1 OF 2 MIAMI RIVER

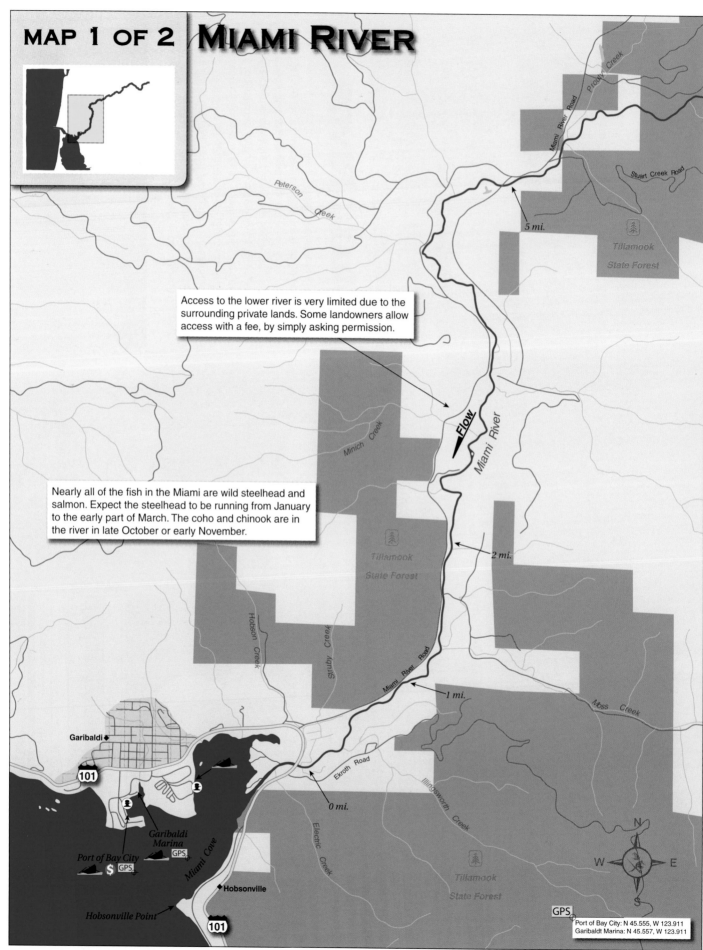

Access to the lower river is very limited due to the surrounding private lands. Some landowners allow access with a fee, by simply asking permission.

Nearly all of the fish in the Miami are wild steelhead and salmon. Expect the steelhead to be running from January to the early part of March. The coho and chinook are in the river in late October or early November.

Port of Bay City: N 45.555, W 123.911
Garibaldt Marina: N 45.557, W 123.911

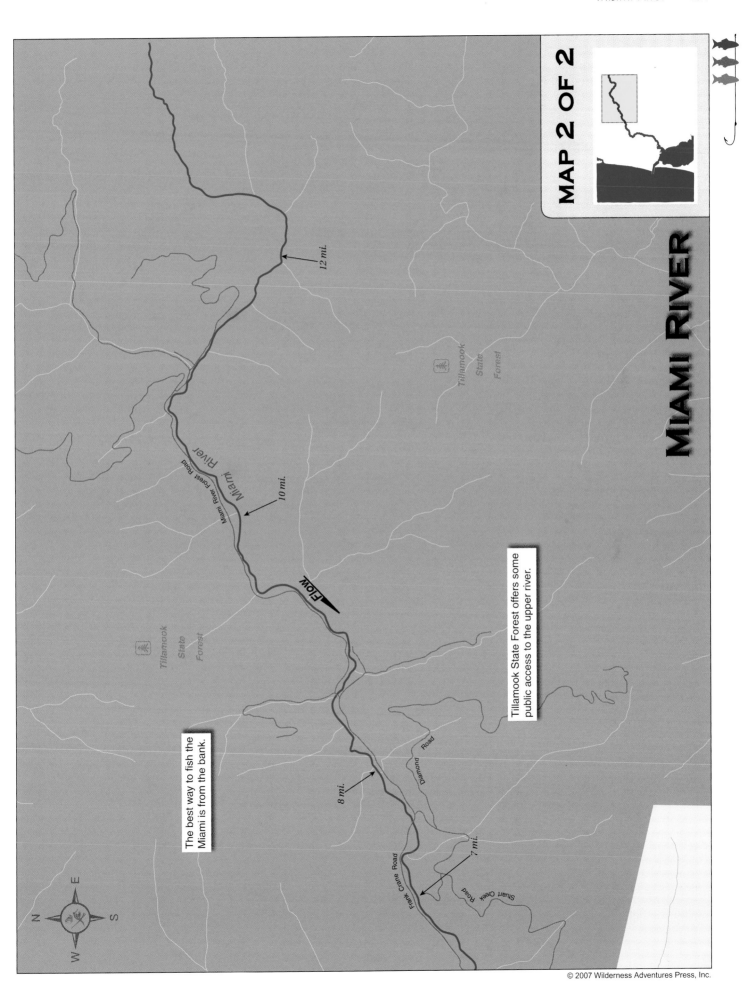

MAP 2 OF 2

MIAMI RIVER

12 mi.

Tillamook
State
Forest

Miami River Forest Road

Miami
River

10 mi.

FLOW

Tillamook State Forest offers some
public access to the upper river.

Tillamook
State
Forest

The best way to fish the
Miami is from the bank.

8 mi.

Diamond
Road

Frank Crane Road

7 mi.

Stuart Creek Road

N
E
W
S

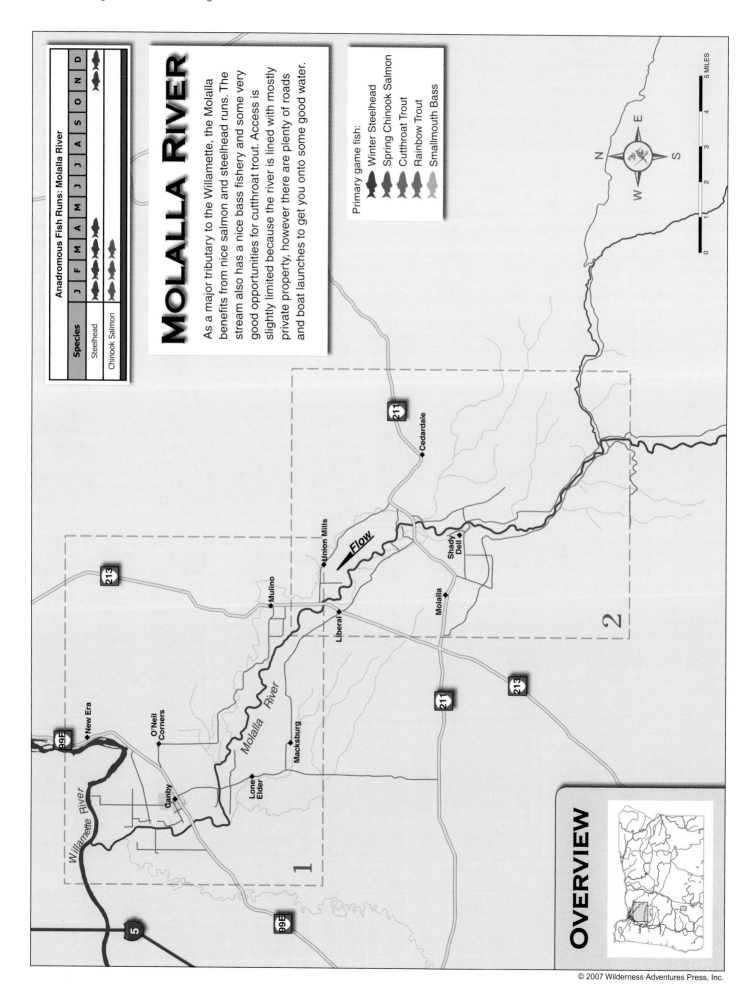

Anadromous Fish Runs: Molalla River

Species	J	F	M	A	M	J	J	A	S	O	N	D
Steelhead												
Chinook Salmon												

MOLALLA RIVER

As a major tributary to the Willamette, the Molalla benefits from nice salmon and steelhead runs. The stream also has a nice bass fishery and some very good opportunities for cutthroat trout. Access is slightly limited because the river is lined with mostly private property, however there are plenty of roads and boat launches to get you onto some good water.

Primary game fish:
Winter Steelhead
Spring Chinook Salmon
Cutthroat Trout
Rainbow Trout
Smallmouth Bass

5 MILES

Cedardale

Union Mills

Flow

Shady Dell

Mulino

Molalla

Liberal

213

211

213

Molalla River

Macksburg

New Era

O'Neil Corners

Lone Elder

Canby

99E

Willamette River

99E

5

2

1

OVERVIEW

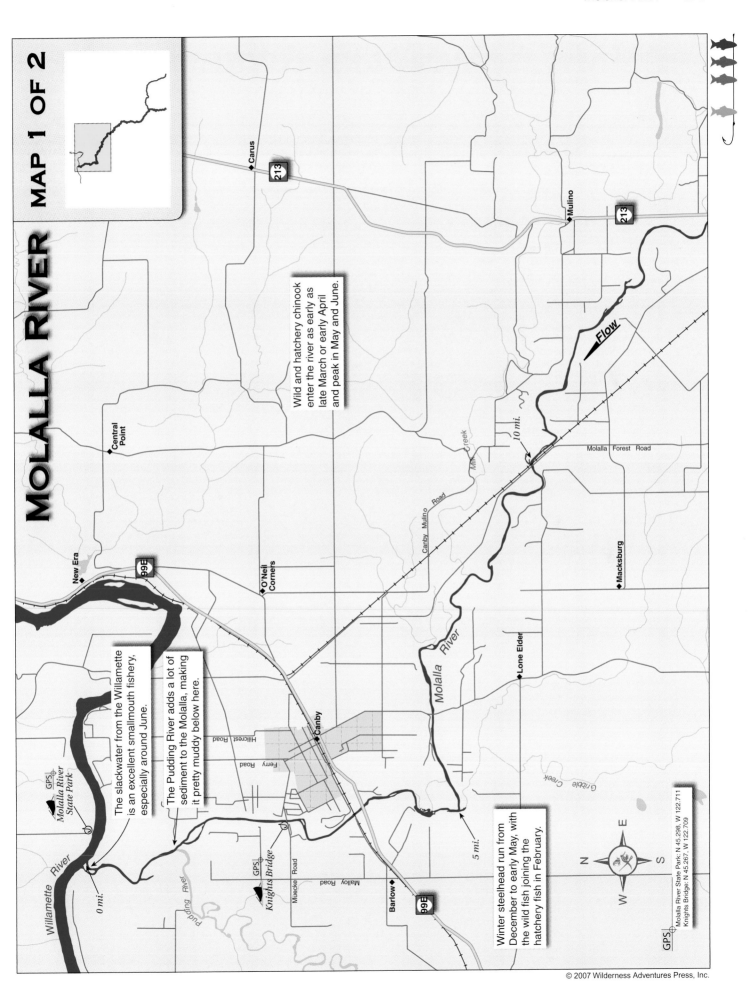

MOLALLA RIVER

MAP 1 OF 2

Carus

213

Mulino

213

Flow

Wild and hatchery chinook enter the river as early as late March or early April and peak in May and June.

Molalla Forest Road

Central Point

Milk Creek

Canby Mulino Road

10 mi.

Macksburg

New Era

99E

O'Neil Corners

Molalla River

Lone Elder

Canby

The slackwater from the Willamette is an excellent smallmouth fishery, especially around June.

The Pudding River adds a lot of sediment to the Molalla, making it pretty muddy below here.

Hillcrest Road

Ferry Road

GPS
Molalla River State Park

Gribble Creek

Willamette River

Pudding River

0 mi.

GPS
Knights Bridge

Muecke Road

Malloy Road

5 mi.

Barlow

99E

Winter steelhead run from December to early May, with the wild fish joining the hatchery fish in February.

N
E
W
S

Molalla River State Park: N 45.298, W 122.711
Knights Bridge: N 45.267, W 122.709

GPS

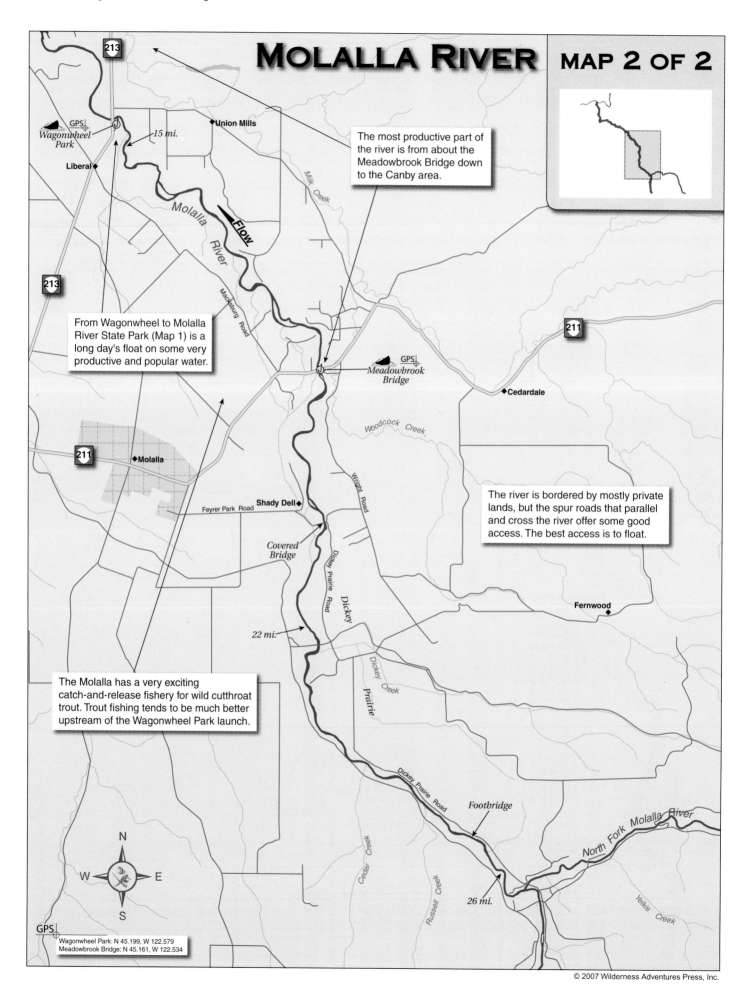

MOLALLA RIVER

MAP 2 OF 2

The most productive part of the river is from about the Meadowbrook Bridge down to the Canby area.

From Wagonwheel to Molalla River State Park (Map 1) is a long day's float on some very productive and popular water.

The river is bordered by mostly private lands, but the spur roads that parallel and cross the river offer some good access. The best access is to float.

The Molalla has a very exciting catch-and-release fishery for wild cutthroat trout. Trout fishing tends to be much better upstream of the Wagonwheel Park launch.

Wagonwheel Park
Liberal
Union Mills
15 mi.
Molalla River
Flow
Madeburg Road
Milk Creek
211
Meadowbrook Bridge
GPS
Cedardale
Molalla
211
Feyrer Park Road
Shady Dell
Covered Bridge
Woodcock Creek
Wright Road
Dickey Prairie Road
Dickey
Prairie
Dickey Creek
Fernwood
22 mi.
Dickey Prairie Road
Footbridge
North Fork Molalla River
Cedar Creek
Russell Creek
26 mi.
Yelkis Creek
213

N
W E
S

GPS
Wagonwheel Park: N 45.199, W 122.579
Meadowbrook Bridge: N 45.161, W 122.534

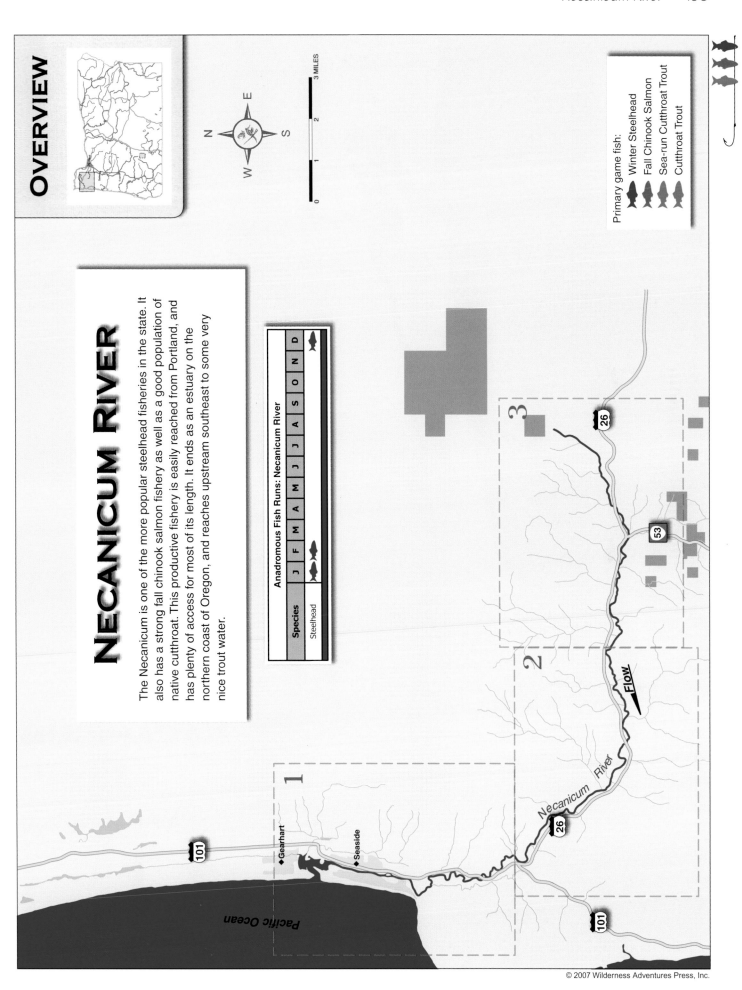

OVERVIEW

NECANICUM RIVER

The Necanicum is one of the more popular steelhead fisheries in the state. It also has a strong fall chinook salmon fishery as well as a good population of native cutthroat. This productive fishery is easily reached from Portland, and has plenty of access for most of its length. It ends as an estuary on the northern coast of Oregon, and reaches upstream southeast to some very nice trout water.

Anadromous Fish Runs: Necanicum River

Species	J	F	M	A	M	J	J	A	S	O	N	D
Steelhead												

Primary game fish:
Winter Steelhead
Fall Chinook Salmon
Sea-run Cutthroat Trout
Cutthroat Trout

Pacific Ocean

Gearhart
Seaside
Necanicum River
Flow

© 2007 Wilderness Adventures Press, Inc.

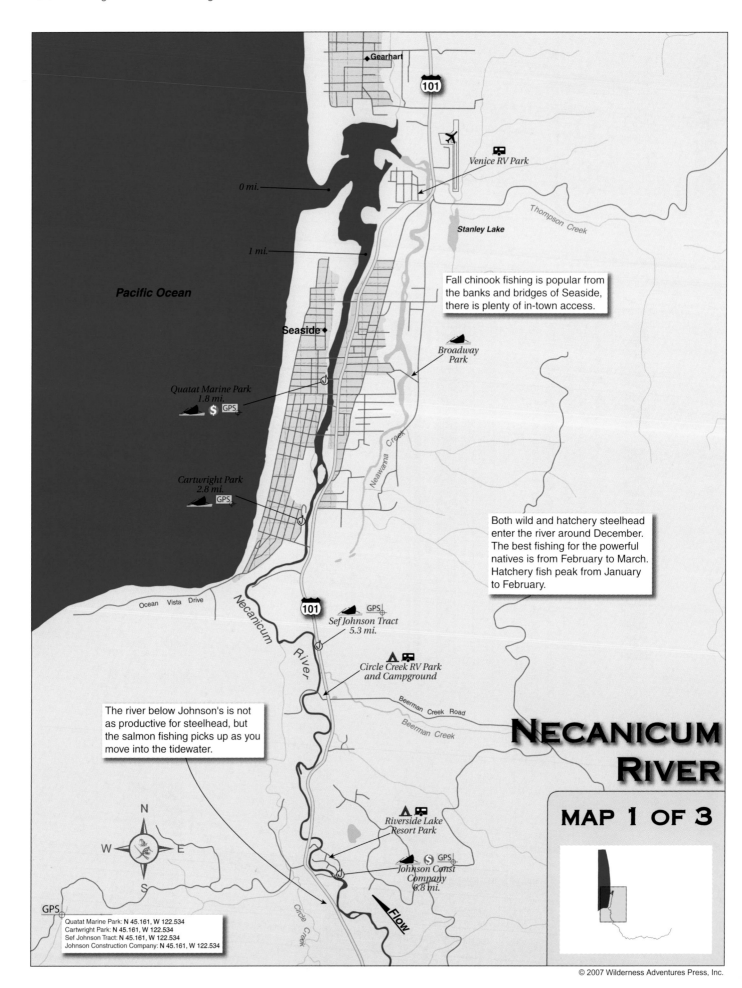

Gearhart

US 101

Venice RV Park

Thompson Creek

0 mi.

1 mi.

Stanley Lake

Pacific Ocean

Fall chinook fishing is popular from the banks and bridges of Seaside, there is plenty of in-town access.

Seaside

Broadway Park

Quatat Marine Park
1.8 mi.
$ GPS

Neawanna Creek

Cartwright Park
2.8 mi.
GPS

Both wild and hatchery steelhead enter the river around December. The best fishing for the powerful natives is from February to March. Hatchery fish peak from January to February.

Ocean Vista Drive

Necanicum River

101

Sef Johnson Tract
5.3 mi.
GPS

Circle Creek RV Park and Campground

Beerman Creek Road

Beerman Creek

The river below Johnson's is not as productive for steelhead, but the salmon fishing picks up as you move into the tidewater.

NECANICUM RIVER

MAP 1 OF 3

N
W   E
S

Riverside Lake Resort Park

Johnson Const Company
6.8 mi.
GPS

Circle Creek

Flow

GPS
Quatat Marine Park: N 45.161, W 122.534
Cartwright Park: N 45.161, W 122.534
Sef Johnson Tract: N 45.161, W 122.534
Johnson Construction Company: N 45.161, W 122.534

© 2007 Wilderness Adventures Press, Inc.

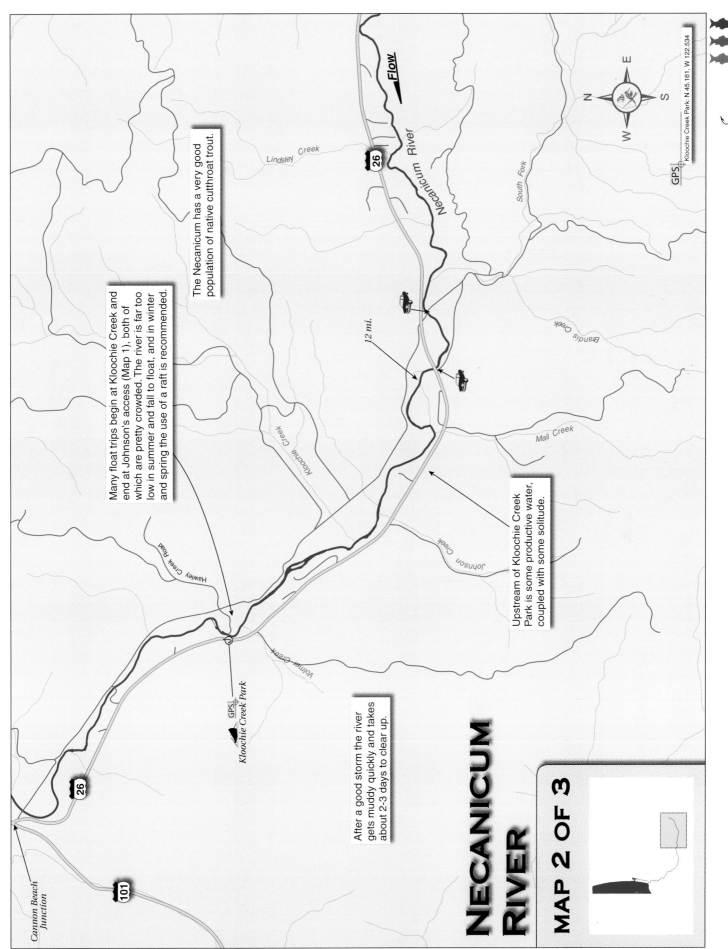

Flow

Lindsley Creek

Necanicum River

South Fork

26

Brandis Creek

12 mi.

Mail Creek

Kloochie Creek

Hawley Creek Road

Johnson Creek

Volmer Creek

GPS
Kloochie Creek Park

26

101

Cannon Beach
Junction

The Necanicum has a very good population of native cutthroat trout.

Many float trips begin at Kloochie Creek and end at Johnson's access (Map 1), both of which are pretty crowded. The river is far too low in summer and fall to float, and in winter and spring the use of a raft is recommended.

Upstream of Kloochie Creek Park is some productive water, coupled with some solitude.

After a good storm the river gets muddy quickly and takes about 2-3 days to clear up.

N E S W

GPS
Kloochie Creek Park: N 45.161, W 122.534

NECANICUM RIVER
MAP 2 OF 3

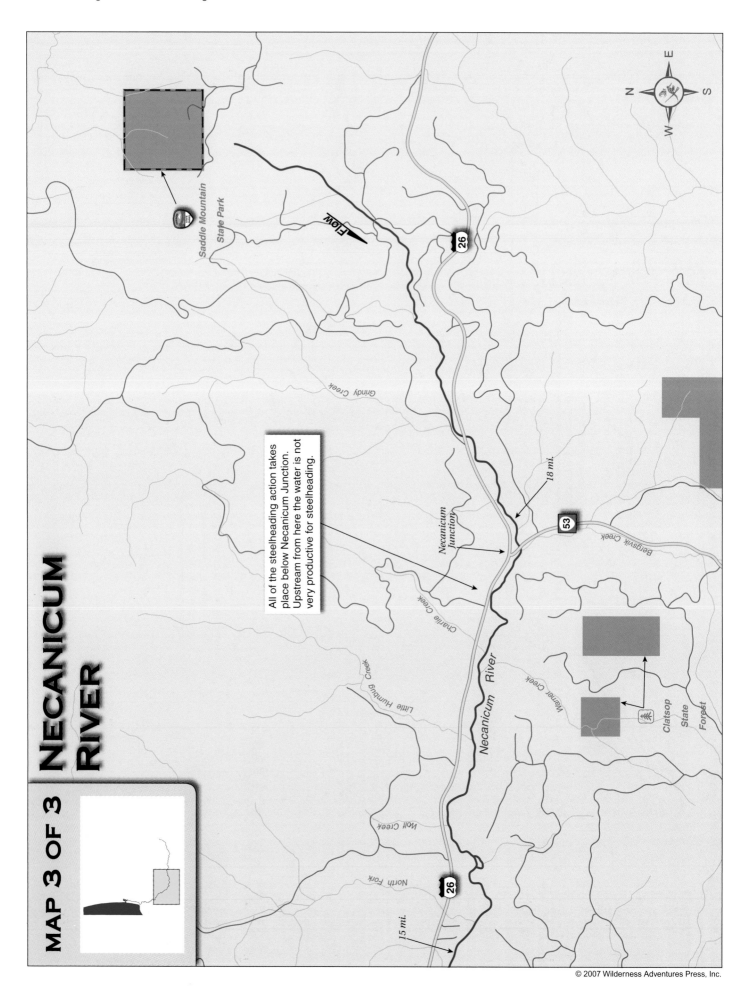

MAP 3 OF 3 NECANICUM RIVER

Saddle Mountain State Park

Flow

26

Grindy Creek

18 mi.

53

Bergsvik Creek

Necanicum Junction

All of the steelheading action takes place below Necanicum Junction. Upstream from here the water is not very productive for steelheading.

Charlie Creek

Little Humbug Creek

Warner Creek

Necanicum River

Clatsop State Forest

Wolf Creek

North Fork

26

15 mi.

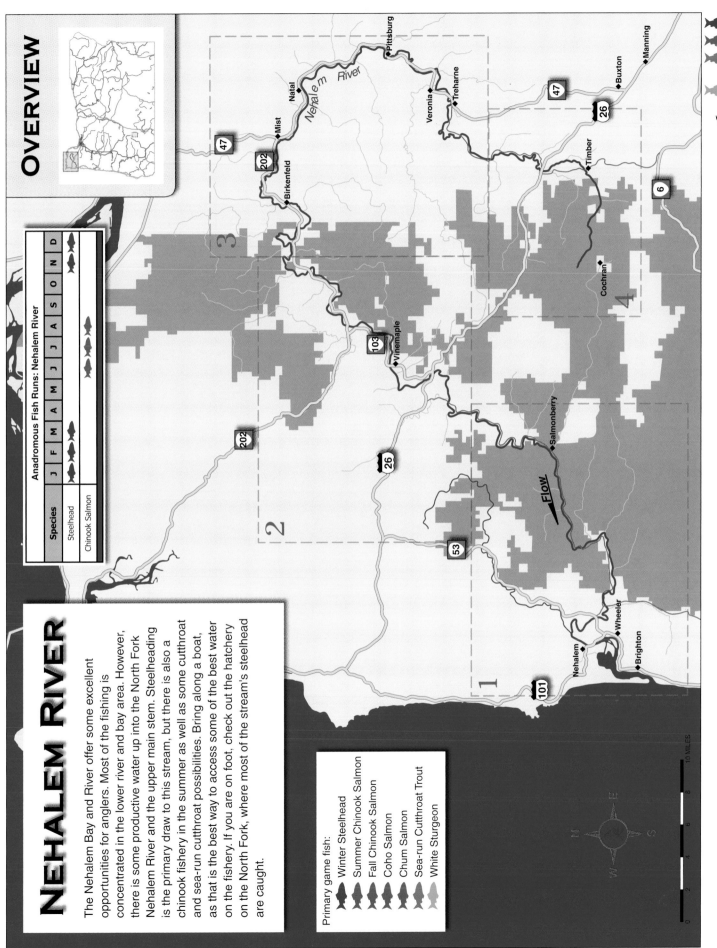

OVERVIEW

NEHALEM RIVER

The Nehalem Bay and River offer some excellent opportunities for anglers. Most of the fishing is concentrated in the lower river and bay area. However, there is some productive water up into the North Fork Nehalem River and the upper main stem. Steelheading is the primary draw to this stream, but there is also a chinook fishery in the summer as well as some cutthroat and sea-run cutthroat possibilities. Bring along a boat, as that is the best way to access some of the best water on the fishery. If you are on foot, check out the hatchery on the North Fork, where most of the stream's steelhead are caught.

Primary game fish:
- Winter Steelhead
- Summer Chinook Salmon
- Fall Chinook Salmon
- Coho Salmon
- Chum Salmon
- Sea-run Cutthroat Trout
- White Sturgeon

Anadromous Fish Runs: Nehalem River

Species	J	F	M	A	M	J	J	A	S	O	N	D
Steelhead												
Chinook Salmon												

10 MILES

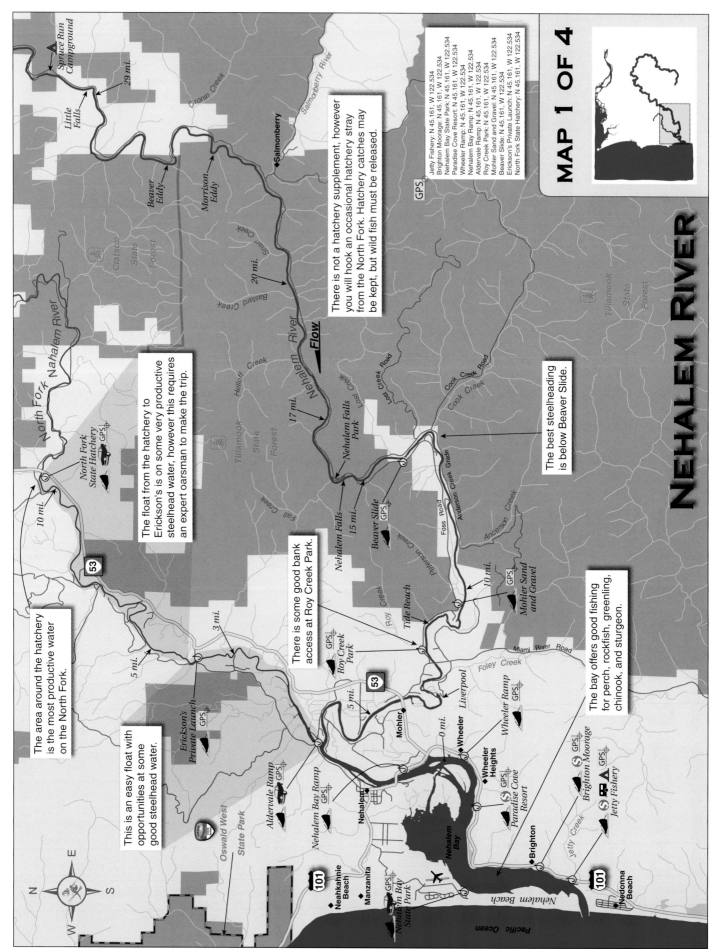

Spruce Run Campground

29 mi.

Little Falls

Cronin Creek

Beaver Eddy

Morrison Eddy

Salmonberry

Salmonberry River

Shart Creek

Clatsop State Forest

20 mi.

There is not a hatchery supplement, however you will hook an occasional hatchery stray from the North Fork. Hatchery catches may be kept, but wild fish must be released.

MAP 1 OF 4

North Fork Nahalem River

North Fork State Hatchery

The float from the hatchery to Erickson's is on some very productive steelhead water, however this requires an expert oarsman to make the trip.

Flow

Nehalem River

17 mi.

Lost Creek

Lost Creek Road

Cook Creek Road

Cook Creek

Tillamook State Forest

Nehalem Falls Park

The best steelheading is below Beaver Slide.

10 mi.

53

Helloff Creek

Nehalem Falls

15 mi.

Beaver Slide

Anderson Creek Grade

Foss Road

Anderson Creek

The area around the hatchery is the most productive water on the North Fork.

Fall Creek

Paterson Creek

5 mi.

3 mi.

Roy Creek

Tide Reach

10 mi.

Mohler Sand and Gravel

This is an easy float with opportunities at some good steelhead water.

Erickson's Private Launch

There is some good bank access at Roy Creek Park.

Roy Creek Park

5 mi.

Liverpool

Foley Creek

Miami River Road

The bay offers good fishing for perch, rockfish, greenling, chinook, and sturgeon.

Oswald West State Park

Aldervale Ramp

Nehalem Bay Ramp

Mohler

0 mi.

Wheeler

Wheeler Ramp

Nehalem

Wheeler Heights

Paradise Cove Resort

Brighton Moorage

Jetty Fishery

N
W E
S

101

Neahkahnie Beach

Manzanita

Nehalem Bay State Park

Nehalem Bay

Brighton

Jetty Creek

101

Nedonna Beach

Nehalem Beach

Pacific Ocean

NEHALEM RIVER

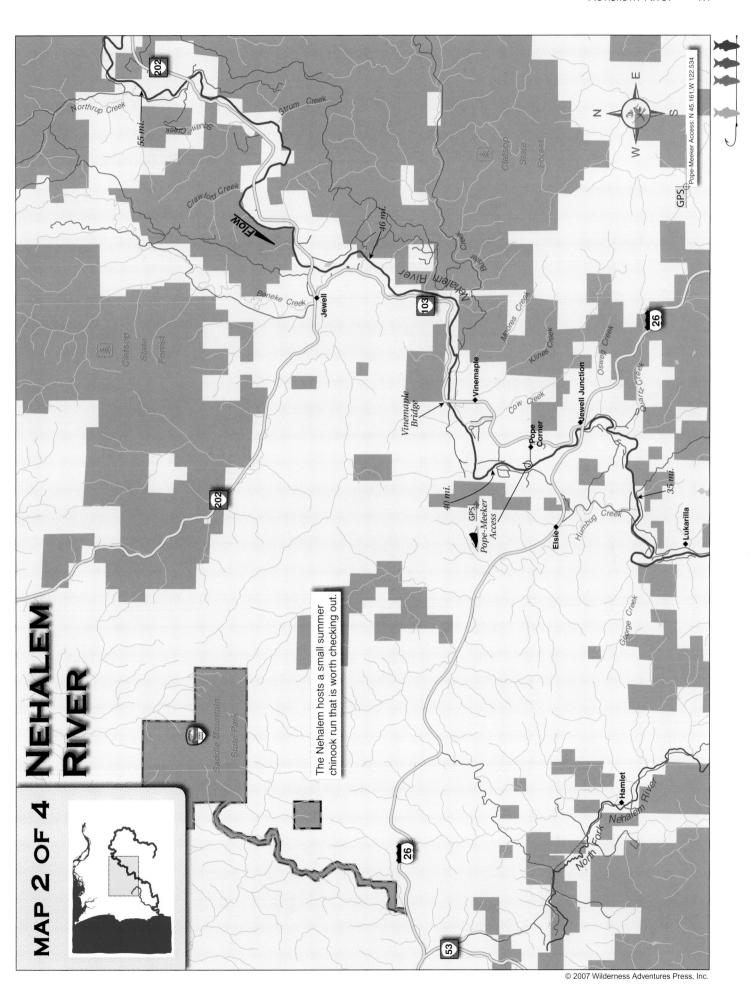

MAP 2 OF 4

NEHALEM RIVER

The Nehalem hosts a small summer chinook run that is worth checking out.

Pope-Meeker Access: N 45.161, W 122.534

© 2007 Wilderness Adventures Press, Inc.

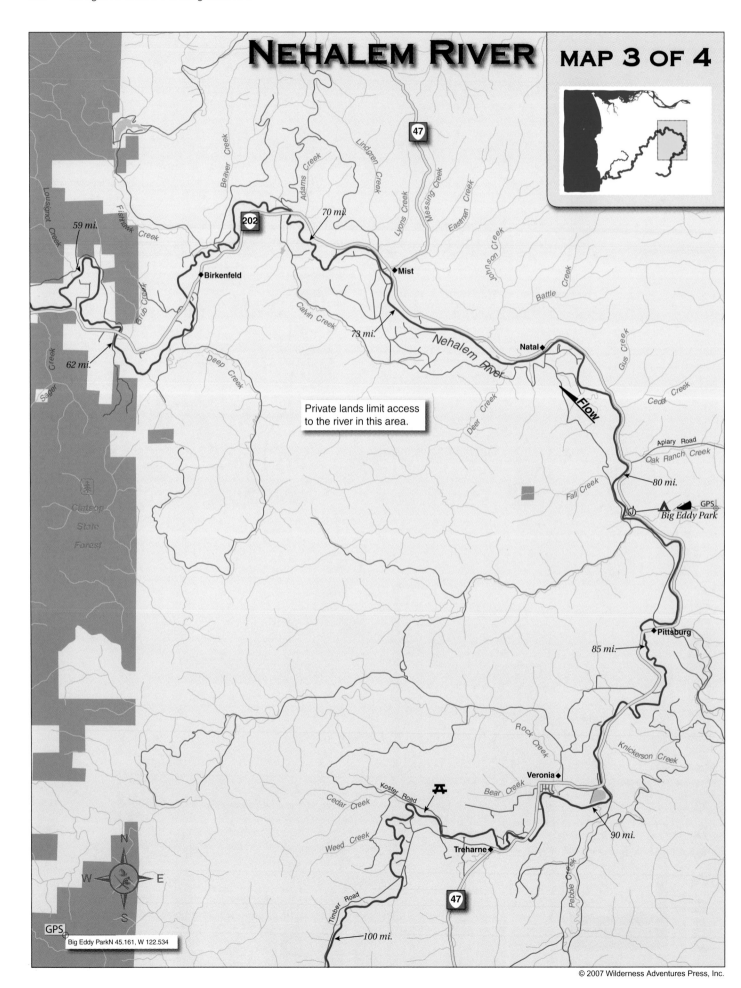

NEHALEM RIVER

MAP 3 OF 4

47

202

Beaver Creek

Adams Creek

Lindgren Creek

Lyons Creek

Messing Creek

Eastman Creek

Johnson Creek

Battle Creek

Gus Creek

Cedar Creek

59 mi.

Louisnof Creek

Fishhawk Creek

Birkenfeld

70 mi.

Mist

Calvin Creek

73 mi.

Nehalem River

Natal

Grub Creek

62 mi.

Sager Creek

Deep Creek

Deer Creek

Deer Creek

Private lands limit access
to the river in this area.

Flow

Apiary Road

Oak Ranch Creek

80 mi.

Fall Creek

GPS
Big Eddy Park

Clatsop State Forest

Pittsburg

85 mi.

Rock Creek

Knickerson Creek

Veronia

Koster Road

Cedar Creek

Bear Creek

90 mi.

Weed Creek

Treharne

N
W   E
S

Pebble Creek

47

100 mi.

GPS
Big Eddy ParkN 45.161, W 122.534

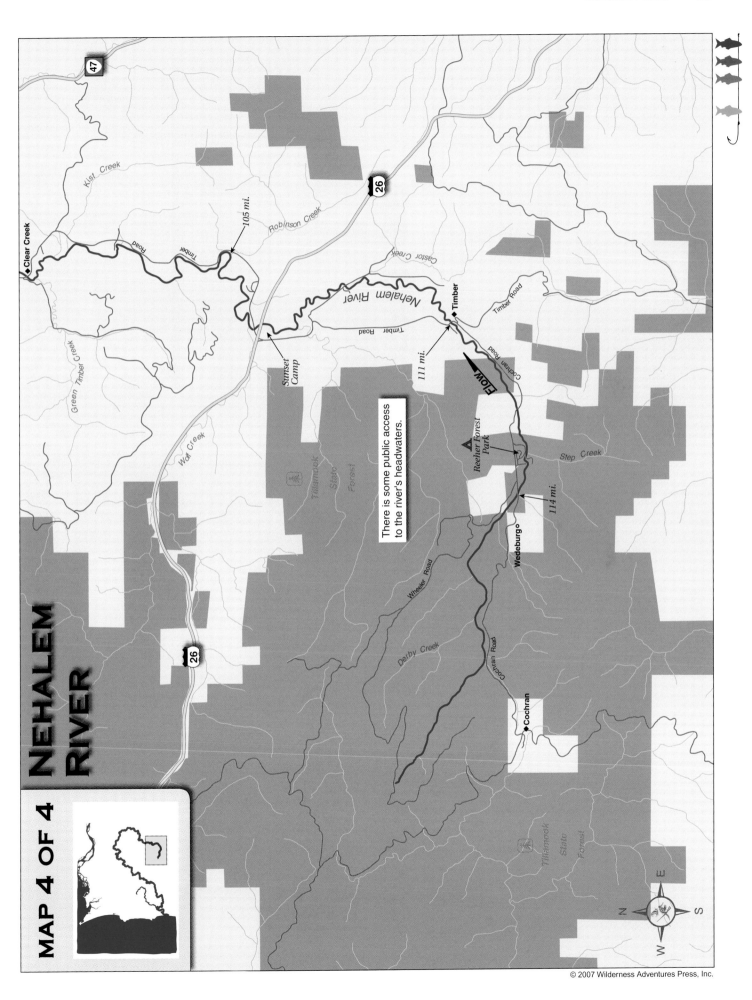

MAP 4 OF 4

NEHALEM
RIVER

There is some public access
to the river's headwaters.

Clear Creek

Kist Creek

Robinson Creek

Timber Road

105 mi.

Sunset Camp

Nehalem River

Castor Creek

Timber

111 mi.

Timber Road

Timber Road

Cochran Road

FLOW

Reeher Forest Park

Step Creek

114 mi.

Green Timber Creek

Wolf Creek

Tillamook State Forest

Wheeler Road

Derby Creek

Wedeburg

Cochran Road

Cochran

Tillamook State Forest

N E W S

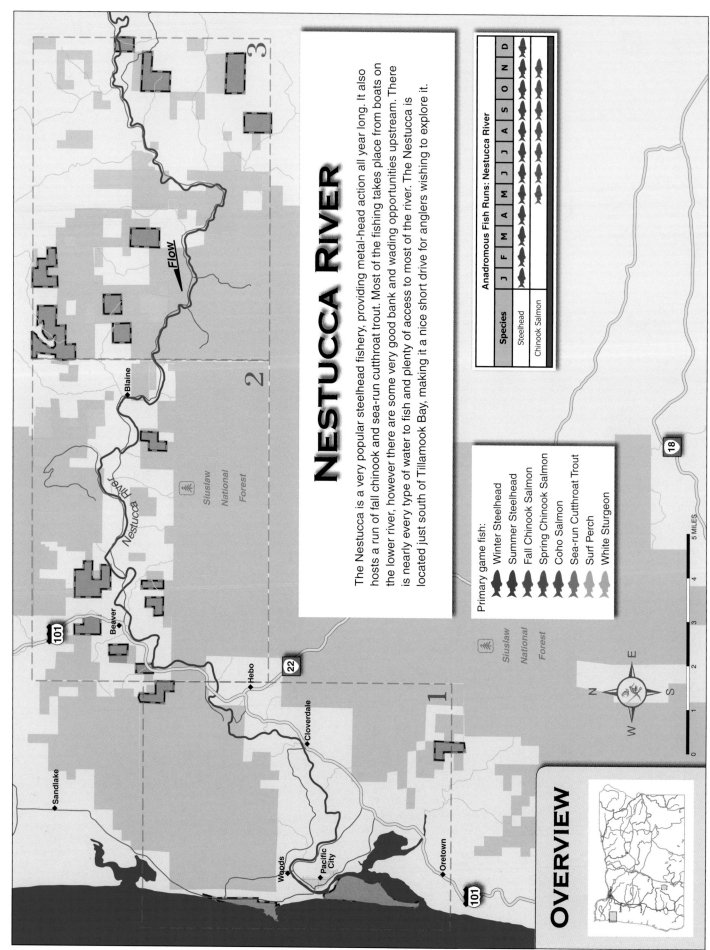

NESTUCCA RIVER

The Nestucca is a very popular steelhead fishery, providing metal-head action all year long. It also hosts a run of fall chinook and sea-run cutthroat trout. Most of the fishing takes place from boats on the lower river, however there are some very good bank and wading opportunities upstream. There is nearly every type of water to fish and plenty of access to most of the river. The Nestucca is located just south of Tillamook Bay, making it a nice short drive for anglers wishing to explore it.

Primary game fish:
- Winter Steelhead
- Summer Steelhead
- Fall Chinook Salmon
- Spring Chinook Salmon
- Coho Salmon
- Sea-run Cutthroat Trout
- Surf Perch
- White Sturgeon

Anadromous Fish Runs: Nestucca River

Species	J	F	M	A	M	J	J	A	S	O	N	D
Steelhead												
Chinook Salmon												

OVERVIEW

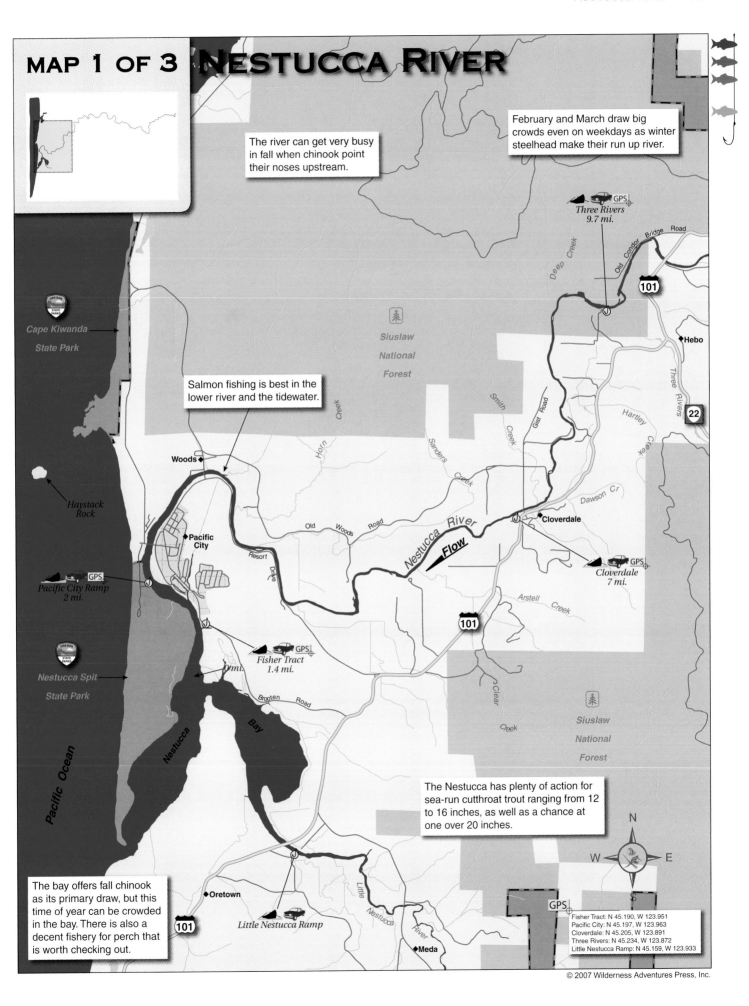

MAP 1 OF 3 NESTUCCA RIVER

The river can get very busy in fall when chinook point their noses upstream.

February and March draw big crowds even on weekdays as winter steelhead make their run up river.

GPS
Three Rivers
9.7 mi.

Old Condor Bridge Road

101

Deep Creek

◆Hebo

Cape Kiwanda State Park

Siuslaw National Forest

Three Rivers

22

Salmon fishing is best in the lower river and the tidewater.

Smith Creek

Gist Road

Hartley Creek

Horn Creek

Sanders Creek

Dawson Cr.

Woods ◆

Haystack Rock

Old Woods Road

Nestucca River

Flow

◆Cloverdale

GPS
Cloverdale
7 mi.

Pacific City

Resort Drive

Arstell Creek

Pacific City Ramp
2 mi.
GPS

101

Fisher Tract
1.4 mi.
GPS

Nestucca Spit State Park

0 mi.

Brooten Road

Clear Creek

Siuslaw National Forest

Nestucca Bay

The Nestucca has plenty of action for sea-run cutthroat trout ranging from 12 to 16 inches, as well as a chance at one over 20 inches.

Pacific Ocean

N
W   E
S

The bay offers fall chinook as its primary draw, but this time of year can be crowded in the bay. There is also a decent fishery for perch that is worth checking out.

◆Oretown

101

Little Nestucca Ramp

Little Nestucca River

◆Meda

GPS

Fisher Tract: N 45.190, W 123.951
Pacific City: N 45.197, W 123.963
Cloverdale: N 45.205, W 123.891
Three Rivers: N 45.234, W 123.872
Little Nestucca Ramp: N 45.159, W 123.933

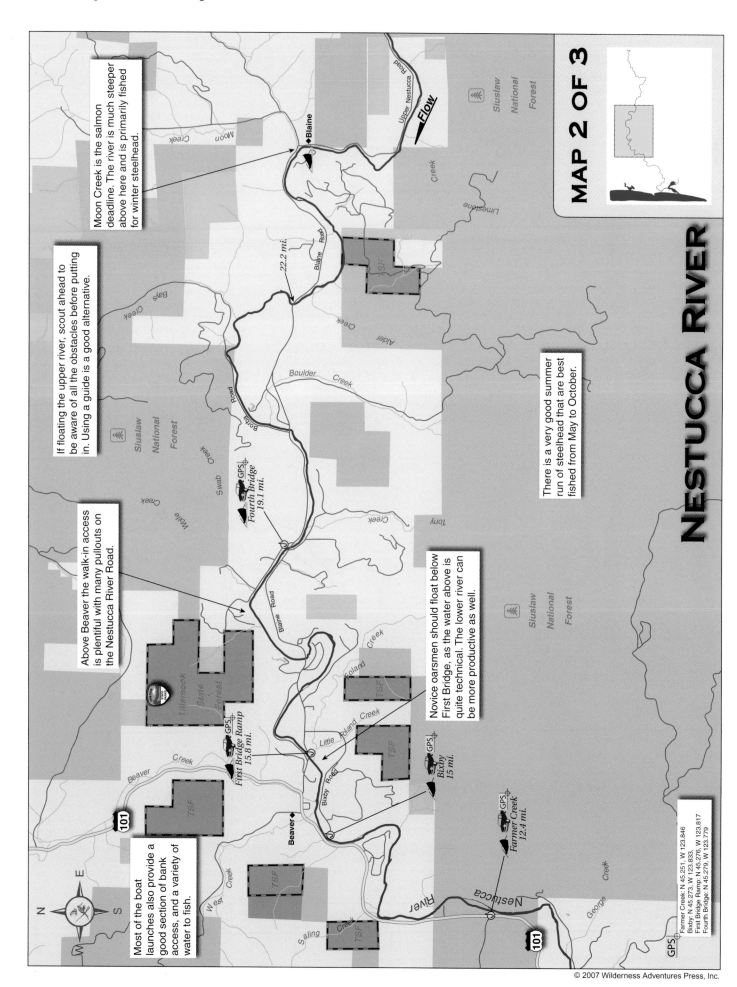

Moon Creek is the salmon deadline. The river is much steeper above here and is primarily fished for winter steelhead.

If floating the upper river, scout ahead to be aware of all the obstacles before putting in. Using a guide is a good alternative.

Above Beaver the walk-in access is plentiful with many pullouts on the Nestucca River Road.

Most of the boat launches also provide a good section of bank access, and a variety of water to fish.

Novice oarsmen should float below First Bridge, as the water above is quite technical. The lower river can be more productive as well.

There is a very good summer run of steelhead that are best fished from May to October.

MAP 2 OF 3

NESTUCCA RIVER

Flow

Upper Nestucca Road

◆Blaine

Moon Creek

Siuslaw National Forest

Limestone Creek

22.2 mi.

Blaine Road

TSF

Alder Creek

Boulder Creek

Bays Creek

Bona Road

Siuslaw National Forest

Swab Creek

GPS Fourth Bridge 19.1 mi.

Wolfe Creek

Tony Creek

Blaine Road

Siuslaw National Forest

Tillamook State Forest

Foland Creek

TSF

First Bridge Ramp 15.8 mi.

Little Foland Creek

Bixby Road

TSF

Beaver Creek

Beaver◆

GPS Bixby 15 mi.

TSF

101

West Creek

GPS Farmer Creek 12.4 mi.

Nestucca River

George Creek

101

Saling Creek

TSF

N E S W

GPS Farmer Creek: N 45.251, W 123.846
Bixby: N 45.273, W 123.833,
First Bridge Ramp: N 45.276, W 123.817
Fourth Bridge: N 45.279, W 123.779

© 2007 Wilderness Adventures Press, Inc.

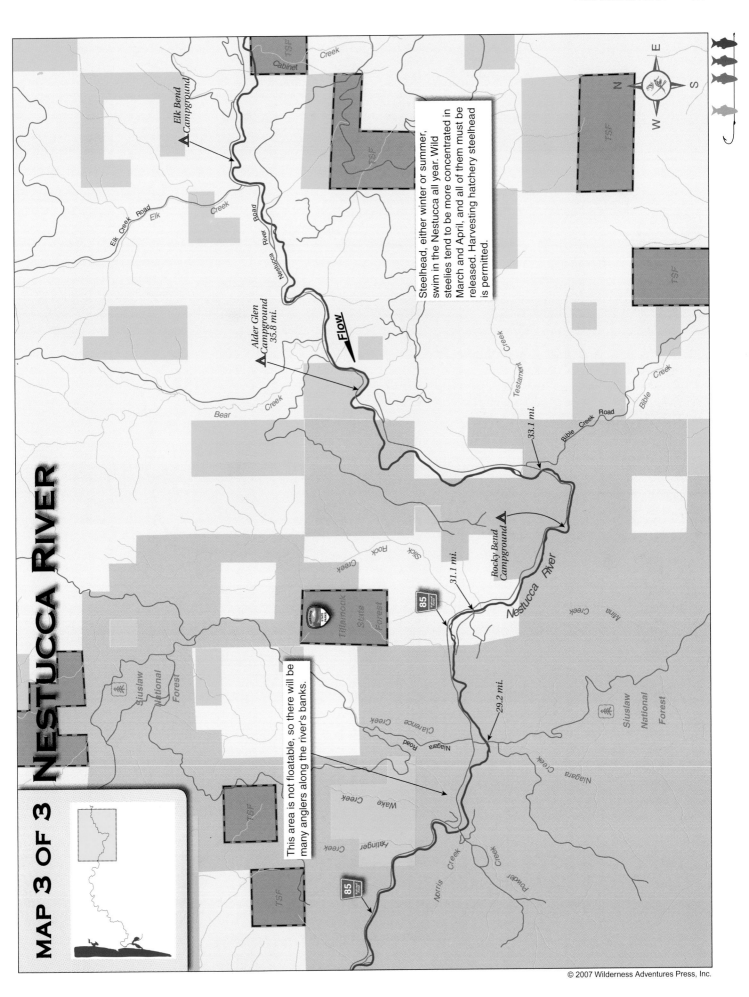

MAP 3 OF 3

NESTUCCA RIVER

Elk Bend Campground

Elk Creek Road

Elk Creek

Nestucca River Road

TSF

Cabinet Creek

Alder Glen Campground 35.8 mi.

Flow

Bear Creek

Steelhead, either winter or summer, swim in the Nestucca all year. Wild steelies tend to be more concentrated in March and April, and all of them must be released. Harvesting hatchery steelhead is permitted.

TSF

TSF

Testament Creek

Bible Creek

Bible Creek Road

33.1 mi.

Rocky Bend Campground

31.1 mi.

Nestucca River

Mina Creek

Slick Rock Creek

Rock Creek

Tillamook State Forest

85

Siuslaw National Forest

This area is not floatable, so there will be many anglers along the river's banks.

Clarence Creek

Niagara Road

29.2 mi.

Niagara Creek

Siuslaw National Forest

TSF

Wake Creek

Fatinger Creek

Norris Creek

Powder Creek

85

TSF

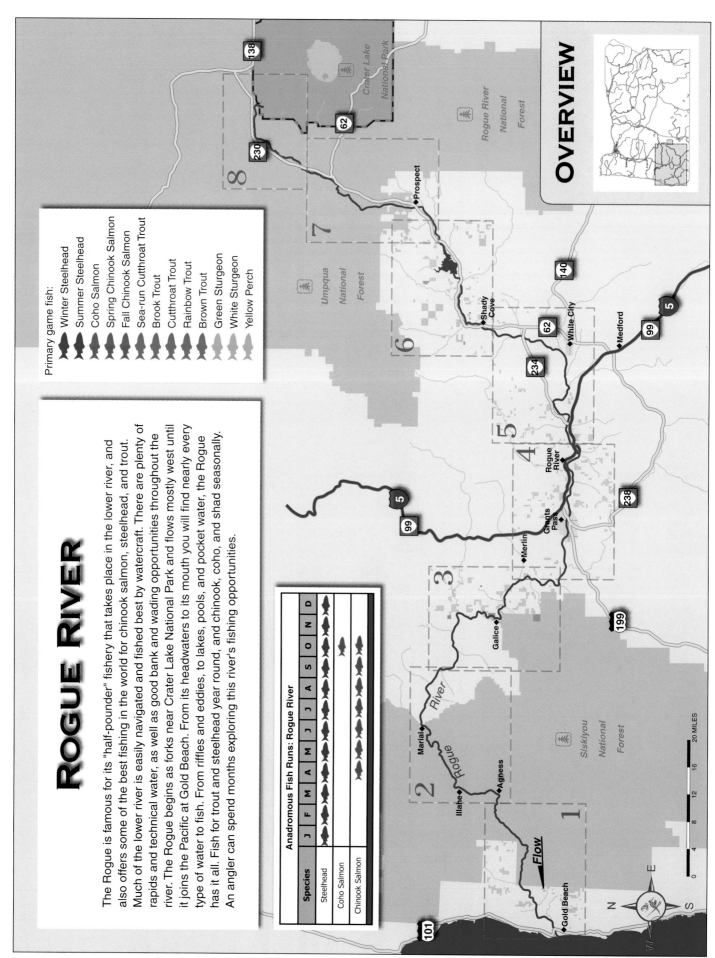

ROGUE RIVER

The Rogue is famous for its "half-pounder" fishery that takes place in the lower river, and also offers some of the best fishing in the world for chinook salmon, steelhead, and trout. Much of the lower river is easily navigated and fished best by watercraft. There are plenty of rapids and technical water, as well as good bank and wading opportunities throughout the river. The Rogue begins as forks near Crater Lake National Park and flows mostly west until it joins the Pacific at Gold Beach. From its headwaters to its mouth you will find nearly every type of water to fish. From riffles and eddies, to lakes, pools, and pocket water, the Rogue has it all. Fish for trout and steelhead year round, and chinook, coho, and shad seasonally. An angler can spend months exploring this river's fishing opportunities.

Primary game fish:
- Winter Steelhead
- Summer Steelhead
- Coho Salmon
- Spring Chinook Salmon
- Fall Chinook Salmon
- Sea-run Cutthroat Trout
- Brook Trout
- Cutthroat Trout
- Rainbow Trout
- Brown Trout
- Green Sturgeon
- White Sturgeon
- Yellow Perch

Anadromous Fish Runs: Rogue River

Species	J	F	M	A	M	J	J	A	S	O	N	D
Steelhead												
Coho Salmon												
Chinook Salmon												

OVERVIEW

© 2007 Wilderness Adventures Press, Inc.

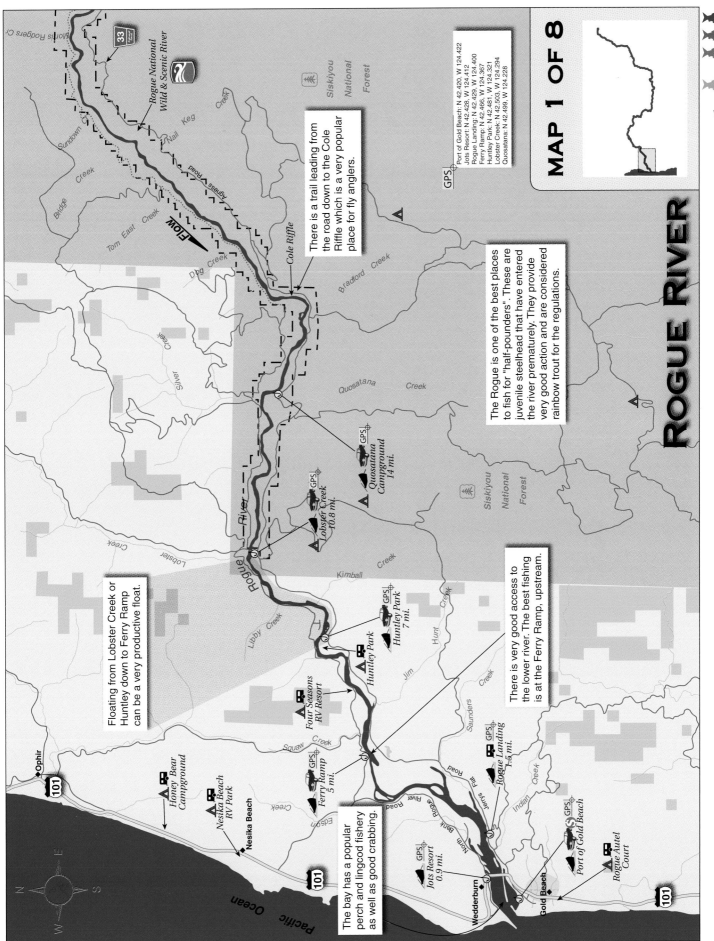

There is a trail leading from the road down to the Cole Riffle which is a very popular place for fly anglers.

The Rogue is one of the best places to fish for "half-pounders". These are juvenile steelhead that have entered the river prematurely. They provide very good action and are considered rainbow trout for the regulations.

GPS

Port of Gold Beach: N 42.420, W 124.422
Jots Resort: N 42.428, W 124.412
Rogue Landing: N 42.429, W 124.400
Ferry Ramp: N 42.466, W 124.367
Huntley Park: N 42.481, W 124.321
Lobster Creek: N 42.503, W 124.294
Quosatana: N 42.499, W 124.228

MAP 1 OF 8

ROGUE RIVER

Floating from Lobster Creek or Huntley down to Ferry Ramp can be a very productive float.

There is very good access to the lower river. The best fishing is at the Ferry Ramp, upstream.

The bay has a popular perch and lingcod fishery as well as good crabbing.

Quosatana Campground
14 mi.

Lobster Creek
10.8 mi.

Huntley Park
Huntley Park
7 mi.

Four Seasons
RV Resort

Ferry Ramp
5 mi.

Honey Bear
Campground

Nesika Beach
RV Park

Nesika Beach

Rogue Landing
1.5 mi.

Port of Gold Beach

Rogue Autel
Court

Jots Resort
0.9 mi.

Wedderburn

Gold Beach

Ophir

Pacific Ocean

Siskiyou National Forest

Rogue National Wild & Scenic River

Cole Riffle

Flow

Morris Rodgers Cr

Nail Keg Creek

Sundown Creek

Bridge Creek

Tom East Creek

Dog Creek

Silver Creek

Bradford Creek

Quosatana Creek

Rogue River

Lobster Creek

Kimball Creek

Libby Creek

Hunt Creek

Jim Creek

Saunders Creek

Squaw Creek

Edson Creek

Indian Creek

North Bank Rogue River Road

Jerrys Flat Road

101

33

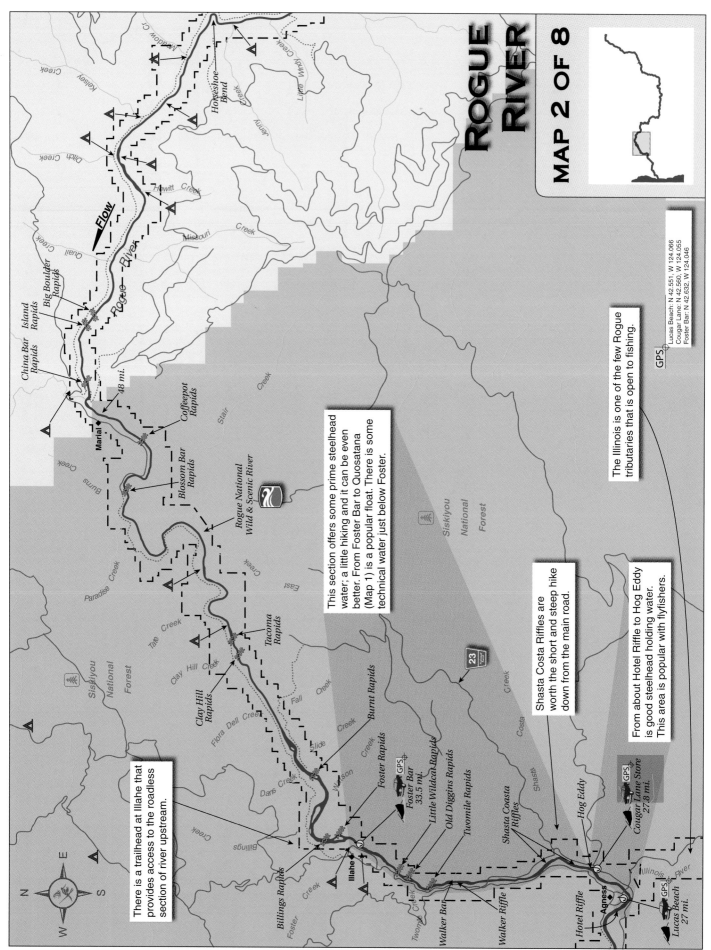

ROGUE RIVER

MAP 2 OF 8

Lucas Beach: N 42.551, W 124.066
Cougar Lane: N 42.560, W 124.055
Foster Bar: N 42.632, W 124.046

The Illinois is one of the few Rogue tributaries that is open to fishing.

This section offers some prime steelhead water; a little hiking and it can be even better. From Foster Bar to Quosatana (Map 1) is a popular float. There is some technical water just below Foster.

Shasta Costa Riffles are worth the short and steep hike down from the main road.

From about Hotel Riffle to Hog Eddy is good steelhead holding water. This area is popular with flyfishers.

There is a trailhead at Illahe that provides access to the roadless section of river upstream.

Flow

Horseshoe Bend

Rogue River

48 mi.

Big Boulder Rapids

Island Rapids

China Bar Rapids

Coffeepot Rapids

Marial

Blossom Bar Rapids

Rogue National Wild & Scenic River

Tacoma Rapids

Clay Hill Rapids

Burnt Rapids

Foster Rapids

Foster Bar 33.5 mi.

Little Wildcat Rapids

Old Diggins Rapids

Twomile Rapids

Shasta Costa Riffles

Hog Eddy

Cougar Lane Store 27.8 mi.

Hotel Riffle

Agness

Lucas Beach 27 mi.

Illinois River

Billings Rapids

Illahe

Walker Bar

Walker Riffle

Siskiyou National Forest

Meadow Cr.

Kelsey Creek

Ditch Creek

Quail Creek

Windy Creek

Little Windy Creek

Jenny Creek

Hewitt Creek

Missouri Creek

Stair Creek

Burns Creek

Paradise Creek

Tate Creek

Clay Hill Creek

East Creek

Flora Dell Creek

Fall Creek

Slide Creek

Dans Creek

Watson Creek

Foster Creek

Billings Creek

Twomile Creek

Shasta Costa Creek

23

© 2007 Wilderness Adventures Press, Inc.

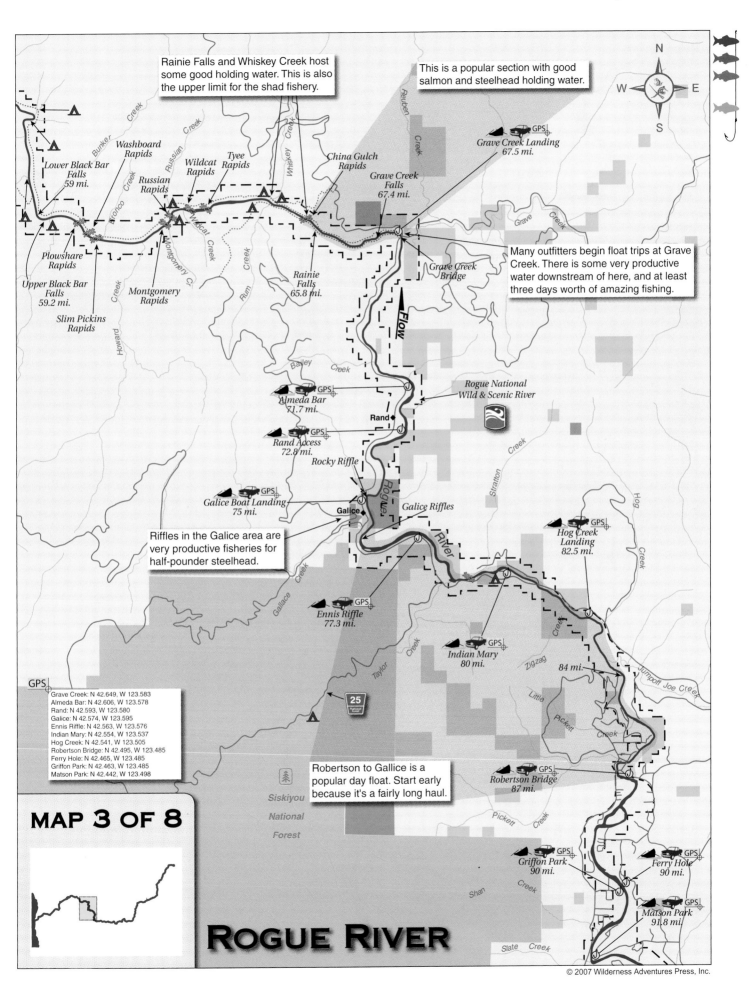

Rainie Falls and Whiskey Creek host some good holding water. This is also the upper limit for the shad fishery.

This is a popular section with good salmon and steelhead holding water.

Grave Creek Landing
67.5 mi.

Lower Black Bar
Falls
59 mi.

Washboard
Rapids

Wildcat
Rapids

Tyee
Rapids

China Gulch
Rapids

Grave Creek
Falls
67.4 mi.

Russian
Rapids

Grave Creek
Bridge

Plowshare
Rapids

Montgomery
Rapids

Rainie
Falls
65.8 mi.

Many outfitters begin float trips at Grave Creek. There is some very productive water downstream of here, and at least three days worth of amazing fishing.

Upper Black Bar
Falls
59.2 mi.

Slim Pickins
Rapids

Flow

Almeda Bar
71.7 mi.

Rand

Rogue National
Wild & Scenic River

Rand Access
72.8 mi.

Rocky Riffle

Galice Boat Landing
75 mi.

Galice

Galice Riffles

Hog Creek
Landing
82.5 mi.

Riffles in the Galice area are very productive fisheries for half-pounder steelhead.

Ennis Riffle
77.3 mi.

Indian Mary
80 mi.

84 mi.

GPS
Grave Creek: N 42.649, W 123.583
Almeda Bar: N 42.606, W 123.578
Rand: N 42.593, W 123.580
Galice: N 42.574, W 123.595
Ennis Riffle: N 42.563, W 123.576
Indian Mary: N 42.554, W 123.537
Hog Creek: N 42.541, W 123.505
Robertson Bridge: N 42.495, W 123.485
Ferry Hole: N 42.465, W 123.485
Griffon Park: N 42.463, W 123.485
Matson Park: N 42.442, W 123.498

Robertson to Gallice is a popular day float. Start early because it's a fairly long haul.

Robertson Bridge
87 mi.

25

Siskiyou

National

Forest

Griffon Park
90 mi.

Ferry Hole
90 mi.

MAP 3 OF 8

Matson Park
91.8 mi.

ROGUE RIVER

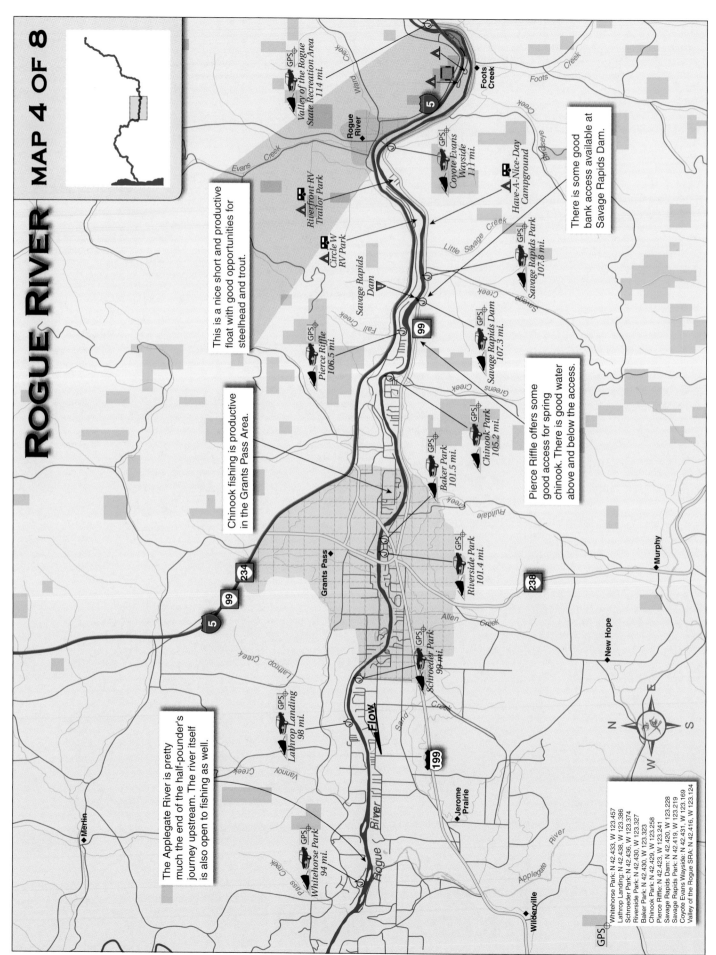

ROGUE RIVER MAP 4 OF 8

Valley of the Rogue State Recreation Area 114 mi.

This is a nice short and productive float with good opportunities for steelhead and trout.

Coyote Evans Wayside 111 mi.

Have-A-Nice-Day Campground

Riverfront RV Trailor Park

There is some good bank access available at Savage Rapids Dam.

Circle W RV Park

Savage Rapids Park 107.8 mi.

Savage Rapids Dam

Savage Rapids Dam 107.3 mi.

Pierce Riffle 106.5 mi.

Pierce Riffle offers some good access for spring chinook. There is good water above and below the access.

Chinook fishing is productive in the Grants Pass Area.

Chinook Park 105.2 mi.

Baker Park 101.5 mi.

Riverside Park 101.4 mi.

Grants Pass

New Hope

Murphy

The Applegate River is pretty much the end of the half-pounder's journey upstream. The river itself is also open to fishing as well.

Schroeder Park 99 mi.

Lathrop Landing 98 mi.

Flow

Merlin

Whitehorse Park 94 mi.

Jerome Prairie

Wilderville

GPS
Whitehorse Park: N 42.433, W 123.457
Lathrop Landing: N 42.438, W 123.386
Schroeder Park: N 42.436, W 123.374
Riverside Park: N 42.430, W 123.327
Baker Park: N 42.430, W 123.323
Chinook Park: N 42.429, W 123.258
Pierce Riffle: N 42.423, W 123.241
Savage Rapids Dam: N 42.420, W 123.228
Savage Rapids Park: N 42.419, W 123.219
Coyote Evans Wayside: N 42.431, W 123.169
Valley of the Rogue SRA: N 42.416, W 123.124

© 2007 Wilderness Adventures Press, Inc.

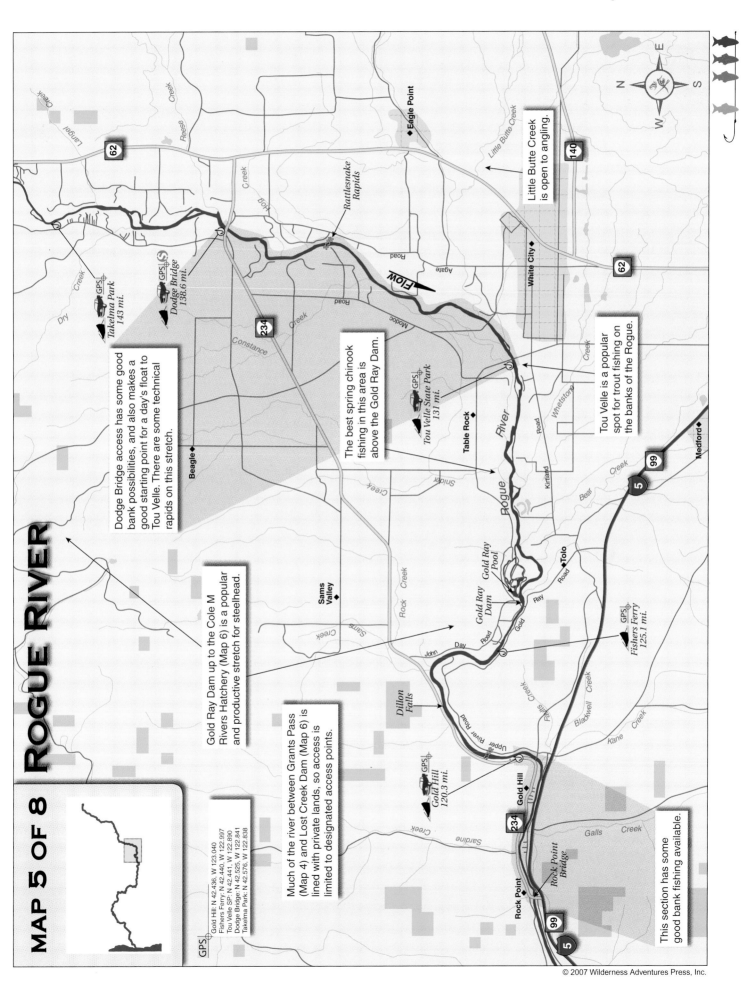

MAP 5 OF 8   ROGUE RIVER

Dodge Bridge access has some good bank possibilities, and also makes a good starting point for a day's float to Tou Velle. There are some technical rapids on this stretch.

Gold Ray Dam up to the Cole M Rivers Hatchery (Map 6) is a popular and productive stretch for steelhead.

Much of the river between Grants Pass (Map 4) and Lost Creek Dam (Map 6) is lined with private lands, so access is limited to designated access points.

The best spring chinook fishing in this area is above the Gold Ray Dam.

Little Butte Creek is open to angling.

Tou Velle is a popular spot for trout fishing on the banks of the Rogue.

This section has some good bank fishing available.

GPS
Gold Hill: N 42.436, W 123.040
Fishers Ferry: N 42.440, W 122.997
Tou Velle SP: N 42.441, W 122.890
Dodge Bridge: N 42.525, W 122.841
Takelma Park: N 42.576, W 122.838

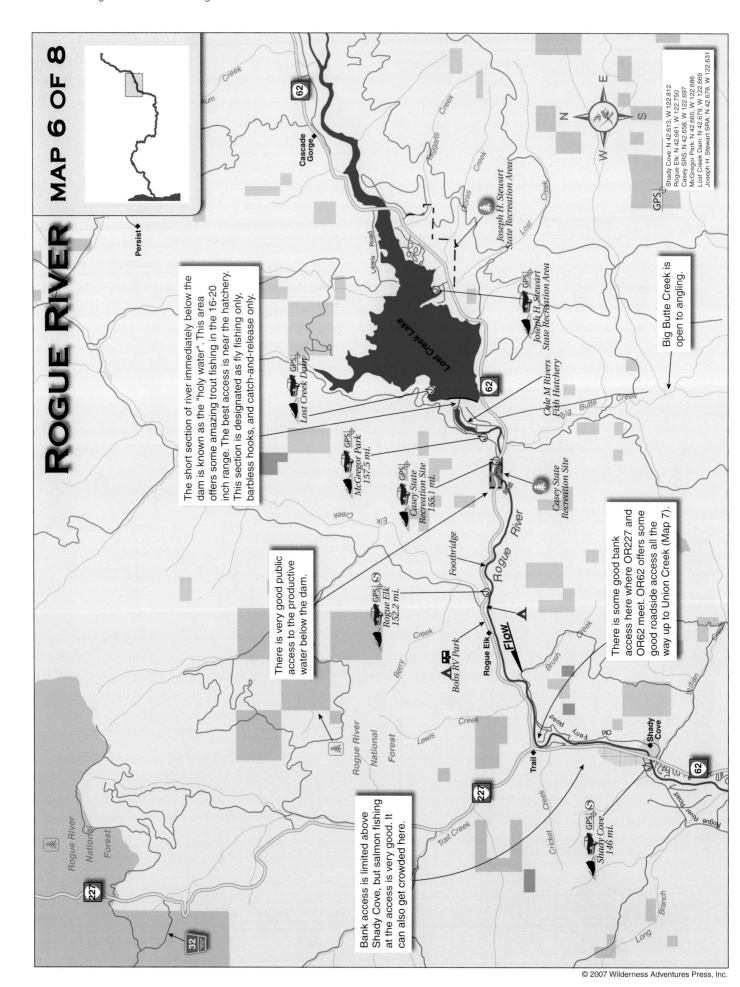

MAP 6 OF 8

ROGUE RIVER

Cascade Gorge

Persist

Ygkum Creek

Creek

62

Joseph H. Stewart State Recreation Area

Haggarts Creek

Lost Creek

Boras Creek

N E S W

GPS

Shady Cove: N 42.613, W 122.812
Rogue Elk: N 42.661, W 122.750
Casey SRS: N 42.658, W 122.697
McGregor Park: N 42.665, W 122.686
Lost Creek Dam: N 42.679, W 122.669
Joseph H. Stewart SRA: N 42.678, W 122.631

The short section of river immediately below the dam is known as the "holy water". This area offers some amazing trout fishing in the 16-20 inch range. The best access is near the hatchery. This section is designated as fly fishing only, barbless hooks, and catch-and-release only.

GPS
Lost Creek Dam

Lost Creek Lake

62

GPS
Joseph H. Stewart State Recreation Area

Cole M Rivers Fish Hatchery

Big Butte Creek

Big Butte Creek is open to angling.

GPS
McGregor Park
157.5 mi.

GPS
Casey State Recreation Site
155.1 mi.

Casey State Recreation Site

Elk Creek

There is very good public access to the productive water below the dam.

Footbridge

Rogue River

GPS S
Rogue Elk
152.2 mi.

Berry Creek

Bobs RV Park

Rogue Elk

FLOW

Brush Creek

There is some good bank access here where OR227 and OR62 meet. OR62 offers some good roadside access all the way up to Union Creek (Map 7).

Rogue River National Forest

Lewis Creek

Trail

Old Ferry Road

Shady Cove

62

227

Bank access is limited above Shady Cove, but salmon fishing at the access is very good. It can also get crowded here.

Trail Creek

Cricket Creek

GPS S
Shady Cove
146 mi.

Rogue River Road

Long Branch

Rogue River National Forest

227

32

© 2007 Wilderness Adventures Press, Inc.

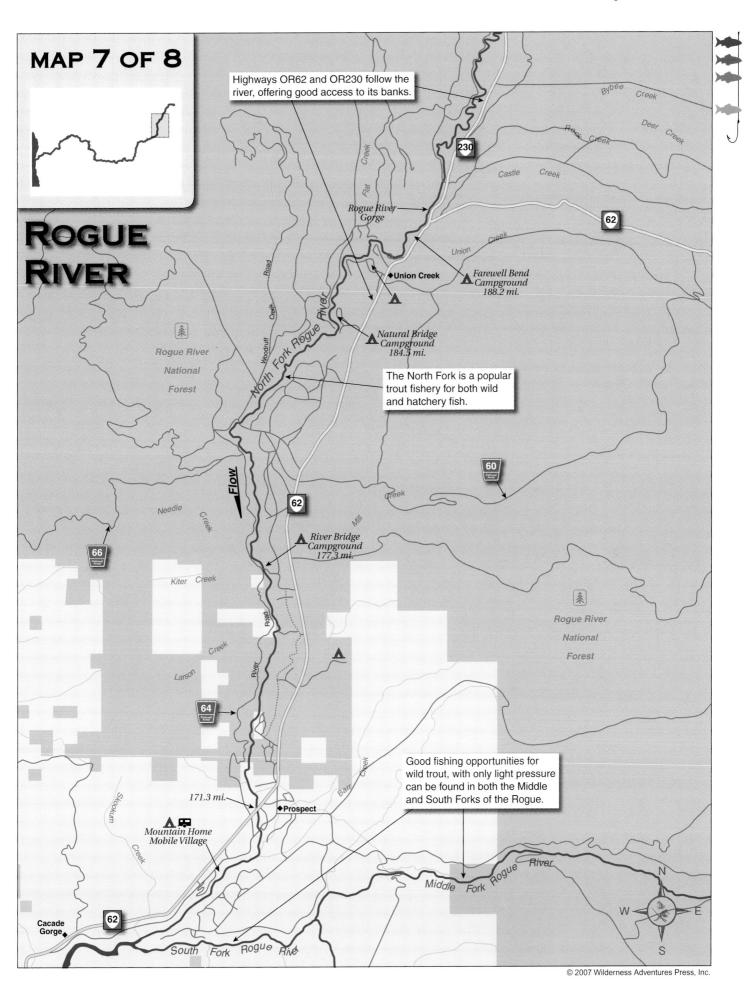

MAP 7 OF 8

ROGUE RIVER

Highways OR62 and OR230 follow the river, offering good access to its banks.

Bybee Creek

Rock Creek

Deer Creek

Castle Creek

230

62

Rogue River Gorge

Union Creek

Union Creek

Farewell Bend Campground 188.2 mi.

Flat Creek

North Fork Rogue River

Woodruff Creek

Road

Rogue River National Forest

Natural Bridge Campground 184.5 mi.

The North Fork is a popular trout fishery for both wild and hatchery fish.

60

National Forest

Mill Creek

Creek

Flow

Needle Creek

66 National Forest

River Bridge Campground 177.3 mi.

62

Kiter Creek

Rogue River National Forest

Larson Creek

River Road

64 National Forest

Barr Creek

Good fishing opportunities for wild trout, with only light pressure can be found in both the Middle and South Forks of the Rogue.

171.3 mi.

Skookum Creek

Prospect

Mountain Home Mobile Village

Middle Fork Rogue River

N

W   E

S

Cacade Gorge

62

South Fork Rogue River

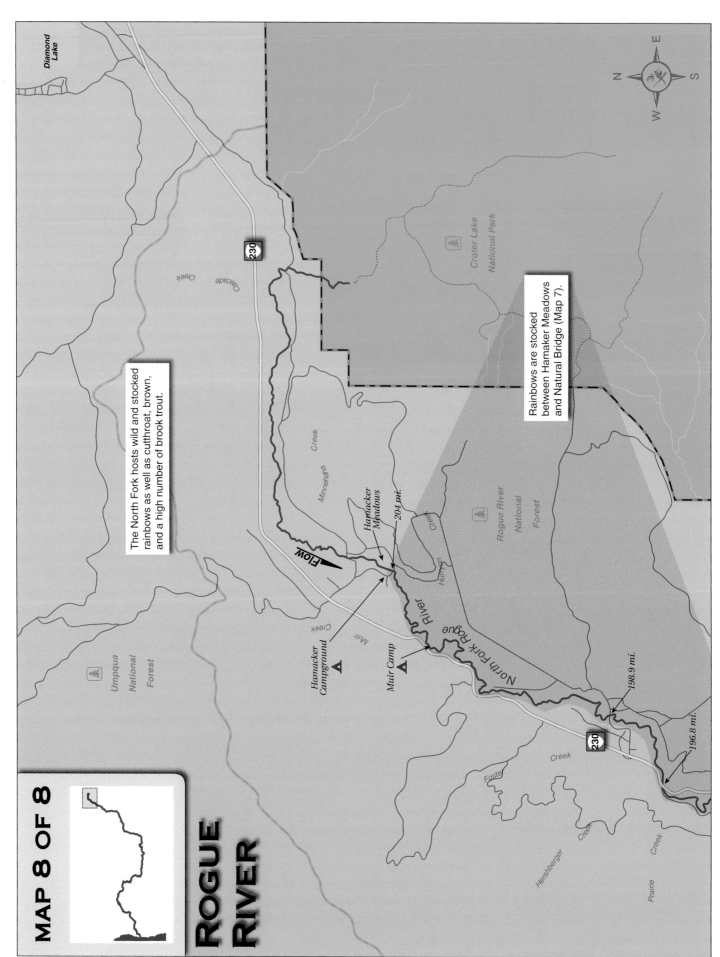

Diamond Lake

230

Cascade Creek

The North Fork hosts wild and stocked rainbows as well as cutthroat, brown, and a high number of brook trout.

Crater Lake National Park

Rainbows are stocked between Hamaker Meadows and Natural Bridge (Map 7).

Minnehaha Creek

Hamacker Meadows

204 mi.

Rogue River National Forest

Flow

Hamacker Campground

Muir Creek

Muir Camp

Umpqua National Forest

Human Creek

North Fork Rogue River

198.9 mi.

230

196.8 mi.

Foster Creek

Hershberger Creek

Prairie Creek

MAP 8 OF 8

ROGUE RIVER

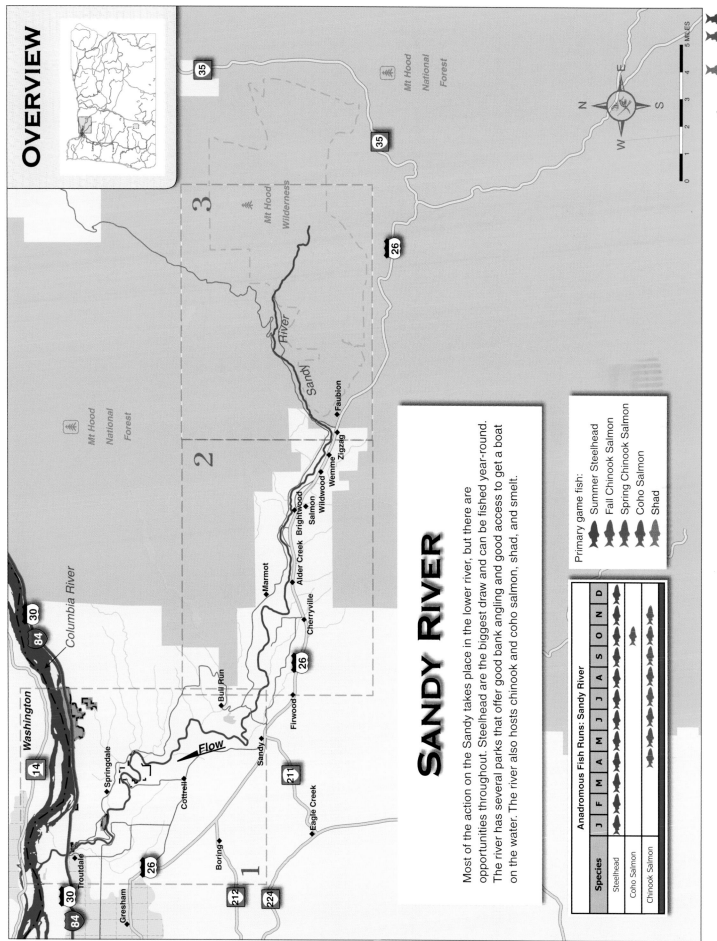

OVERVIEW

SANDY RIVER

Most of the action on the Sandy takes place in the lower river, but there are opportunities throughout. Steelhead are the biggest draw and can be fished year-round. The river has several parks that offer good bank angling and good access to get a boat on the water. The river also hosts chinook and coho salmon, shad, and smelt.

Primary game fish:

Summer Steelhead
Fall Chinook Salmon
Spring Chinook Salmon
Coho Salmon
Shad

Anadromous Fish Runs: Sandy River												
Species	J	F	M	A	M	J	J	A	S	O	N	D
Steelhead												
Coho Salmon												
Chinook Salmon												

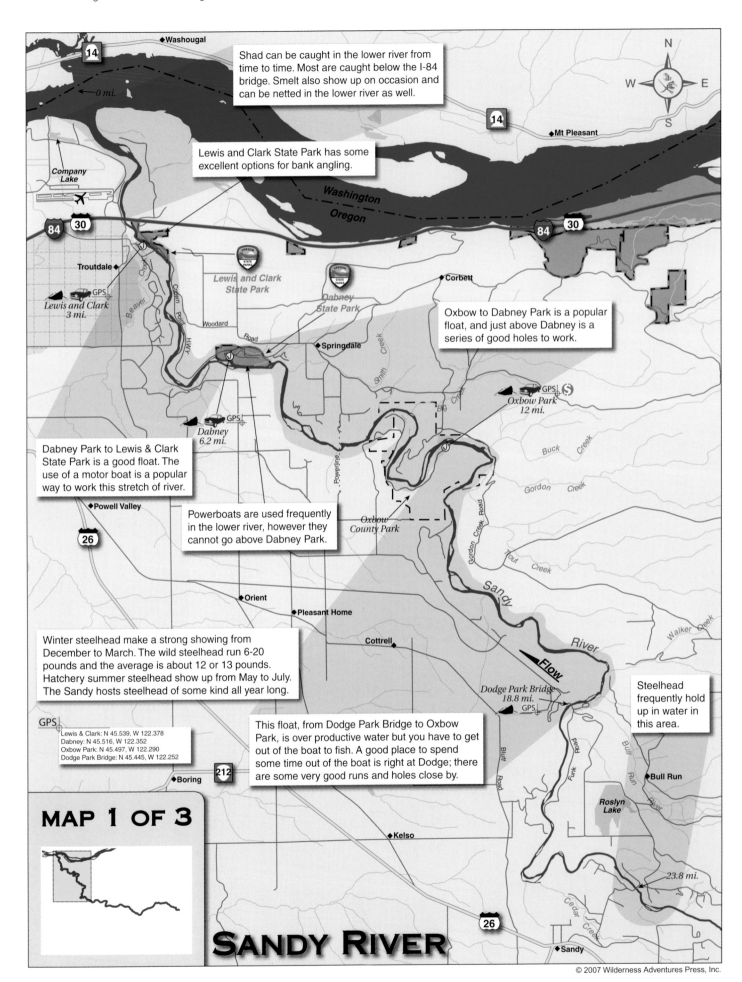

Shad can be caught in the lower river from time to time. Most are caught below the I-84 bridge. Smelt also show up on occasion and can be netted in the lower river as well.

Lewis and Clark State Park has some excellent options for bank angling.

Oxbow to Dabney Park is a popular float, and just above Dabney is a series of good holes to work.

Dabney Park to Lewis & Clark State Park is a good float. The use of a motor boat is a popular way to work this stretch of river.

Powerboats are used frequently in the lower river, however they cannot go above Dabney Park.

Winter steelhead make a strong showing from December to March. The wild steelhead run 6-20 pounds and the average is about 12 or 13 pounds. Hatchery summer steelhead show up from May to July. The Sandy hosts steelhead of some kind all year long.

GPS
Lewis & Clark: N 45.539, W 122.378
Dabney: N 45.516, W 122.352
Oxbow Park: N 45.497, W 122.290
Dodge Park Bridge: N 45.445, W 122.252

This float, from Dodge Park Bridge to Oxbow Park, is over productive water but you have to get out of the boat to fish. A good place to spend some time out of the boat is right at Dodge; there are some very good runs and holes close by.

Steelhead frequently hold up in water in this area.

MAP 1 OF 3

SANDY RIVER

© 2007 Wilderness Adventures Press, Inc.

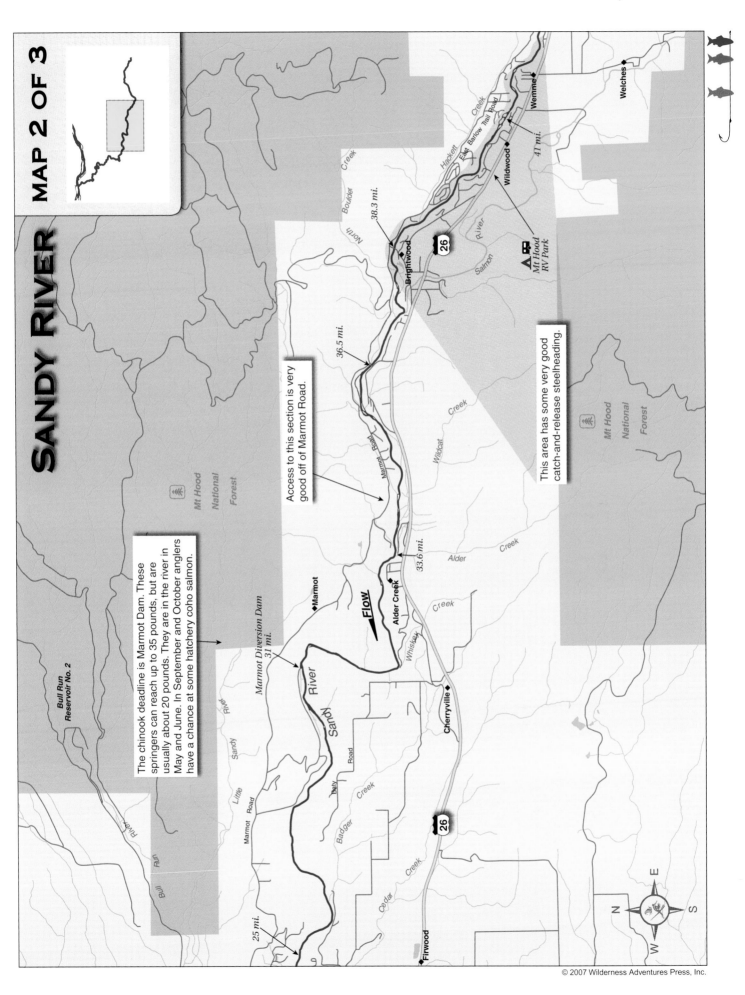

MAP 2 OF 3

SANDY RIVER

The chinook deadline is Marmot Dam. These springers can reach up to 35 pounds, but are usually about 20 pounds. They are in the river in May and June. In September and October anglers have a chance at some hatchery coho salmon.

Access to this section is very good off of Marmot Road.

This area has some very good catch-and-release steelheading.

Bull Run Reservoir No. 2

Mt Hood National Forest

Marmot

Marmot Diversion Dam

31 mi.

Sandy River

Little Sandy River

Marmot Road

Baty Road

Badger Creek

Cedar Creek

25 mi.

Firwood

Cherryville

Whiskey Creek

Alder Creek

Flow

33.6 mi.

Alder Creek

Wildcat Creek

Marmot Road

36.5 mi.

38.3 mi.

North Boulder Creek

Brightwood

26

Salmon River

Mt Hood RV Park

Wildwood

41 mi.

East Barlow Trail Road

Hackett Creek

Welches

Wemme

Mt Hood National Forest

26

Bull Run River

N E W S

© 2007 Wilderness Adventures Press, Inc.

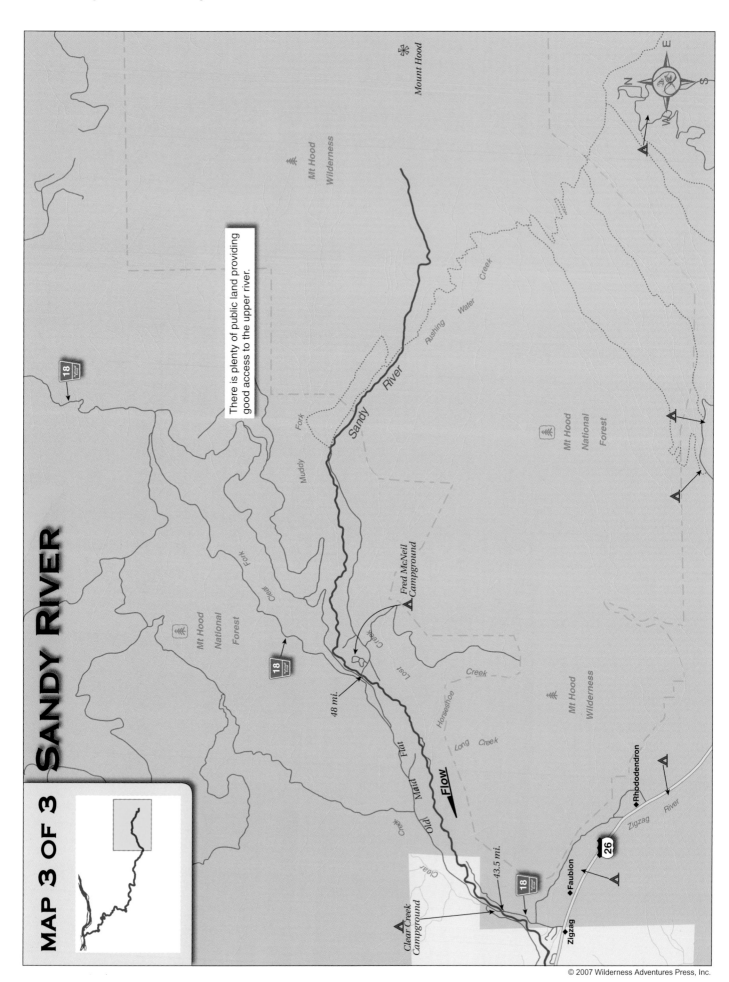

MAP 3 OF 3 SANDY RIVER

There is plenty of public land providing good access to the upper river.

Mount Hood

Mt Hood Wilderness

Sandy River

Rushing Water Creek

Muddy Fork

Clear Fork

Mt Hood National Forest

Mt Hood National Forest

Fred McNeil Campground

Lost Creek

Horseshoe Creek

Long Creek

Mt Hood Wilderness

48 mi.

FLOW

Old Maid Flat

Clear Creek

43.5 mi.

Clear Creek Campground

Faubion

Zigzag

Rhododendron

Zigzag River

© 2007 Wilderness Adventures Press, Inc.

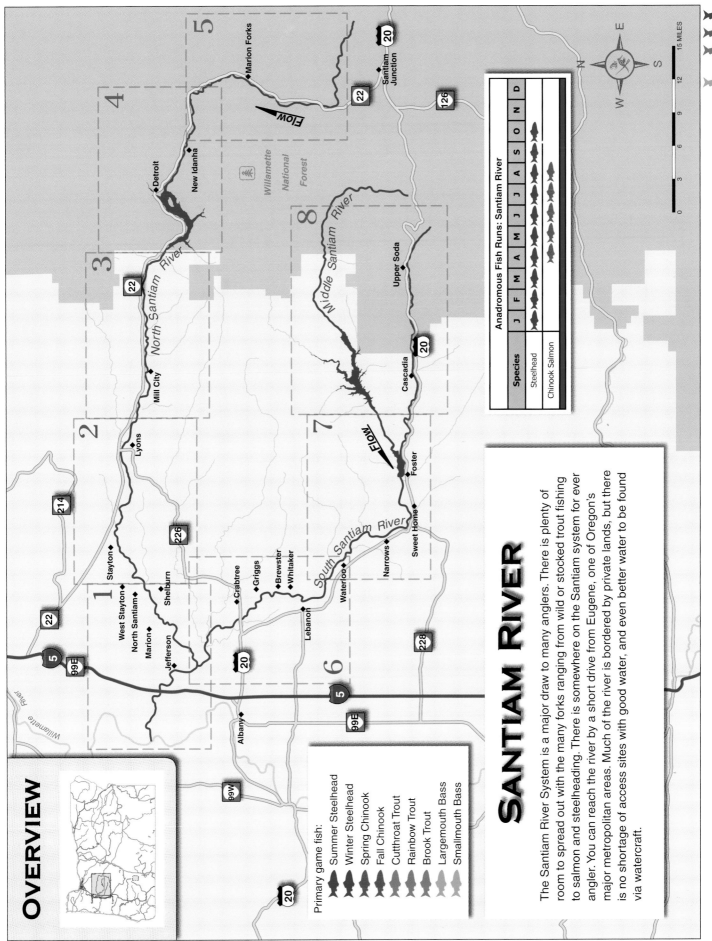

SANTIAM RIVER

The Santiam River System is a major draw to many anglers. There is plenty of room to spread out with the many forks ranging from wild or stocked trout fishing to salmon and steelhead. There is somewhere on the Santiam system for ever angler. You can reach the river by a short drive from Eugene, one of Oregon's major metropolitan areas. Much of the river is bordered by private lands, but there is no shortage of access sites with good water, and even better water to be found via watercraft.

Primary game fish:
- Summer Steelhead
- Winter Steelhead
- Spring Chinook
- Fall Chinook
- Cutthroat Trout
- Rainbow Trout
- Brook Trout
- Largemouth Bass
- Smallmouth Bass

OVERVIEW

Anadromous Fish Runs: Santiam River

Species	J	F	M	A	M	J	J	A	S	O	N	D
Steelhead												
Chinook Salmon												

Willamette National Forest

North Santiam River

Middle Santiam River

South Santiam River

Willamette River

Marion Forks
Santiam Junction
Detroit
New Idanha
Mill City
Lyons
Upper Soda
Cascadia
Foster
Sweet Home
Narrows
Waterloo
Whitaker
Brewster
Griggs
Crabtree
Lebanon
Shelburn
Stayton
West Stayton
North Santiam
Marion
Jefferson
Albany

15 MILES

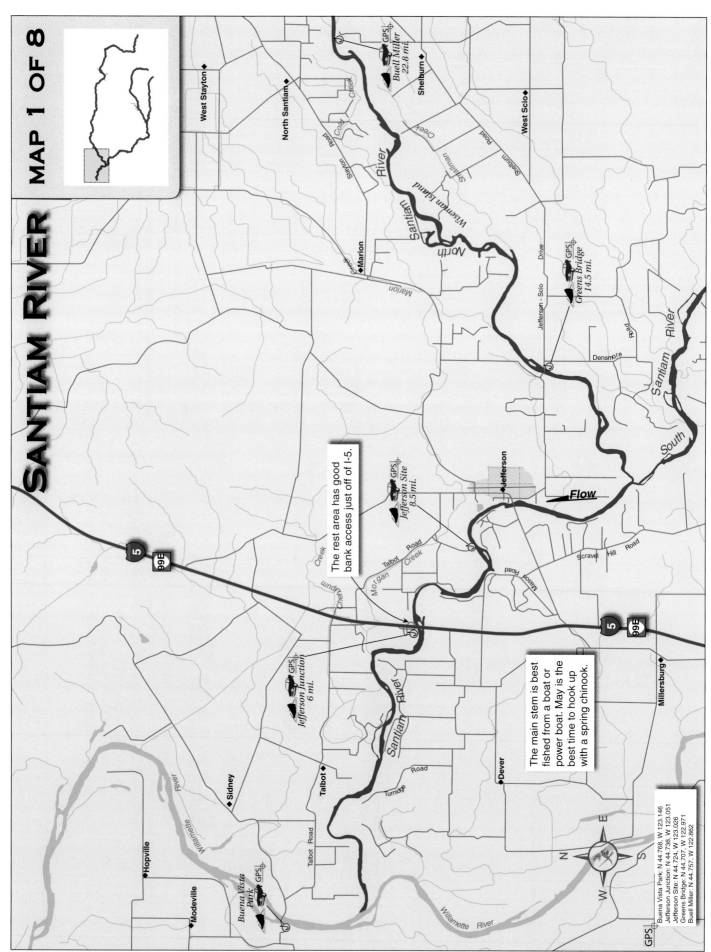

MAP 1 OF 8

SANTIAM RIVER

The rest area has good bank access just off of I-5.

The main stem is best fished from a boat or power boat. May is the best time to hook up with a spring chinook.

West Stayton ◆

North Santiam ◆

Marion ◆

Buell Miller 22.8 mi.

Shelburn ◆

West Scio ◆

Greens Bridge 14.5 mi.

Jefferson Site 8.5 mi.

Jefferson ◆

Densmore

Flow

Scravel Hill Road

Jefferson Junction 6 mi.

Dever ◆

Millersburg ◆

Talbot ◆

Sidney ◆

Hopville ◆

Modeville ◆

Buena Vista Park

Willamette River

Santiam River

South Santiam River

North Santiam River

Wisentham Island

Crabtree Creek

Thomas Creek

Jefferson - Scio Drive

Talbot Road

Morgan Creek

Mason Road

Turnidge Road

Talbot Road

GPS
Buena Vista Park: N 44.768, W 123.146
Jefferson Junction: N 44.738, W 123.051
Jefferson Site: N 44.724, W 123.026
Greens Bridge: N 44.707, W 122.971
Buell Miller: N 44.757, W 122.862

N
E
S
W

© 2007 Wilderness Adventures Press, Inc.

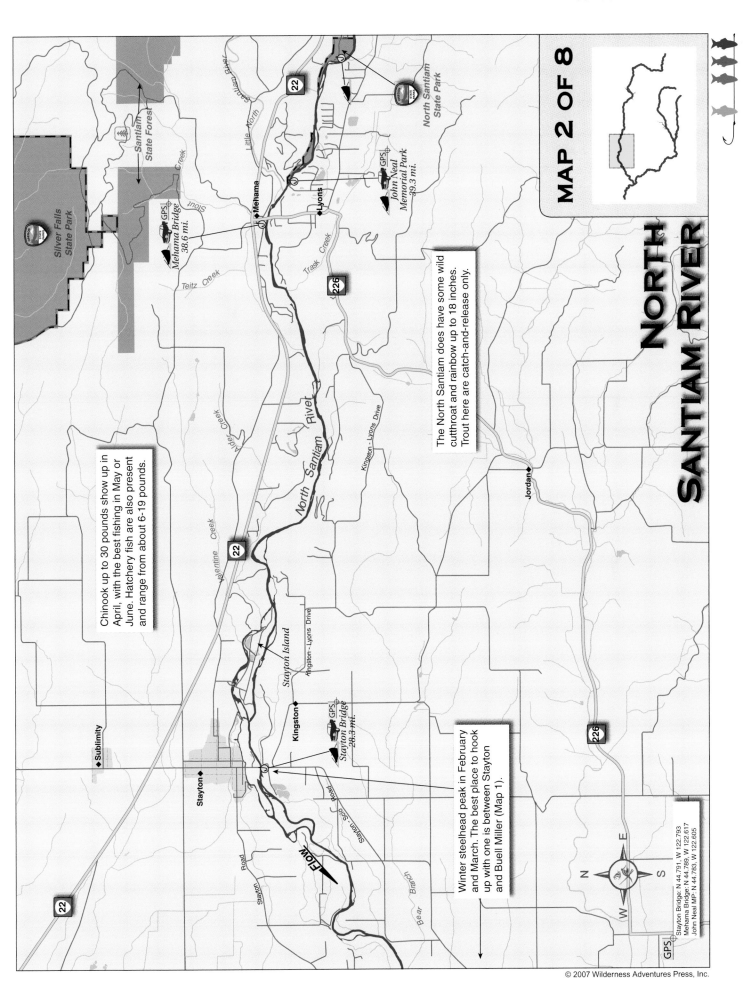

MAP 2 OF 8

NORTH
SANTIAM RIVER

Chinook up to 30 pounds show up in April, with the best fishing in May or June. Hatchery fish are also present and range from about 6-19 pounds.

The North Santiam does have some wild cutthroat and rainbow up to 18 inches. Trout here are catch-and-release only.

Winter steelhead peak in February and March. The best place to hook up with one is between Stayton and Buell Miller (Map 1).

Silver Falls State Park

Santiam State Forest

North Santiam State Park

John Neal Memorial Park 39.3 mi.

Mehama Bridge 38.6 mi.

Stayton Bridge 28.3 mi.

Mehama
Lyons
Stayton
Kingston
Sublimity
Jordan

Stayton Island

North Santiam River

Valentine Creek

Alder Creek

Teitz Creek
Trask Creek

Stout Creek

Little North Santiam River

Kingston - Lyons Drive

Stayton - Scio Road

FLOW

GPS Stayton Bridge: N 44.791, W 122.793
Mehama Bridge: N 44.789, W 122.617
John Neal MP: N 44.783, W 122.605

© 2007 Wilderness Adventures Press, Inc.

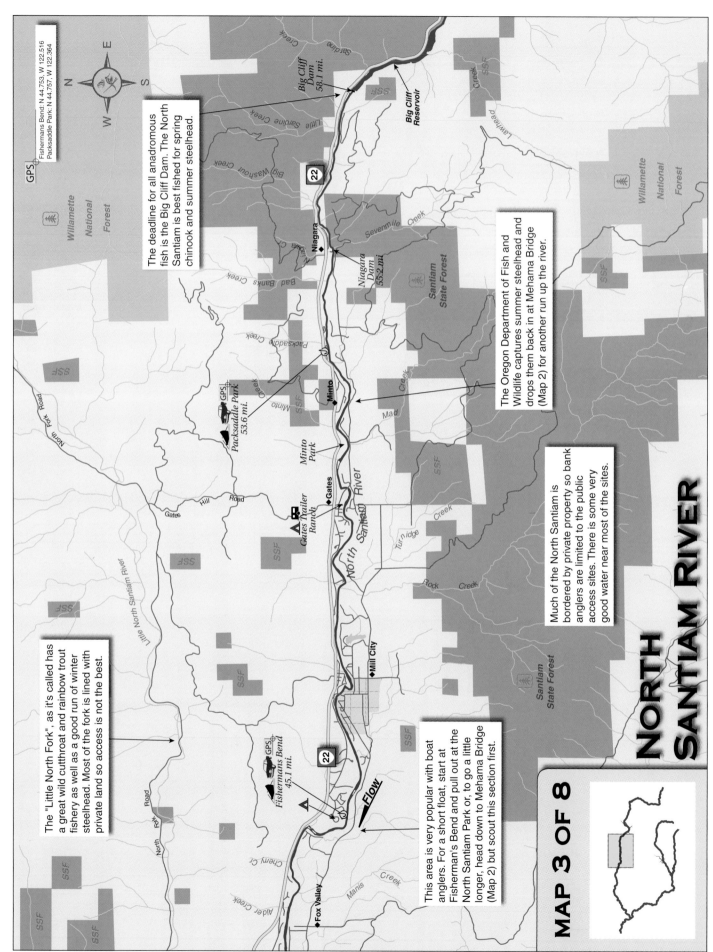

© 2007 Wilderness Adventures Press, Inc.

GPS | Fishermans Bend: N 44.753, W 122.516
Packsaddle Park: N 44.757, W 122.364

The deadline for all anadromous fish is the Big Cliff Dam. The North Santiam is best fished for spring chinook and summer steelhead.

The Oregon Department of Fish and Wildlife captures summer steelhead and drops them back in at Mehama Bridge (Map 2) for another run up the river.

Much of the North Santiam is bordered by private property so bank anglers are limited to the public access sites. There is some very good water near most of the sites.

The "Little North Fork", as it's called has a great wild cutthroat and rainbow trout fishery as well as a good run of winter steelhead. Most of the fork is lined with private land so access is not the best.

This area is very popular with boat anglers. For a short float, start at Fisherman's Bend and pull out at the North Santiam Park or, to go a little longer, head down to Mehama Bridge (Map 2) but scout this section first.

Big Cliff Dam
58.1 mi.

Big Cliff Reservoir

Niagara

Niagara Dam
55.2 mi.

Packsaddle Park
53.6 mi.

Minto

Minto Park

Gates

Gates Trailer Ranch

Mill City

Fishermans Bend
45.1 mi.

Fox Valley

North Santiam River

Flow

Willamette National Forest

Santiam State Forest

NORTH SANTIAM RIVER

MAP 3 OF 8

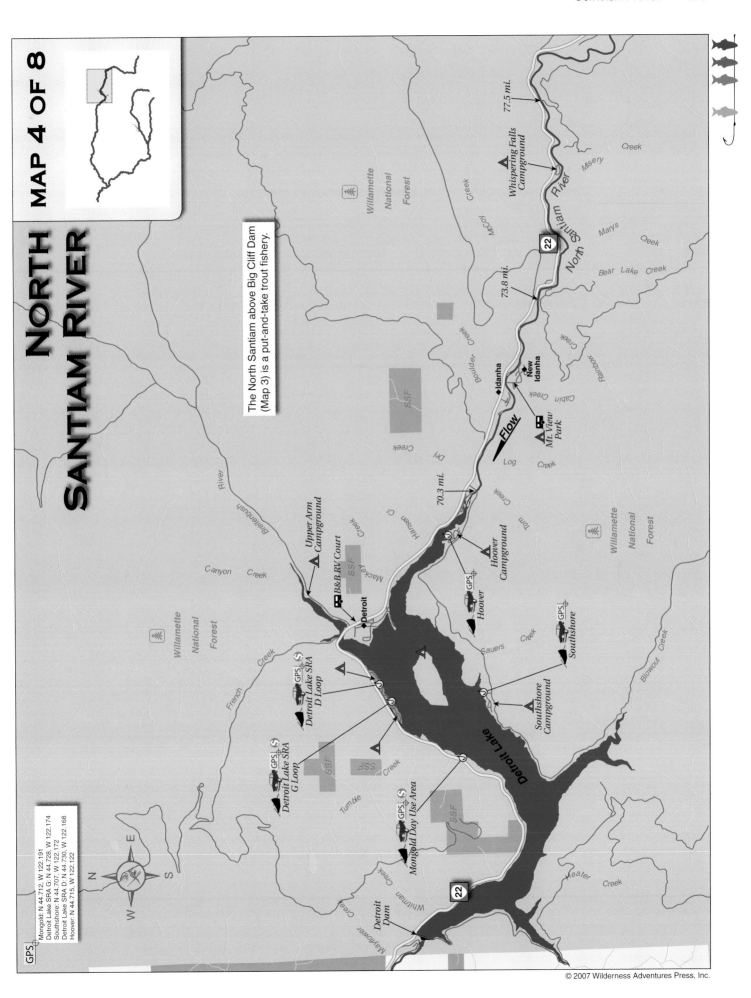

NORTH
SANTIAM RIVER

MAP 4 OF 8

The North Santiam above Big Cliff Dam (Map 3) is a put-and-take trout fishery.

GPS
Mongold: N 44.712, W 122.191
Detroit Lake SRA G: N 44.728, W 122.174
Southshore: N 44.707, W 122.172
Detroit Lake SRA D: N 44.730, W 122.168
Hoover: N 44.715, W 122.122

77.5 mi.

Whispering Falls
Campground

Misery   Creek

McCoy   Creek

73.8 mi.

North Santiam River

22

Marys   Creek

Bear Lake Creek

Rainbow   Creek

Idanha

New
Idanha

Cabin   Creek

Flow

Mt. View
Park

Boulder   Creek

Log   Creek

70.3 mi.

Willamette
National
Forest

Dry   Creek

SSF

Tom   Creek

Hoover
Campground

Hoover

Gauers   Creek

Southshore

Willamette
National
Forest

Blowout   Creek

Hansen   Cr.

Mackey   Creek

SSF

Southshore
Campground

Breitenbush   River

Upper Arm
Campground

B&B RV Court

Detroit

Canyon   Creek

French   Creek

Willamette
National
Forest

GPS
Detroit Lake SRA
D Loop

GPS
Detroit Lake SRA
G Loop

SSF

SSF   Creek

Tumble   Creek

GPS
Mongold Day Use Area

Detroit Lake

22

Whitman   Creek

Detroit
Dam

Mayflower   Creek

Heater   Creek

N
W   E
S

© 2007 Wilderness Adventures Press, Inc.

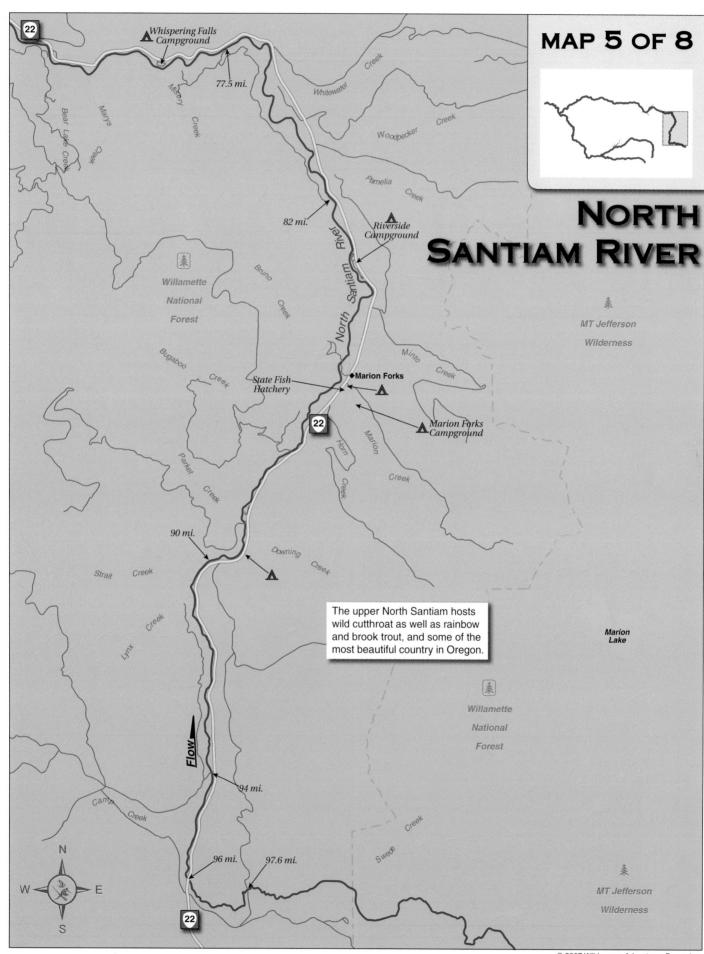

MAP 5 OF 8

NORTH SANTIAM RIVER

Whispering Falls Campground

77.5 mi.

Whitewater Creek

Woodpecker Creek

Pamelia Creek

82 mi.

Riverside Campground

Misery Creek

Marys Creek

Bear Lake Creek

Bruno Creek

Willamette National Forest

MT Jefferson Wilderness

Bugaboo Creek

Minto Creek

State Fish Hatchery

◆Marion Forks

Marion Forks Campground

22

Horn Creek

Marion Creek

Parket Creek

90 mi.

Downing Creek

Strait Creek

The upper North Santiam hosts wild cutthroat as well as rainbow and brook trout, and some of the most beautiful country in Oregon.

Marion Lake

Lynx Creek

Flow

Willamette National Forest

94 mi.

Camp Creek

Swede Creek

96 mi.   97.6 mi.

N
W   E
S

MT Jefferson Wilderness

22

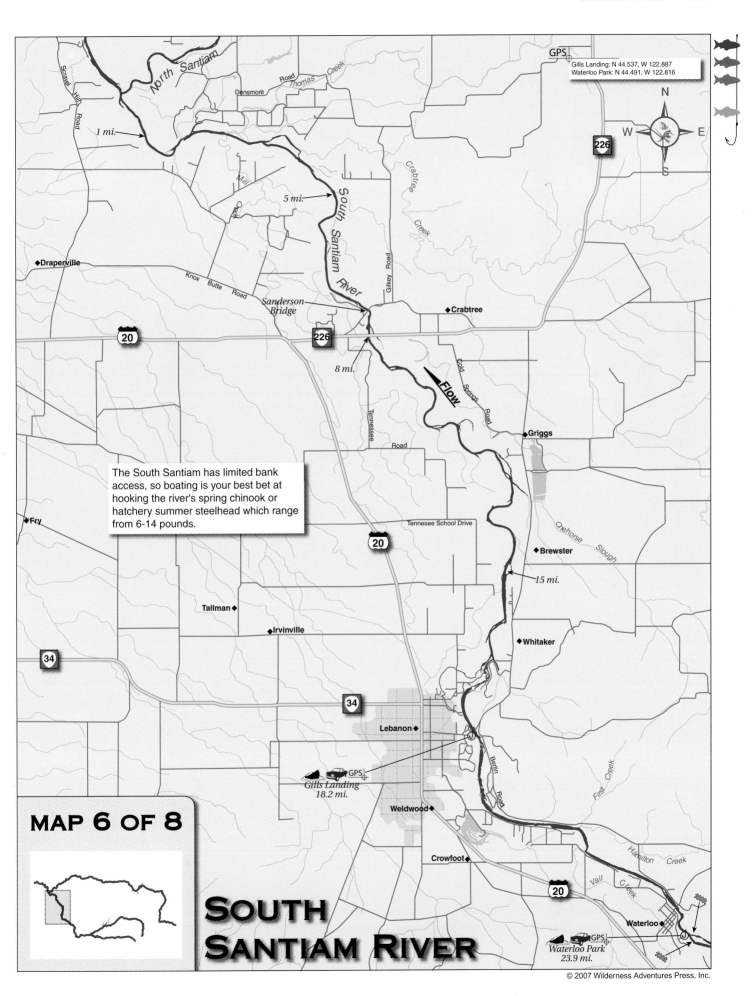

GPS
Gills Landing: N 44.537, W 122.887
Waterloo Park: N 44.491, W 122.816

North Santiam

Scravel Hill Road

1 mi.

Densmore

Road Thomas Creek

Crabtree Creek

226

South Santiam River

5 mi.

◆Draperville

Knox Butte Road

Sanderson Bridge

226

Gilkey Road

◆Crabtree

20

8 mi.

Flow

Cold Springs Road

◆Griggs

Tennessee Road

The South Santiam has limited bank access, so boating is your best bet at hooking the river's spring chinook or hatchery summer steelhead which range from 6-14 pounds.

◆Fry

Tennesee School Drive

20

Onehorse Slough

◆Brewster

15 mi.

◆Tallman

◆Irvinville

◆Whitaker

34

34

Lebanon◆

Berlin Road

GPS
Gills Landing
18.2 mi.

Weldwood◆

First Creek

Crowfoot◆

Hamilton Creek

20

Vail Creek

Waterloo◆

GPS
Waterloo Park
23.9 mi.

MAP 6 OF 8

SOUTH SANTIAM RIVER

© 2007 Wilderness Adventures Press, Inc.

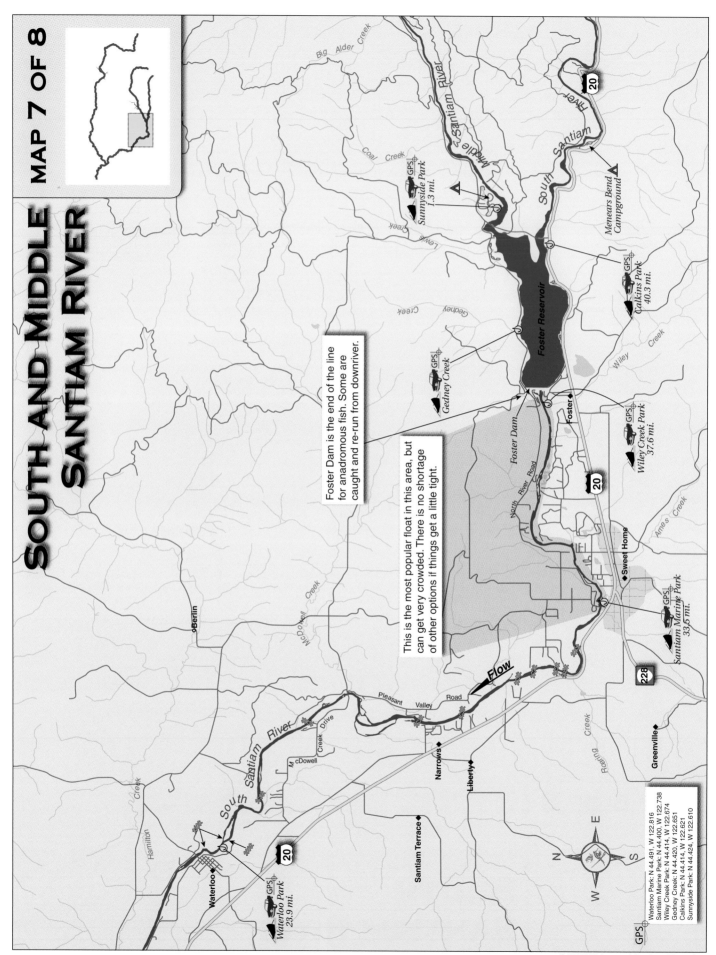

SOUTH AND MIDDLE SANTIAM RIVER

MAP 7 OF 8

Big Alder Creek

Coal Creek

Middle Santiam River

South Santiam River

20

Menears Bend Campground

GPS Sunnyside Park 1.3 mi.

Lewis Creek

Foster Reservoir

GPS Calkins Park 40.3 mi.

Gedney Creek

GPS Gedney Creek

Wiley Creek

Foster Dam is the end of the line for anadromous fish. Some are caught and re-run from downriver.

This is the most popular float in this area, but can get very crowded. There is no shortage of other options if things get a little tight.

Foster

GPS Wiley Creek Park 37.6 mi.

20

Foster Dam

North River Road

Ames' Creek

Sweet Home

GPS Santiam Marine Park 33.5 mi.

Berlin

McDowell Creek

228

Flow

Pleasant Valley Road

Roaring Creek

Creek Drive

McDowell

Narrows

Liberty

Greenville

South Santiam River

Hamilton Creek

Santiam Terrace

N E W S

Waterloo

20

GPS Waterloo Park 23.9 mi.

GPS
Waterloo Park: N 44.491, W 122.816
Santiam Marine Park: N 44.400, W 122.738
Wiley Creek Park: N 44.414, W 122.674
Gedney Creek: N 44.420, W 122.651
Calkins Park: N 44.414, W 122.621
Sunnyside Park: N 44.424, W 122.610

© 2007 Wilderness Adventures Press, Inc.

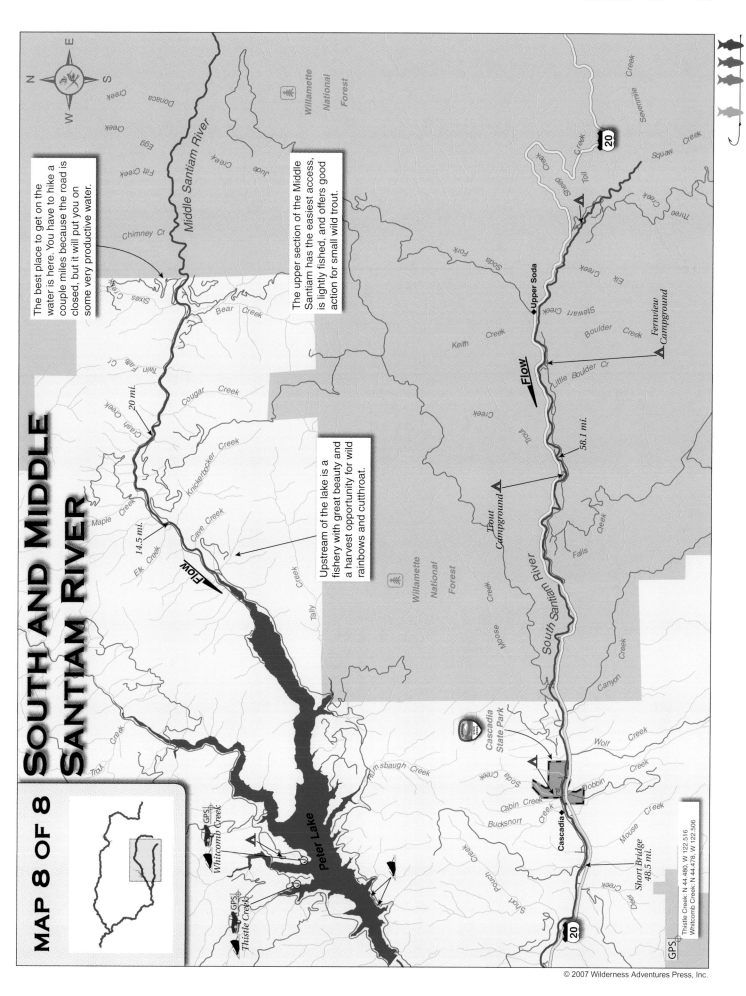

MAP 8 OF 8 SOUTH AND MIDDLE SANTIAM RIVER

The best place to get on the water is here. You have to hike a couple miles because the road is closed, but it will put you on some very productive water.

The upper section of the Middle Santiam has the easiest access, is lightly fished, and offers good action for small wild trout.

Upstream of the lake is a fishery with great beauty and a harvest opportunity for wild rainbows and cutthroat.

Middle Santiam River

Willamette National Forest

Donaca Creek

Egg Creek

Fitt Creek

Jude Creek

Chimney Cr

Sixes Creek

Bear Creek

Twin Falls Cr

Crash Creek

20 mi.

Cougar Creek

Knickerbocker Creek

Maple Creek

Cave Creek

14.5 mi.

Elk Creek

Flow

Tally Creek

Willamette National Forest

Trout Creek

Moose Creek

Rumsbaugh Creek

Soda Creek

Cabin Creek

Bucksnort Creek

Short Pouch Creek

Deer Creek

Peter Lake

GPS
Whitcomb Creek

GPS
Thistle Creek

Trout Creek

Sheep Creek

Toll Creek

Sevenmile Creek

Squaw Creek

Three Creek

20

Upper Soda

Soda Fork

Keith Creek

Stewart Creek

Elk Creek

Boulder Creek

Fernview Campground

Little Boulder Cr

Flow

58.1 mi.

Trout Creek

Trout Campground

South Santiam River

Falls

Canyon Creek

Cascadia State Park

Wolf Creek

Dobbin Creek

Cascadia

Mouse Creek

Short Bridge
48.5 mi.

20

GPS | Thistle Creek: N 44.480, W 122.516
Whitcomb Creek: N 44.478, W 122.506

© 2007 Wilderness Adventures Press, Inc.

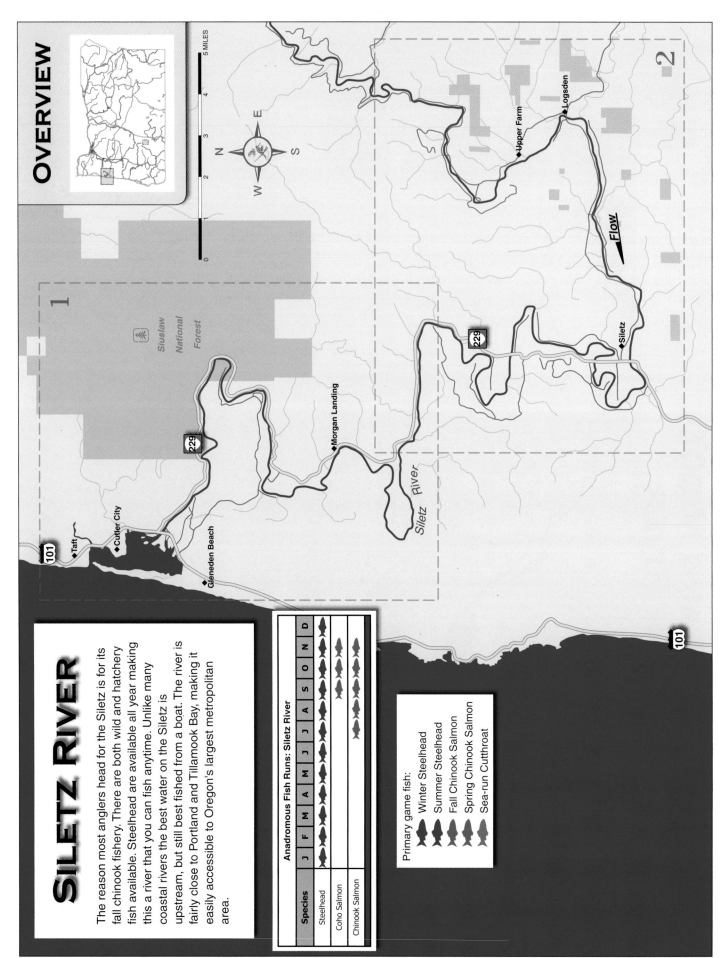

OVERVIEW

5 MILES

SILETZ RIVER

The reason most anglers head for the Siletz is for its fall chinook fishery. There are both wild and hatchery fish available. Steelhead are available all year making this a river that you can fish anytime. Unlike many coastal rivers the best water on the Siletz is upstream, but still best fished from a boat. The river is fairly close to Portland and Tillamook Bay, making it easily accessible to Oregon's largest metropolitan area.

Anadromous Fish Runs: Siletz River

Species	J	F	M	A	M	J	J	A	S	O	N	D
Steelhead	🐟	🐟	🐟	🐟	🐟	🐟	🐟	🐟	🐟	🐟	🐟	🐟
Coho Salmon									🐟	🐟	🐟	
Chinook Salmon								🐟	🐟	🐟	🐟	🐟

Primary game fish:

Winter Steelhead
Summer Steelhead
Fall Chinook Salmon
Spring Chinook Salmon
Sea-run Cutthroat

Siuslaw National Forest

Taft
Cutler City
Gleneden Beach
Morgan Landing
Siletz
Logsden
Upper Farm

Siletz River

Flow

SILETZ RIVER

MAP 1 OF 2

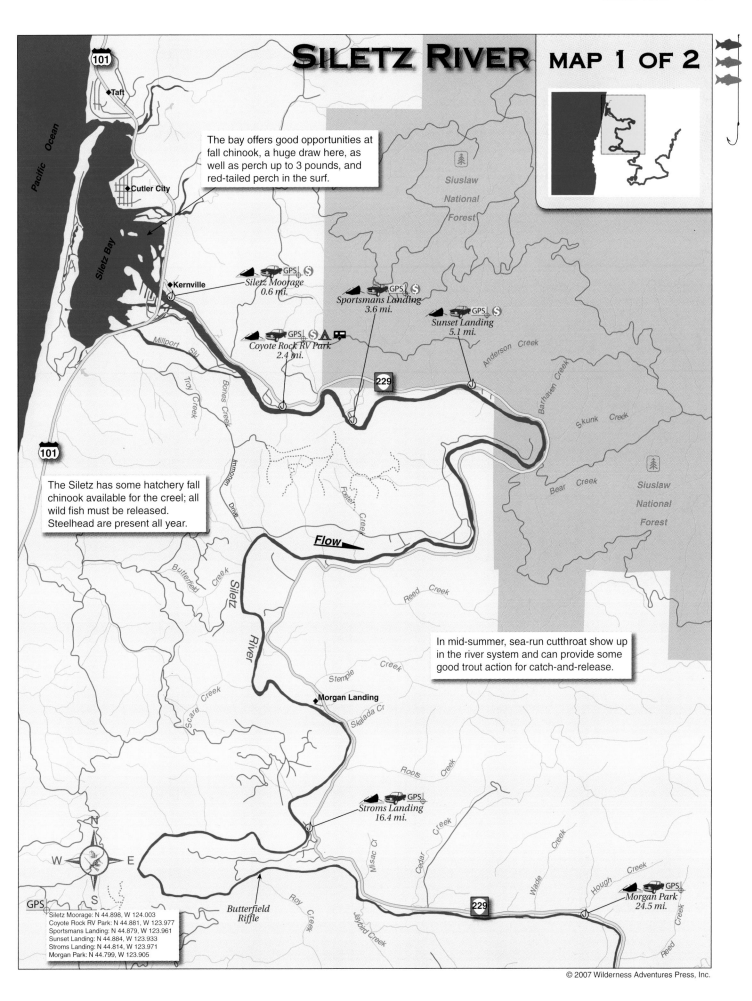

The bay offers good opportunities at fall chinook, a huge draw here, as well as perch up to 3 pounds, and red-tailed perch in the surf.

The Siletz has some hatchery fall chinook available for the creel; all wild fish must be released. Steelhead are present all year.

In mid-summer, sea-run cutthroat show up in the river system and can provide some good trout action for catch-and-release.

Pacific Ocean

Siletz Bay

Taft

Cutler City

Kernville

Siletz Moorage 0.6 mi.

Sportsmans Landing 3.6 mi.

Sunset Landing 5.1 mi.

Coyote Rock RV Park 2.4 mi.

Siuslaw National Forest

Anderson Creek

Barhaven Creek

Skunk Creek

Bear Creek

Siuslaw National Forest

Millport Slu

Troy Creek

Bones Creek

Immonen Drive

Foster Creek

Flow

Reed Creek

Butterfield Creek

Siletz River

Stemple Creek

Morgan Landing

Skalada Cr

Scare Creek

Roots Creek

Creek

Misac Cr

Cedar Creek

Wade Creek

Hough Creek

Strons Landing 16.4 mi.

Butterfield Riffle

Roy Creek

Jaybird Creek

Morgan Park 24.5 mi.

Reed Creek

101

101

229

229

N
W E
S

GPS

Siletz Moorage: N 44.898, W 124.003
Coyote Rock RV Park: N 44.881, W 123.977
Sportsmans Landing: N 44.879, W 123.961
Sunset Landing: N 44.884, W 123.933
Strons Landing: N 44.814, W 123.971
Morgan Park: N 44.799, W 123.905

© 2007 Wilderness Adventures Press, Inc.

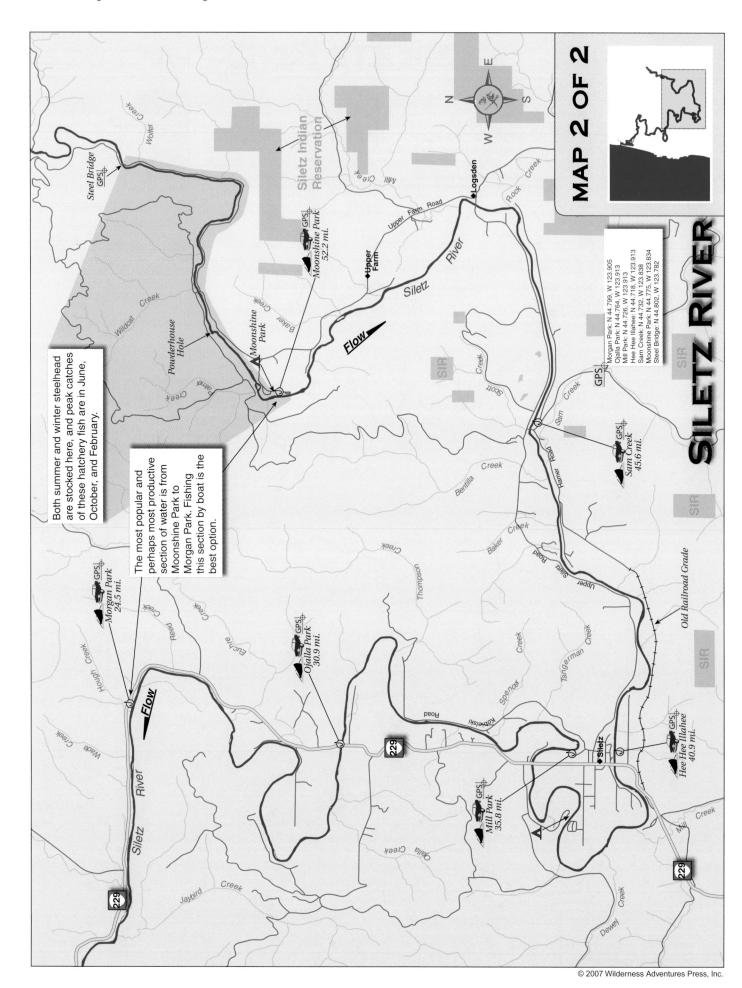

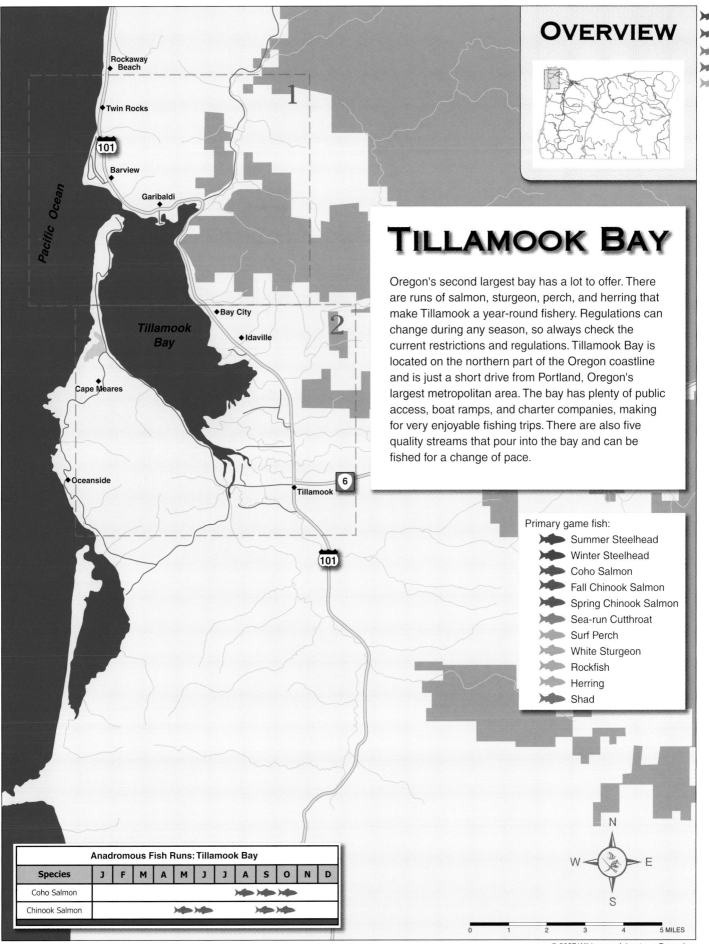

TILLAMOOK BAY

Oregon's second largest bay has a lot to offer. There are runs of salmon, sturgeon, perch, and herring that make Tillamook a year-round fishery. Regulations can change during any season, so always check the current restrictions and regulations. Tillamook Bay is located on the northern part of the Oregon coastline and is just a short drive from Portland, Oregon's largest metropolitan area. The bay has plenty of public access, boat ramps, and charter companies, making for very enjoyable fishing trips. There are also five quality streams that pour into the bay and can be fished for a change of pace.

Primary game fish:
- Summer Steelhead
- Winter Steelhead
- Coho Salmon
- Fall Chinook Salmon
- Spring Chinook Salmon
- Sea-run Cutthroat
- Surf Perch
- White Sturgeon
- Rockfish
- Herring
- Shad

Anadromous Fish Runs: Tillamook Bay												
Species	J	F	M	A	M	J	J	A	S	O	N	D
Coho Salmon								✦	✦	✦		
Chinook Salmon				✦	✦				✦	✦		

© 2007 Wilderness Adventures Press, Inc.

TILLAMOOK BAY

MAP 1 OF 2

Chinook have both a spring and fall run. In the spring, expect an average of 19 or 20 pounds, and in fall about 26 pounds.

Hobsonville Point is popular and productive for perch.

The best sturgeon fishing throughout the season is consistently in the Ghost Hole to Bay City area.

Ghost Hole is a popular salmon hot spot, as well as a productive sturgeon fishery. If the fishing is good, expect a crowd here.

Sturgeon show up in the bay in winter and can be found near Bay City. They continue to increase in numbers until spring when they can be found in almost any of the deep channels.

The best and safest way to fish offshore halibut, coho, and chinook salmon is to charter a boat and plan on a full day.

The Garibaldi Coast Guard Pier is popular for crabbing as well as offering a chance at some chinook.

Anglers fishing from the South Jetty can catch ling cod and chinook. This is also a popular place for night fishing for sea bass.

Flow

Miami River

Moss Creek

Illingsworth Creek

Tillamook State Forest

Patterson Creek

Bay City

Larson Creek

Electric Creek

Ghost Hole

Hobsonville

Oregon Coast Highway

Bay City Channel

Larson Cove

Sandstone Point

Hobsonville Point

Tidal Flat

Port of Bay City

GPS

Tillamook Bay

Main Channel

Seal Channel

South Channel

Miami Cove

101

Garibaldi Marina

GPS

Garibaldi

Old Coast Guard Pier

Painted Rocks

Smith Creek

Enright Road

Miami River Road

Hobson Creek

Struby Creek

Tillamook State Forest

Twin Rocks

Watseco

Shorewood Travel Trailer Village

Smith Lake

Bareview Park

Barview

101

Crab Harbor

Kincheloe Point

Dike Road

Tidal Flat

Bayocean Peninsula

Bayocean

N

E

S

W

Pacific Ocean

North Jetty

South Jetty

Oregon Islands National Wildlife Refuge

1 MILE

0

GPS

Port of Bay City: N 45.555, W 123.911
Garibaldi Marina: N 45.557, W 123.911

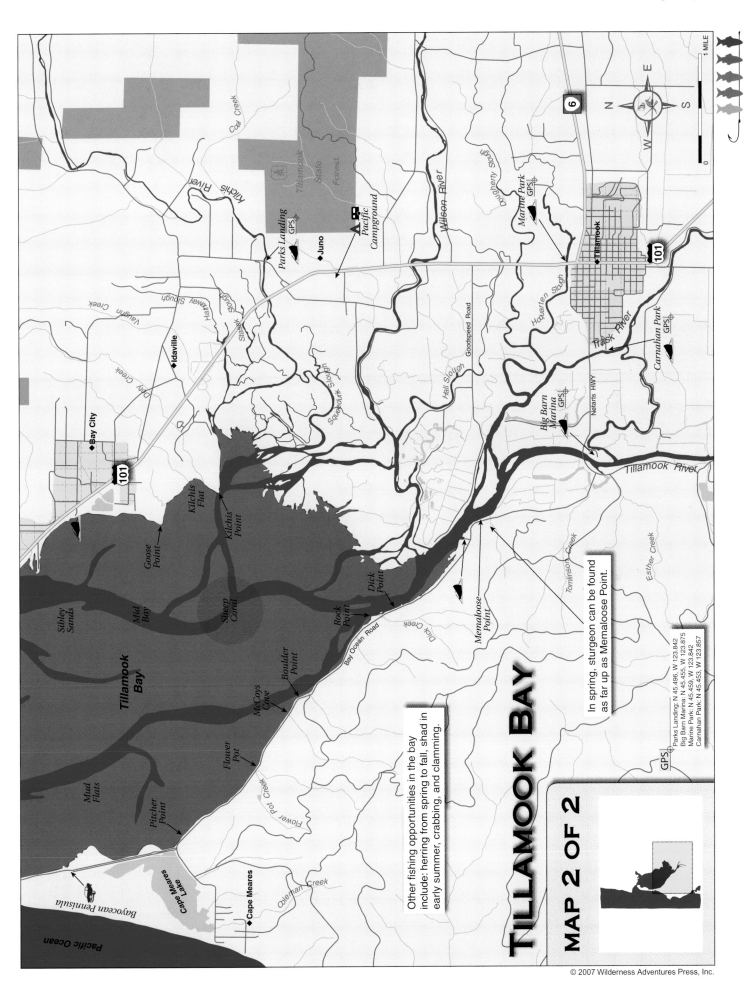

Pacific Ocean

Bayocean Peninsula

Cape Meares Lake

♦ Cape Meares

Coleman Creek

Flower Pot Creek

Mud Flats

Pitcher Point

Flower Pot

Tillamook Bay

Sibley Sands

Mid Bay

McCoys Cove

Boulder Point

Sheep Corral

Rock Point

Bay Ocean Road

Dick Creek

Dick Point

Memaloose Point

Goose Point

Kilchis Flat

Kilchis Point

Vaughn Creek

Dry Creek

♦ Bay City

101

Idaville ♦

Hathaway Slough

Stasek Slough

Squeedunk Slough

Hall Slough

Goodspeed Road

Netarts HWY

Tomlinson Creek

Esther Creek

Coal Creek

Kilchis River

Tillamook State Forest

Parks Landing
GPS

Juno ♦

Pacific Campground

Wilson River

Dougherty Slough

Marine Park
GPS

Hoquarten Slough

♦ Tillamook

101

6

Trask River

Carnahan Park
GPS

Big Barn Marina
GPS

Tillamook River

In spring, sturgeon can be found
as far up as Memaloose Point.

Other fishing opportunities in the bay
include: herring from spring to fall, shad in
early summer, crabbing, and clamming.

GPS   Parks Landing: N 45.496, W 123.842
Big Barn Marina: N 45.455, W 123.875
Marine Park: N 45.459, W 123.842
Carnahan Park: N 45.453, W 123.857

Tillamook Bay

Map 2 of 2

N
E   W
S

1 MILE

0

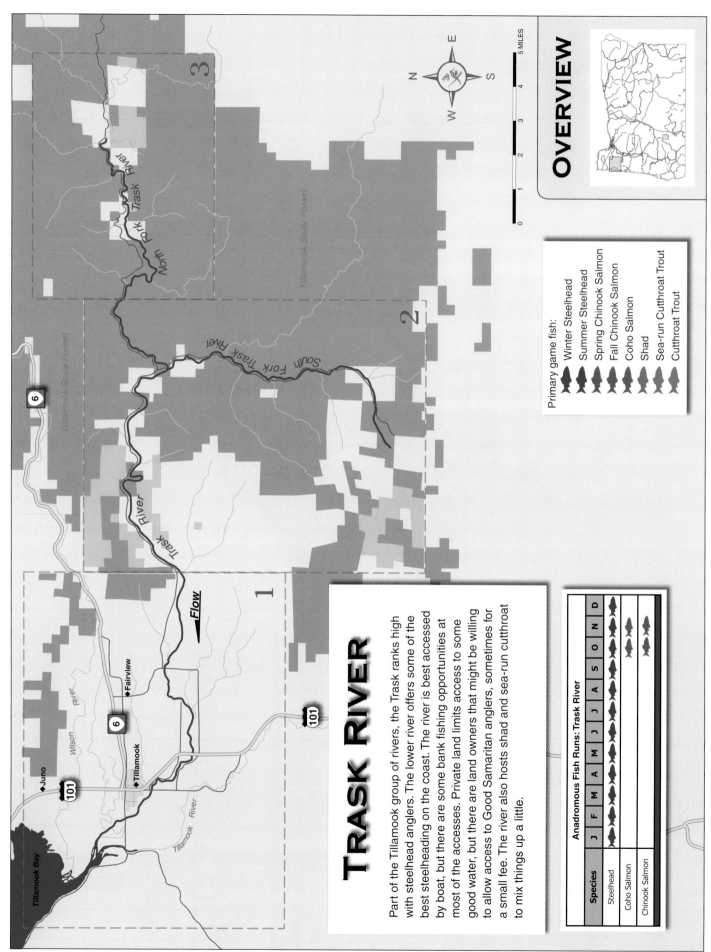

OVERVIEW

TRASK RIVER

Part of the Tillamook group of rivers, the Trask ranks high with steelhead anglers. The lower river offers some of the best steelheading on the coast. The river is best accessed by boat, but there are some bank fishing opportunities at most of the accesses. Private land limits access to some good water, but there are land owners that might be willing to allow access to Good Samaritan anglers, sometimes for a small fee. The river also hosts shad and sea-run cutthroat to mix things up a little.

Anadromous Fish Runs: Trask River

Species	J	F	M	A	M	J	J	A	S	O	N	D
Steelhead												
Coho Salmon												
Chinook Salmon												

Primary game fish:

- Winter Steelhead
- Summer Steelhead
- Spring Chinook Salmon
- Fall Chinook Salmon
- Coho Salmon
- Shad
- Sea-run Cutthroat Trout
- Cutthroat Trout

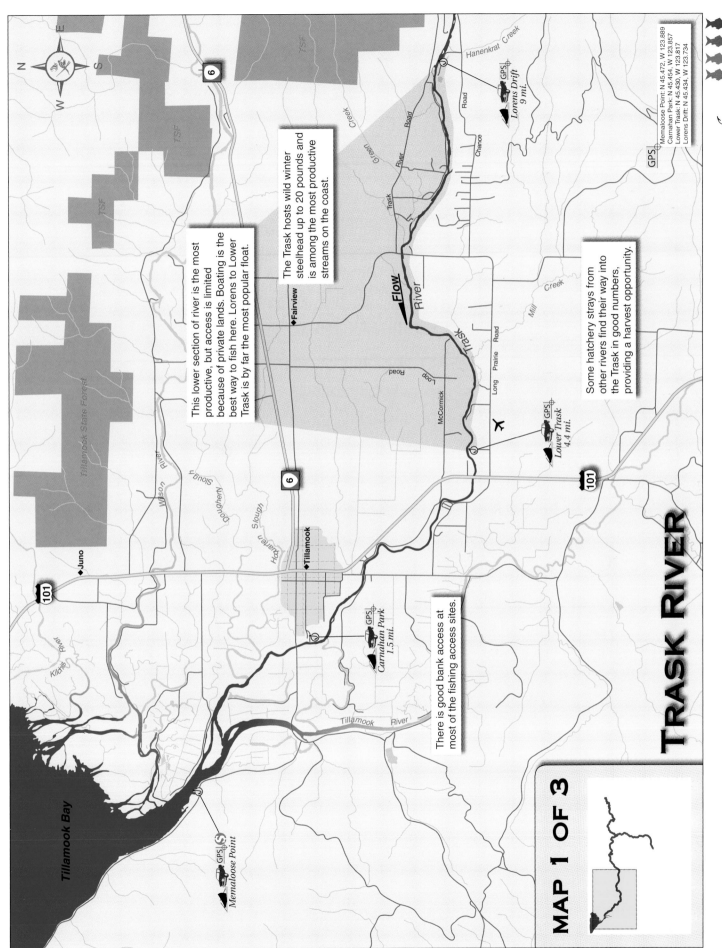

This lower section of river is the most productive, but access is limited because of private lands. Boating is the best way to fish here. Lorens to Lower Trask is by far the most popular float.

The Trask hosts wild winter steelhead up to 20 pounds and is among the most productive streams on the coast.

Some hatchery strays from other rivers find their way into the Trask in good numbers, providing a harvest opportunity.

There is good bank access at most of the fishing access sites.

Memaloose Point: N 45.472, W 123.889
Carnahan Park: N 45.454, W 123.857
Lower Trask: N 45.430, W 123.817
Lorens Drift: N 45.434, W 123.734

Lorens Drift 9 mi.

Lower Trask 4.4 mi.

Carnahan Park 1.5 mi.

Memaloose Point

TRASK RIVER

MAP 1 OF 3

© 2007 Wilderness Adventures Press, Inc.

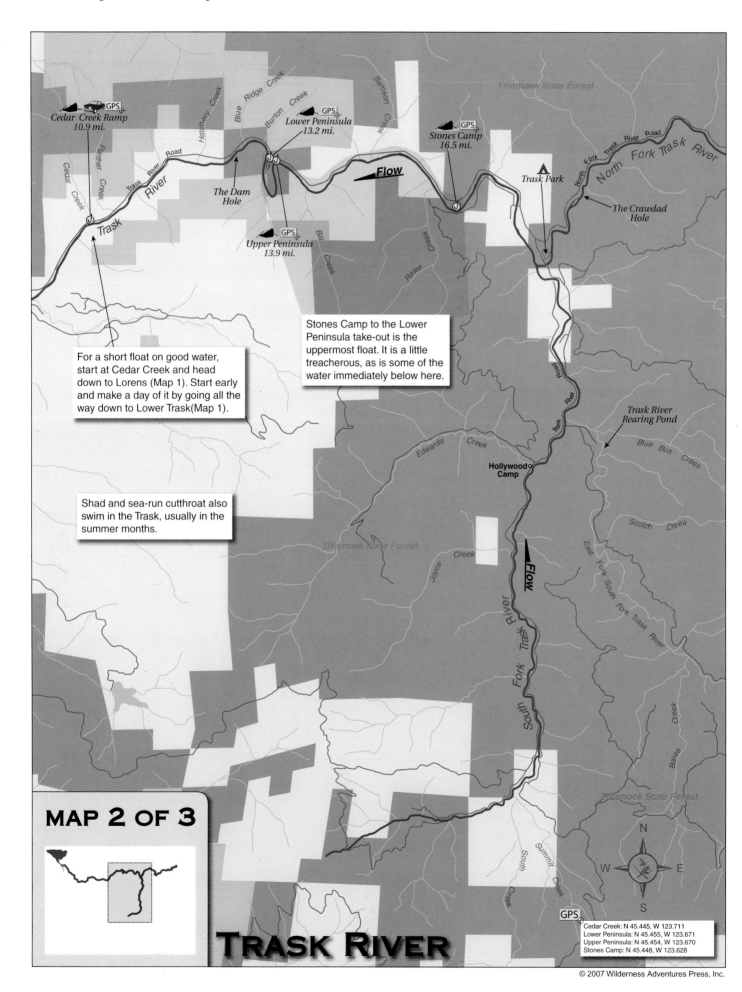

Cedar Creek Ramp
10.9 mi.

GPS

Panther Creek

Cedar Creek

Hatchery Creek

Blue Ridge Creek

Burton Creek

Trask River Road

Trask River

Lower Peninsula
13.2 mi.

GPS

The Dam
Hole

Upper Peninsula
13.9 mi.

GPS

Bill Creek

Samson Creek

Flow

Stones Camp
16.5 mi.

GPS

Rawe Creek

Trask Park

North Fork Trask River Road

North Fork Trask River

The Crawdad
Hole

For a short float on good water,
start at Cedar Creek and head
down to Lorens (Map 1). Start early
and make a day of it by going all the
way down to Lower Trask(Map 1).

Stones Camp to the Lower
Peninsula take-out is the
uppermost float. It is a little
treacherous, as is some of the
water immediately below here.

Trask River
Rearing Pond

Blue Bus Creek

Edwards Creek

Hollywood
Camp

Trask River

Scotch Creek

Shad and sea-run cutthroat also
swim in the Trask, usually in the
summer months.

Tillamook State Forest

Joyce Creek

Creek

South Fork Trask River

Flow

East Fork South Fork Trask River

Bales Creek

Tillamook State Forest

MAP 2 OF 3

South Creek

Summit Creek

N
W   E
S

GPS

TRASK RIVER

Cedar Creek: N 45.445, W 123.711
Lower Peninsula: N 45.455, W 123.671
Upper Peninsula: N 45.454, W 123.670
Stones Camp: N 45.448, W 123.628

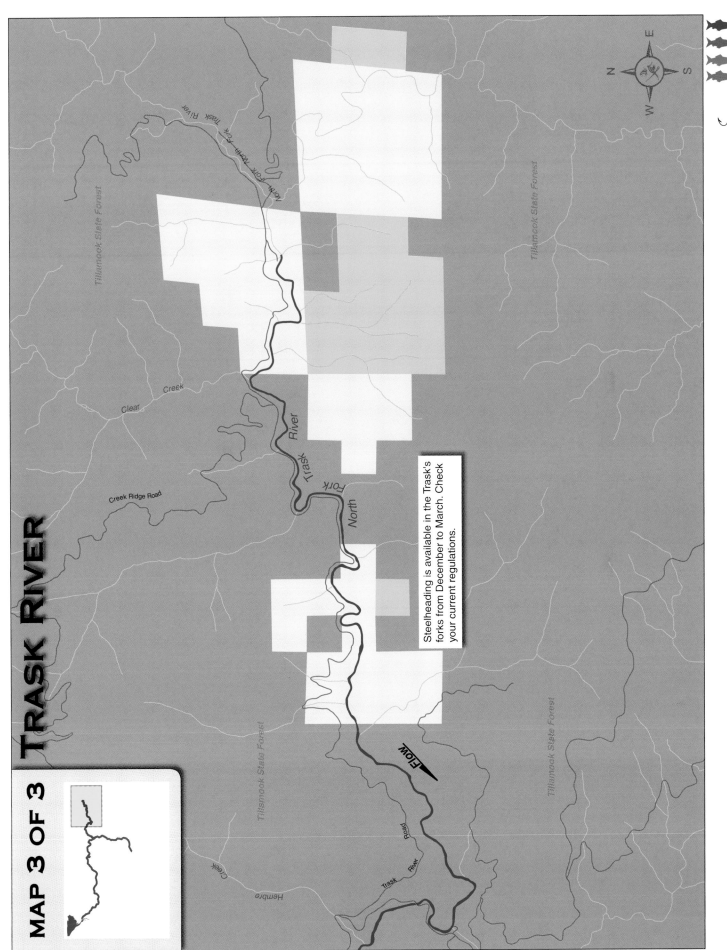

TRASK RIVER

MAP 3 OF 3

Steelheading is available in the Trask's forks from December to March. Check your current regulations.

FLOW

Tillamook State Forest

Tillamook State Forest

Tillamook State Forest

Tillamook State Forest

North Fork Trask River

Trask River

North Fork

Clear Creek

Creek Ridge Road

Hembre Creek

Trask River Road

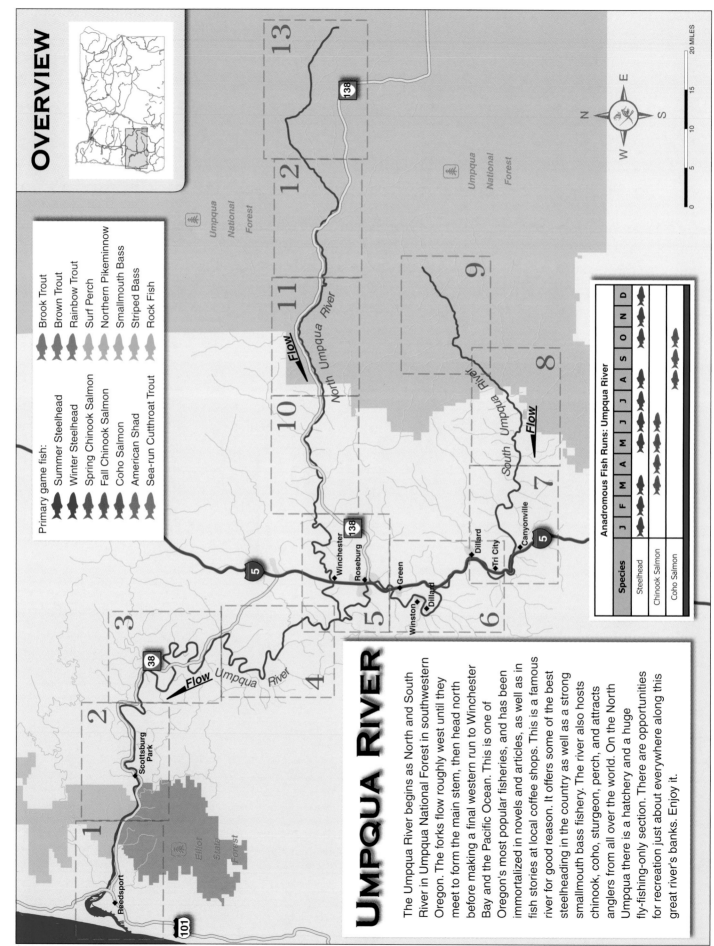

OVERVIEW

Primary game fish:

- Brook Trout
- Brown Trout
- Rainbow Trout
- Surf Perch
- Northern Pikeminnow
- Smallmouth Bass
- Striped Bass
- Rock Fish
- Summer Steelhead
- Winter Steelhead
- Spring Chinook Salmon
- Fall Chinook Salmon
- Coho Salmon
- American Shad
- Sea-run Cutthroat Trout

Anadromous Fish Runs: Umpqua River

Species	J	F	M	A	M	J	J	A	S	O	N	D
Steelhead												
Chinook Salmon												
Coho Salmon												

UMPQUA RIVER

The Umpqua River begins as North and South River in Umpqua National Forest in southwestern Oregon. The forks flow roughly west until they meet to form the main stem, then head north before making a final western run to Winchester Bay and the Pacific Ocean. This is one of Oregon's most popular fisheries, and has been immortalized in novels and articles, as well as in fish stories at local coffee shops. This is a famous river for good reason. It offers some of the best steelheading in the country as well as a strong smallmouth bass fishery. The river also hosts chinook, coho, sturgeon, perch, and attracts anglers from all over the world. On the North Umpqua there is a hatchery and a huge fly-fishing-only section. There are opportunities for recreation just about everywhere along this great river's banks. Enjoy it.

North Umpqua River

South Umpqua River

Umpqua River

Flow

Reedsport

Scottsburg Park

Elliott State Forest

Winchester

Roseburg

Green

Winston

Dillard

Tri City

Canyonville

Umpqua National Forest

20 MILES

N E S W

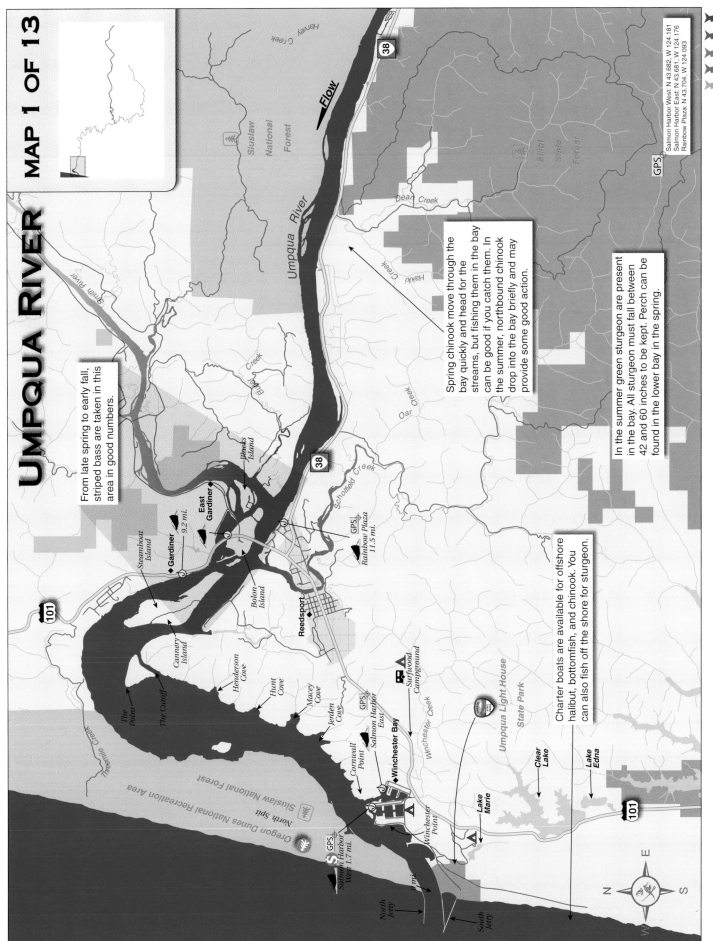

UMPQUA RIVER

MAP 1 OF 13

From late spring to early fall, striped bass are taken in this area in good numbers.

Spring chinook move through the bay quickly and head for the streams, but fishing them in the bay can be good if you catch them. In the summer, northbound chinook drop into the bay briefly and may provide some good action.

In the summer green sturgeon are present in the bay. All sturgeon must fall between 42 and 60 inches to be kept. Perch can be found in the lower bay in the spring.

Charter boats are available for offshore halibut, bottomfish, and chinook. You can also fish off the shore for sturgeon.

Salmon Harbor West: N 43.682, W 124.181
Salmon Harbor East: N 43.681, W 124.176
Rainbow Plaza: N 43.704, W 124.093

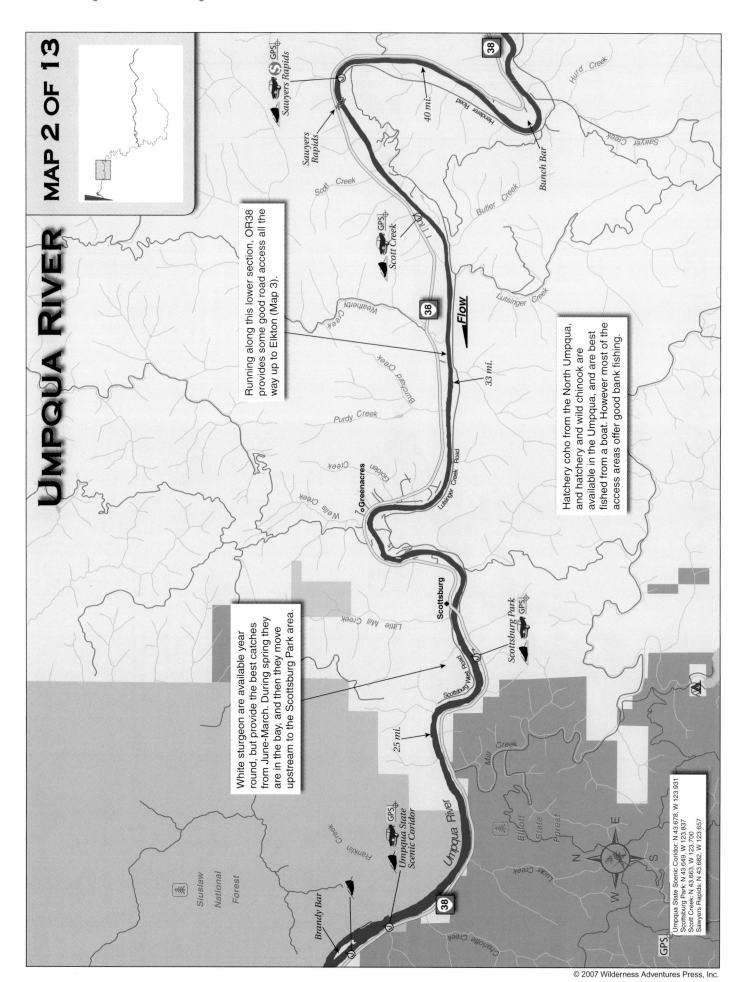

UMPQUA RIVER

MAP 2 OF 13

Running along this lower section, OR38 provides some good road access all the way up to Elkton (Map 3).

Hatchery coho from the North Umpqua, and hatchery and wild chinook are available in the Umpqua, and are best fished from a boat. However most of the access areas offer good bank fishing.

White sturgeon are available year round, but provide the best catches from June-March. During spring they are in the bay, and then they move upstream to the Scottsburg Park area.

Sauyers Rapids

Sauyers Rapids

Scott Creek

Greenacres

Scottsburg

Scottsburg Park

Umpqua State Scenic Coridor

Brandy Bar

Flow

40 mi.

33 mi.

25 mi.

Siuslaw National Forest

Elliott State Forest

Umpqua River

GPS
Umpqua State Scenic Corridor: N 43.678, W 123.931
Scottsburg Park: N 43.649, W 123.837
Scott Creek: N 43.663, W 123.700
Sauyers Rapids: N 43.682, W 123.657

© 2007 Wilderness Adventures Press, Inc.

UMPQUA RIVER

MAP 3 OF 13

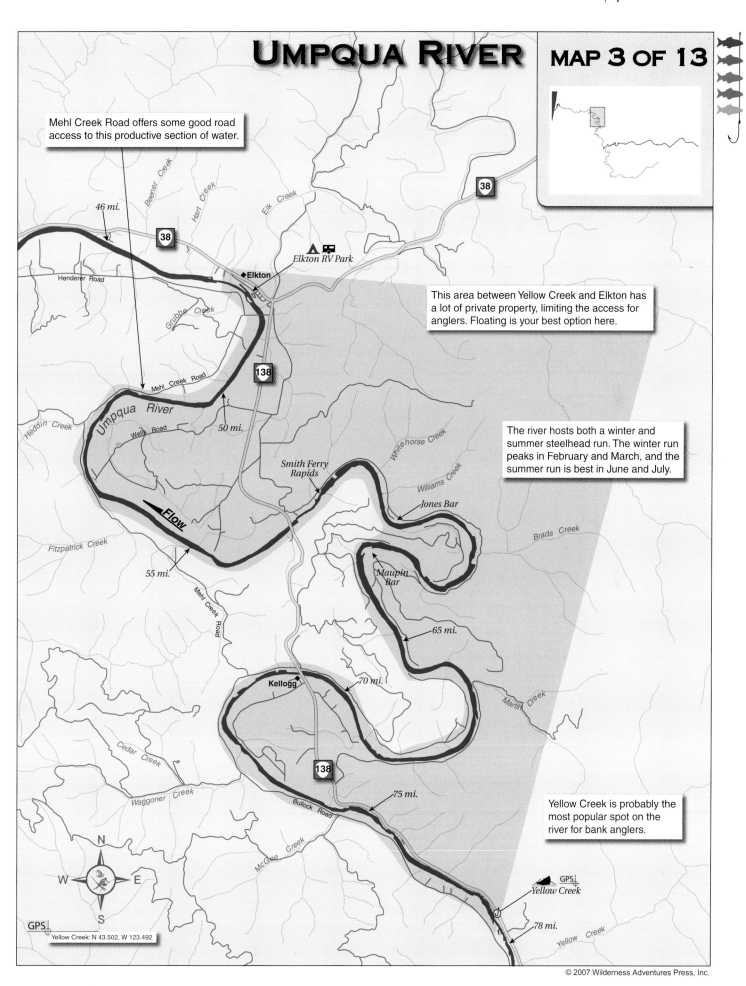

Mehl Creek Road offers some good road access to this productive section of water.

This area between Yellow Creek and Elkton has a lot of private property, limiting the access for anglers. Floating is your best option here.

The river hosts both a winter and summer steelhead run. The winter run peaks in February and March, and the summer run is best in June and July.

Yellow Creek is probably the most popular spot on the river for bank anglers.

38

38

Henderer Road

Be.... Creek

Hart Creek

Elk Creek

Elkton RV Park

◆Elkton

Grubbe Creek

138

Mehl Creek Road

50 mi.

Umpqua River

Wells Road

Heddin Creek

46 mi.

Fitzpatrick Creek

Flow

55 mi.

Mehl Creek Road

Smith Ferry Rapids

Whitehorse Creek

Williams Creek

Jones Bar

Brads Creek

Maupin Bar

65 mi.

Kellogg ◆

70 mi.

Martin Creek

Cedar Creek

138

Waggoner Creek

Bullock Road

75 mi.

McGee Creek

GPS
Yellow Creek

N
W   E
S

GPS

78 mi.

Yellow Creek

Yellow Creek: N 43.502, W 123.492

© 2007 Wilderness Adventures Press, Inc.

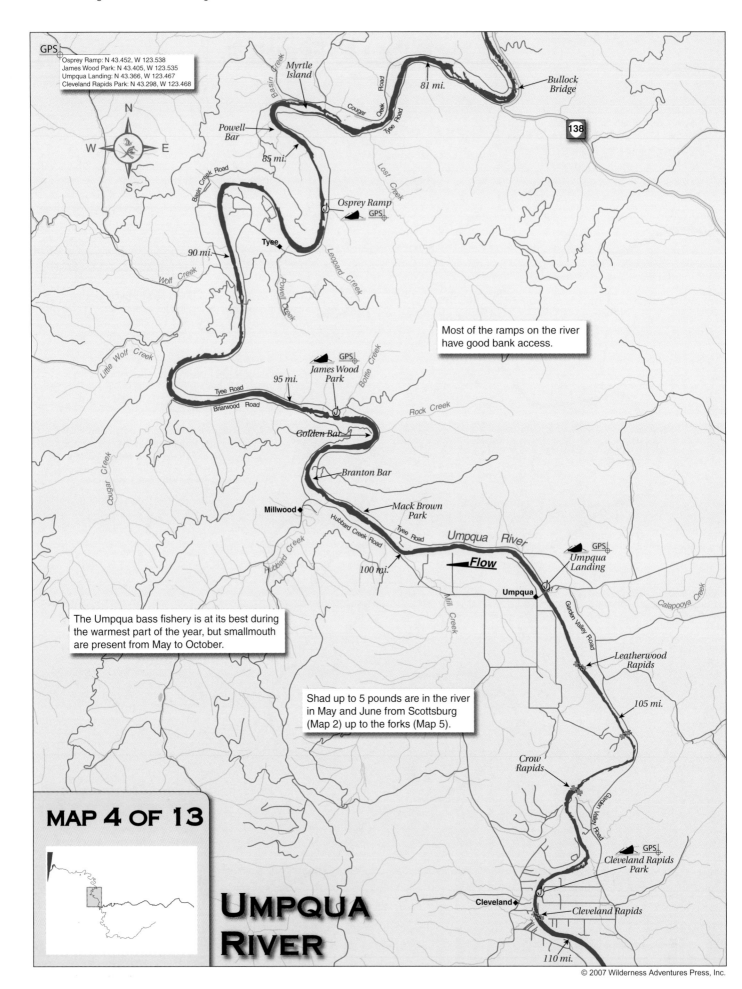

GPS
Osprey Ramp: N 43.452, W 123.538
James Wood Park: N 43.405, W 123.535
Umpqua Landing: N 43.366, W 123.467
Cleveland Rapids Park: N 43.298, W 123.468

Myrtle Island

81 mi.

Bullock Bridge

138

Powell Bar

85 mi.

Osprey Ramp
GPS

Tyee

90 mi.

Most of the ramps on the river have good bank access.

GPS
James Wood Park

95 mi.

Golden Bar

Branton Bar

Mack Brown Park

Millwood

Umpqua River

Flow

GPS
Umpqua Landing

100 mi.

Umpqua

The Umpqua bass fishery is at its best during the warmest part of the year, but smallmouth are present from May to October.

Leatherwood Rapids

105 mi.

Shad up to 5 pounds are in the river in May and June from Scottsburg (Map 2) up to the forks (Map 5).

Crow Rapids

GPS
Cleveland Rapids Park

Cleveland

Cleveland Rapids

MAP 4 OF 13

UMPQUA RIVER

110 mi.

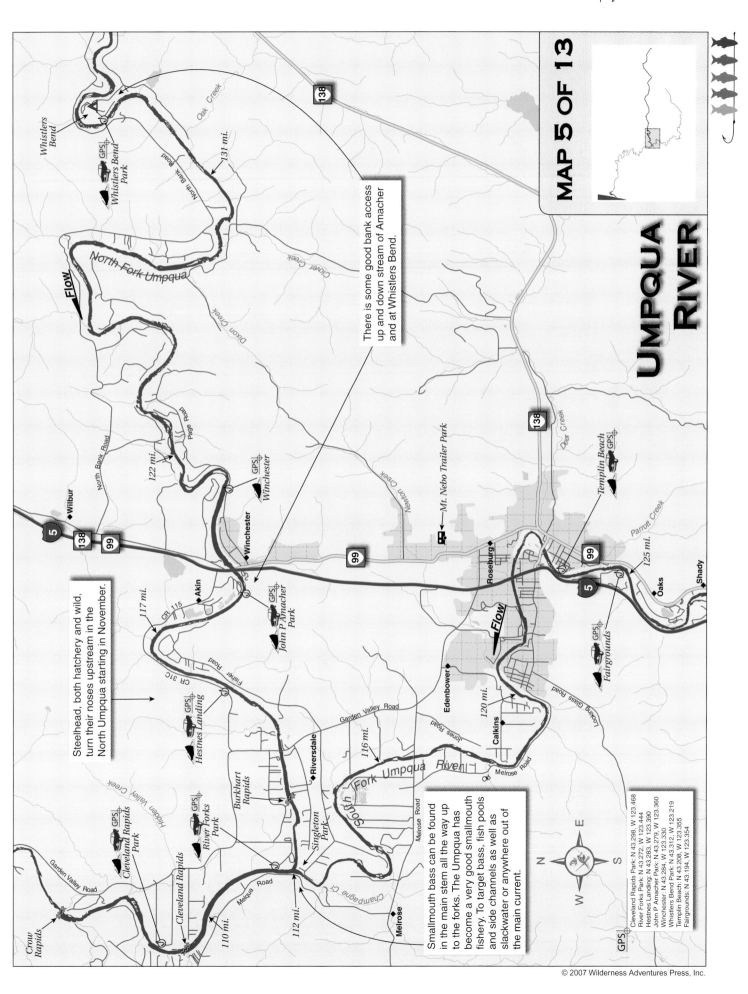

MAP **5** OF **13**

UMPQUA RIVER

There is some good bank access up and down stream of Amacher and at Whistlers Bend.

Steelhead, both hatchery and wild, turn their noses upstream in the North Umpqua starting in November.

Smallmouth bass can be found in the main stem all the way up to the forks. The Umpqua has become a very good smallmouth fishery. To target bass, fish pools and side channels as well as slackwater or anywhere out of the main current.

GPS

Cleveland Rapids Park: N 43.298, W 123.468
River Forks Park: N 43.272, W 123.444
Hestnes Landing: N 43.283, W 123.390
John P Amacher Park: N 43.279, W 123.360
Winchester: N 43.284, W 123.330
Whistlers Bend Park: N 43.312, W 123.219
Templin Beach: N 43.208, W 123.355
Fairgrounds: N 43.194, W 123.354

© 2007 Wilderness Adventures Press, Inc.

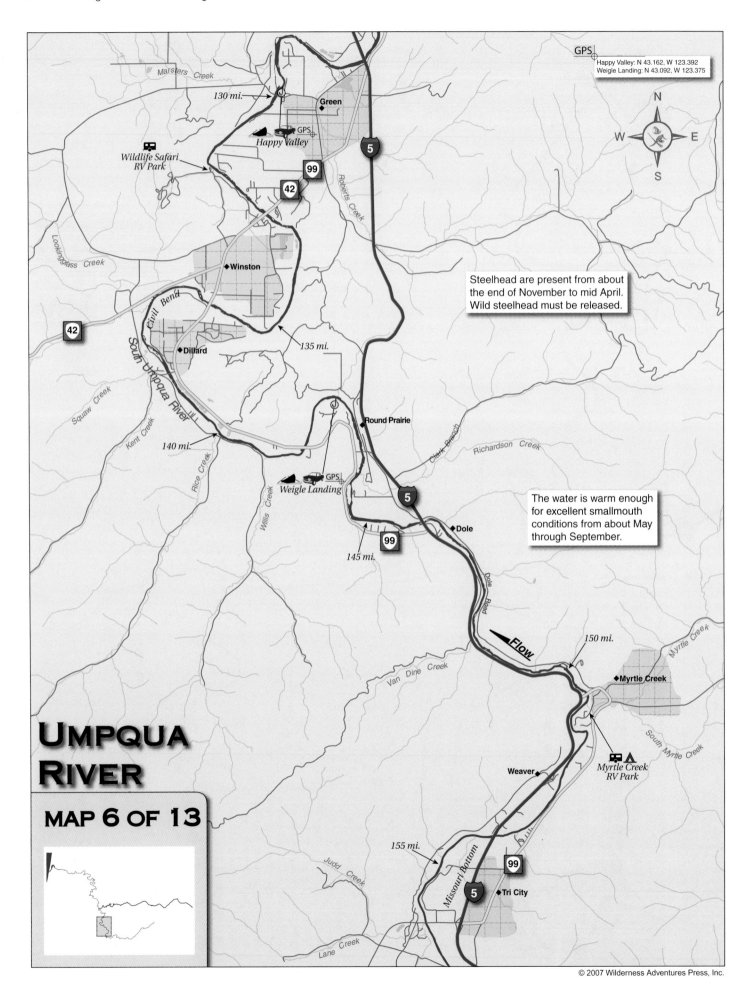

GPS
Happy Valley: N 43.162, W 123.392
Weigle Landing: N 43.092, W 123.375

130 mi.

Green

GPS
Happy Valley

5

99

42

Wildlife Safari
RV Park

Marsters Creek

Roberts Creek

Lookingglass Creek

Winston

Civil Bend

South Umpqua River

Dillard

135 mi.

Steelhead are present from about
the end of November to mid April.
Wild steelhead must be released.

Squaw Creek

Kent Creek

Rice Creek

140 mi.

Round Prairie

Clark Branch

Richardson Creek

Willis Creek

GPS
Weigle Landing

5

The water is warm enough
for excellent smallmouth
conditions from about May
through September.

99

145 mi.

Dole

Dole Road

Flow

150 mi.

Van Dine Creek

Myrtle Creek

South Myrtle Creek

Myrtle Creek
RV Park

UMPQUA
RIVER

MAP 6 OF 13

Weaver

155 mi.

Missouri Bottom

Judd Creek

5

99

Tri City

Lane Creek

© 2007 Wilderness Adventures Press, Inc.

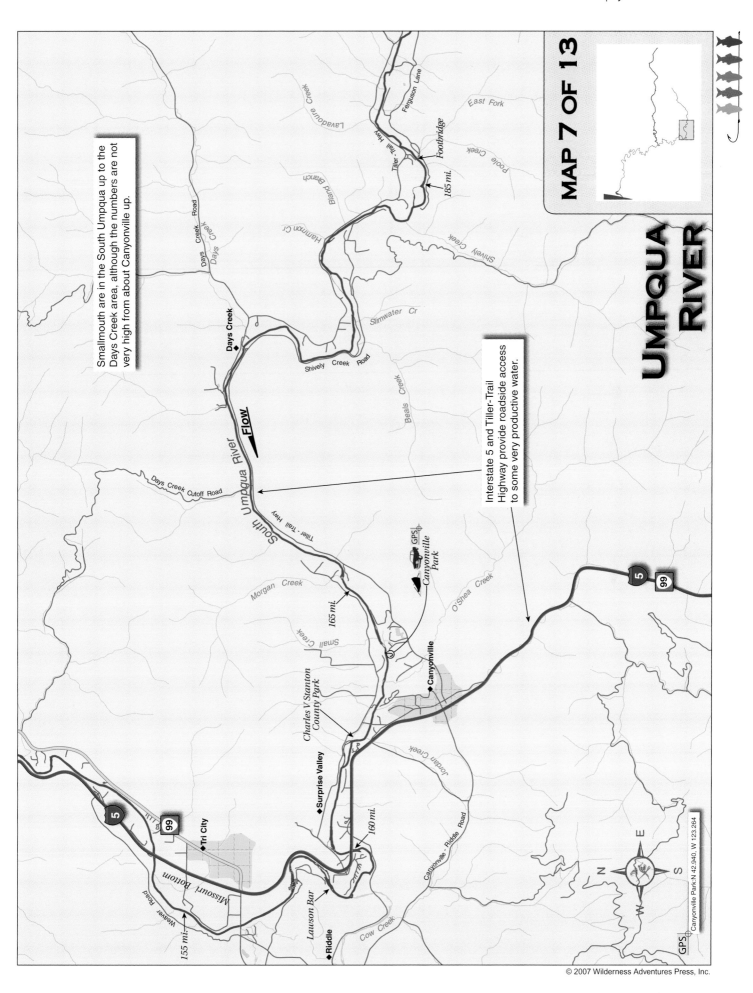

MAP 7 OF 13

UMPQUA RIVER

Smallmouth are in the South Umpqua up to the Days Creek area, although the numbers are not very high from about Canyonville up.

Interstate 5 and Tiller-Trail Highway provide roadside access to some very productive water.

East Fork

Footbridge

185 mi.

Poole Creek

Ferguson Lane

Tiller - Trail Hwy

Lavadoure Creek

Bland Branch

Hammon Cr.

Shively Creek

Days Creek Road

Days Creek

Days Creek

Slimwater Cr

Shively Creek Road

Beals Creek

FLOW

South Umpqua River

Days Creek Cutoff Road

Tiller - Trail Hwy

Morgan Creek

Small Creek

165 mi.

GPS

Canyonville Park

O'Shea Creek

Canyonville

Charles V Stanton County Park

Surprise Valley

Jordan Creek

Canyonville - Riddle Road

160 mi.

5

99

Tri City

Missouri Bottom

Weaver Road

99

5

155 mi.

Lawson Bar

Cow Creek

Riddle

N

E

S

W

GPS Canyonville Park: N 42.940, W 123.264

© 2007 Wilderness Adventures Press, Inc.

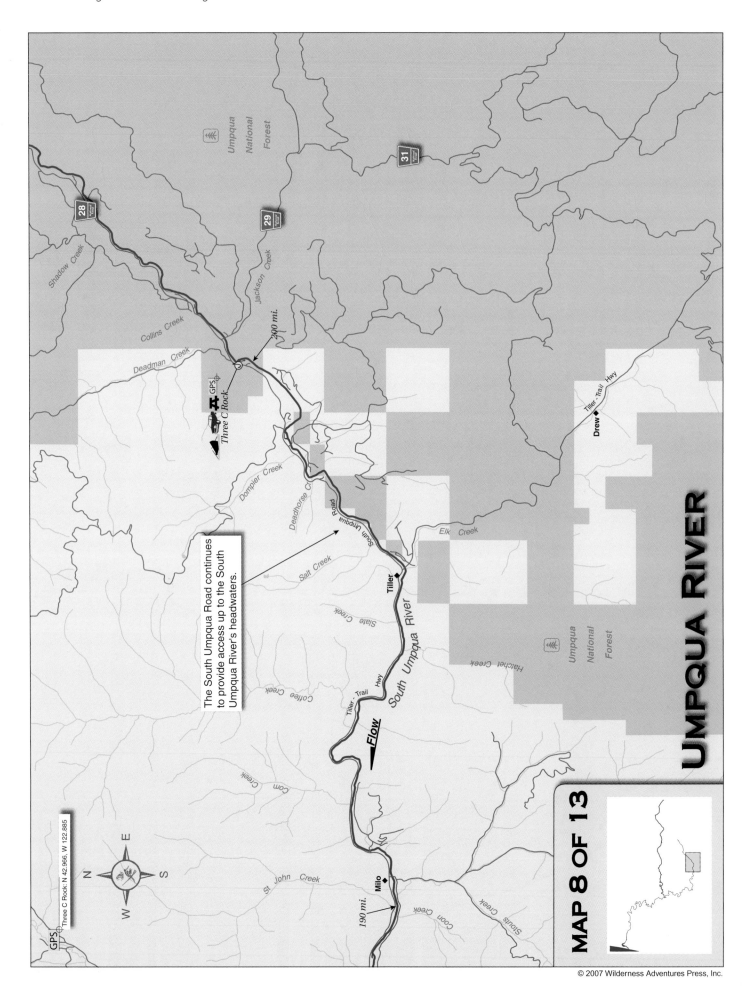

Umpqua National Forest

31

28

29

Shadow Creek

Collins Creek

Deadman Creek

200 mi.

GPS

Three C Rock

Jackson Creek

Dompier Creek

Deadhorse Cr

South Umpqua Road

The South Umpqua Road continues to provide access up to the South Umpqua River's headwaters.

Salt Creek

Slate Creek

Coffee Creek

Corn Creek

St John Creek

Milo

190 mi.

Coon Creek

Stouts Creek

Elk Creek

Tiller

South Umpqua River

Tiller - Trail Hwy

Flow

Hatchet Creek

Umpqua National Forest

Drew

Tiller - Trail Hwy

UMPQUA RIVER

MAP 8 OF 13

GPS

Three C Rock: N 42.966, W 122.885

N
E
S
W

© 2007 Wilderness Adventures Press, Inc.

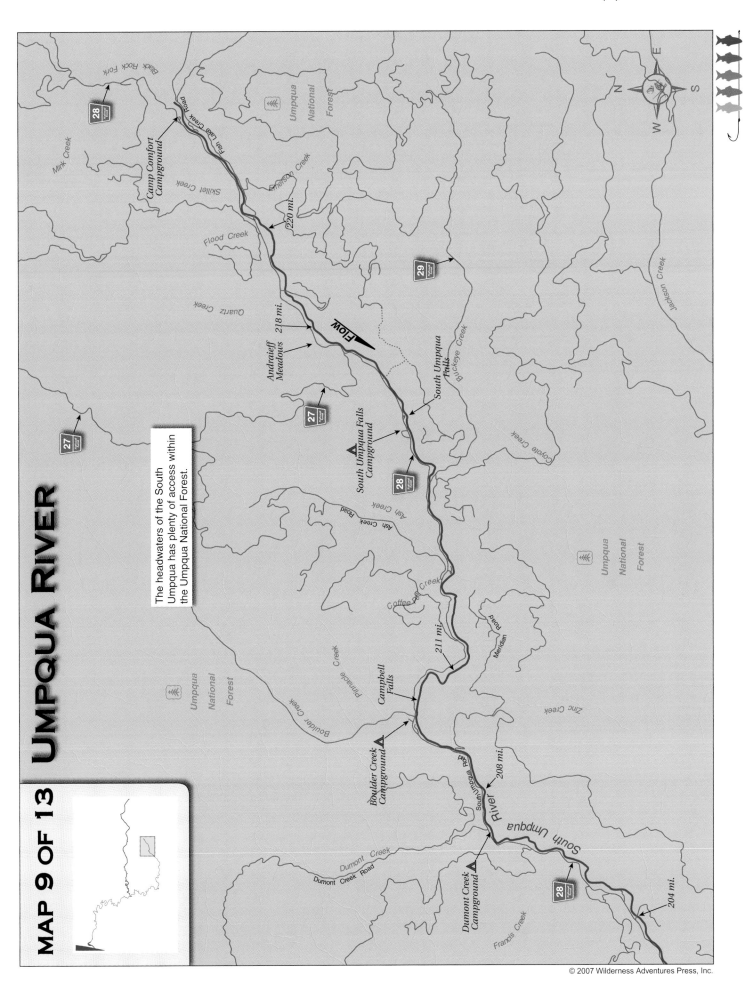

MAP 9 OF 13 | UMPQUA RIVER

The headwaters of the South Umpqua has plenty of access within the Umpqua National Forest.

© 2007 Wilderness Adventures Press, Inc.

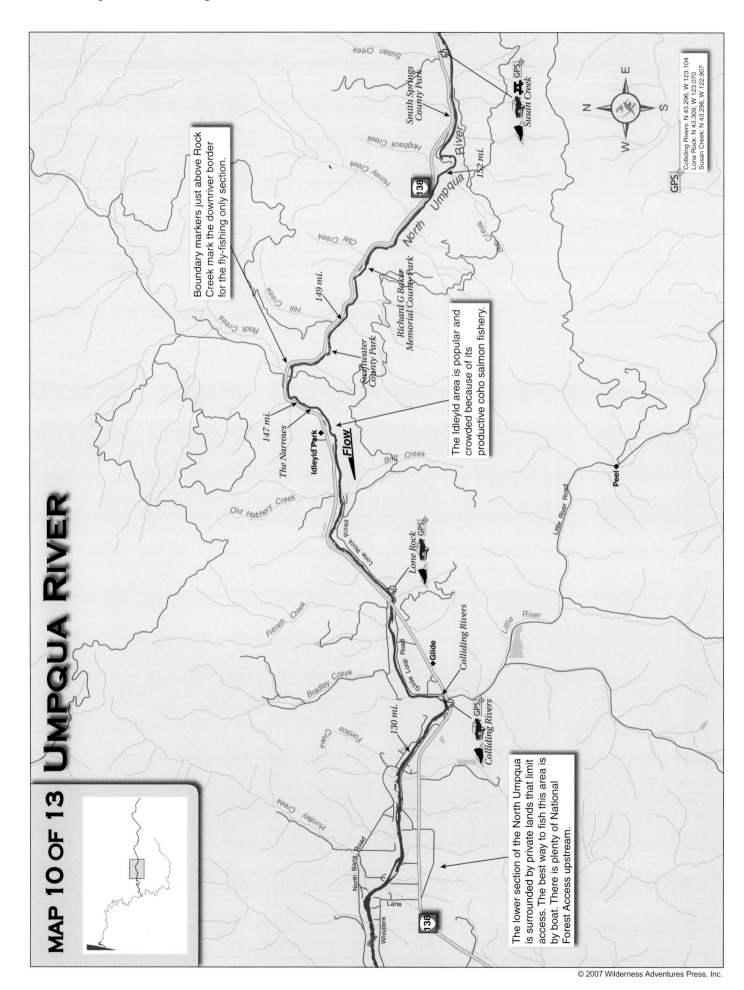

MAP 10 OF 13 UMPQUA RIVER

Boundary markers just above Rock Creek mark the downriver border for the fly-fishing only section.

Smith Springs County Park

Susan Creek

152 mi.

149 mi.

Richard G Baker Memorial County Park

Swiftwater County Park

147 mi.

The Narrows

Idleyld Park

Flow

Britt Creek

The Idleyld area is popular and crowded because of its productive coho salmon fishery.

Old Hatchery Creek

Lone Rock

Colliding Rivers

Glide

Colliding Rivers

Peel

Little River Road

Little River

130 mi.

Colliding Rivers

The lower section of the North Umpqua is surrounded by private lands that limit access. The best way to fish this area is by boat. There is plenty of National Forest Access upstream.

North Bank Road

Lane

Whistlers

Colliding Rivers: N 43.296, W 123.104
Lone Rock: N 43.309, W 123.070
Susan Creek: N 43.296, W 122.907

GPS

N E S W

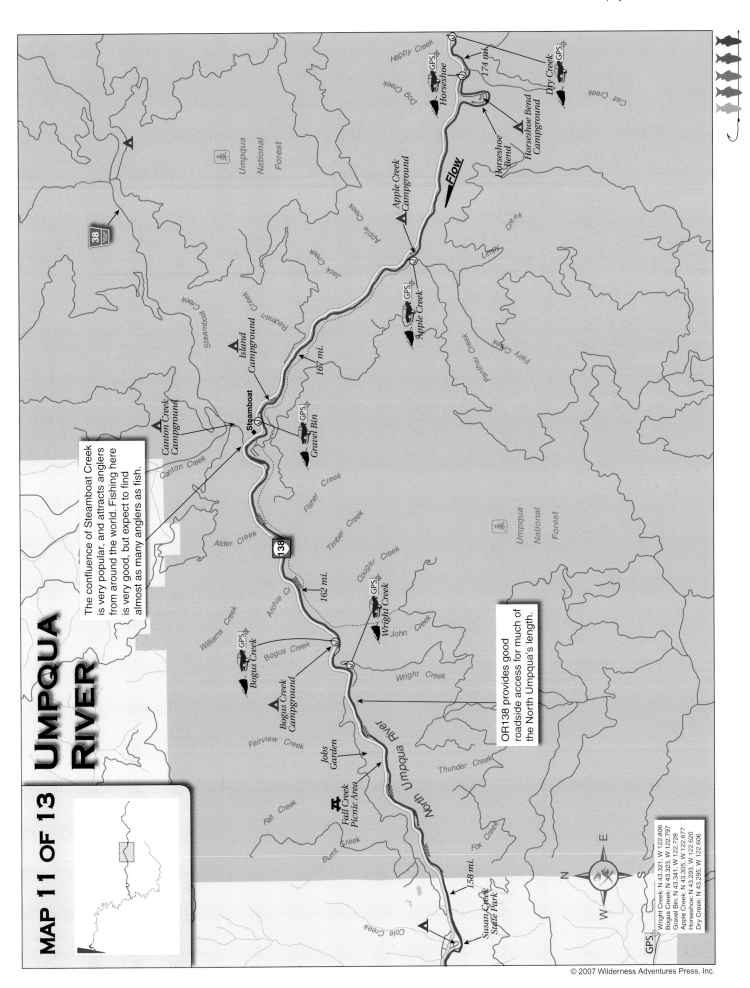

MAP 11 OF 13

UMPQUA RIVER

The confluence of Steamboat Creek is very popular, and attracts anglers from around the world. Fishing here is very good, but expect to find almost as many anglers as fish.

OR138 provides good roadside access for much of the North Umpqua's length.

Canton Creek Campground

Canton Creek

Steamboat

Steamboat Creek

Island Campground

Gravel Bin GPS

167 mi.

Redman Creek

Jack Creek

Apple Creek

Apple Creek Campground

GPS Apple Creek

Limpy Creek

Creek

Flow

Happy Creek

Dog Creek

Horseshoe GPS

174 mi.

Horseshoe Bend

Horseshoe Bend Campground

Dry Creek GPS

Cat Creek

Panther Creek

Fairy Creek

Umpqua National Forest

Umpqua National Forest

38

138

Alder Creek

Fisher Creek

Timber Creek

Williams Creek

Archie Cr

162 mi.

Bogus Creek GPS

Bogus Creek

Bogus Creek Campground

Fairview Creek

Cougar Creek

Wright Creek GPS

Wright Creek

John Creek

Wright Creek

Thunder Creek

Jobs Garden

Fall Creek Picnic Area

Fall Creek

Burnt Creek

North Umpqua River

Fox Creek

158 mi.

Cole Creek

Susan Creek State Park

N W E S

GPS
Wright Creek: N 43.321, W 122.806
Bogus Creek: N 43.323, W 122.797
Gravel Bin: N 43.341, W 122.728
Apple Creek: N 43.305, W 122.677
Horseshoe: N 43.293, W 122.620
Dry Creek: N 43.295, W 122.606

© 2007 Wilderness Adventures Press, Inc.

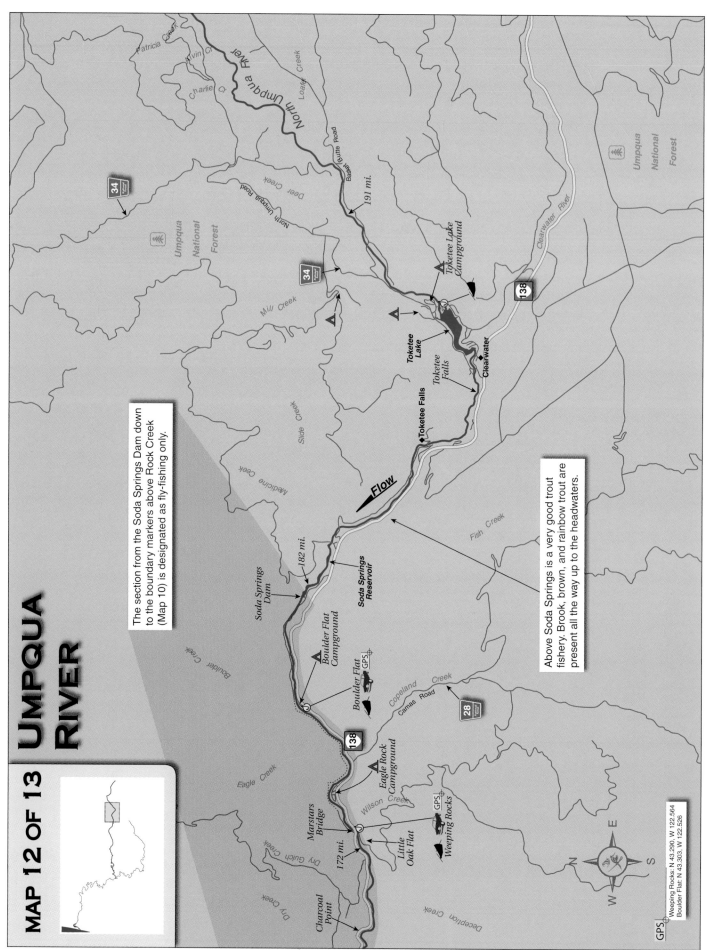

MAP 12 OF 13 | **UMPQUA RIVER**

The section from the Soda Springs Dam down to the boundary markers above Rock Creek (Map 10) is designated as fly-fishing only.

Above Soda Springs is a very good trout fishery. Brook, brown, and rainbow trout are present all the way up to the headwaters.

GPS | Weeping Rocks: N 43.290, W 122.564
Boulder Flat: N 43.303, W 122.526

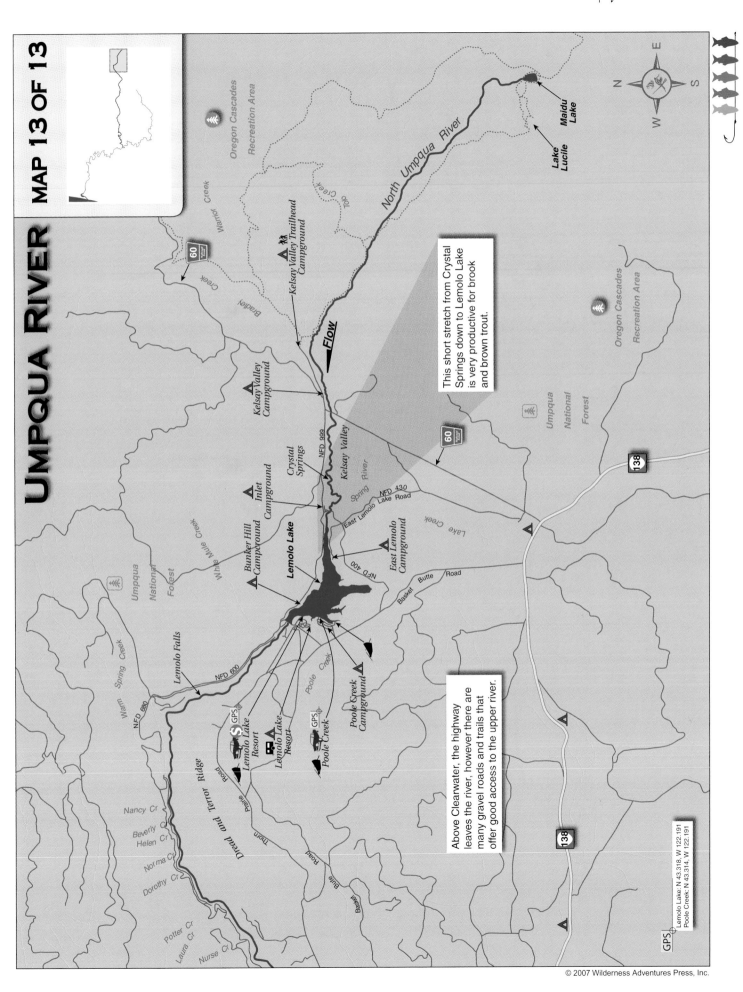

UMPQUA RIVER

MAP 13 OF 13

This short stretch from Crystal Springs down to Lemolo Lake is very productive for brook and brown trout.

Above Clearwater, the highway leaves the river, however there are many gravel roads and trails that offer good access to the upper river.

GPS Lemolo Lake: N 43.318, W 122.191
Poole Creek: N 43.314, W 122.191

© 2007 Wilderness Adventures Press, Inc.

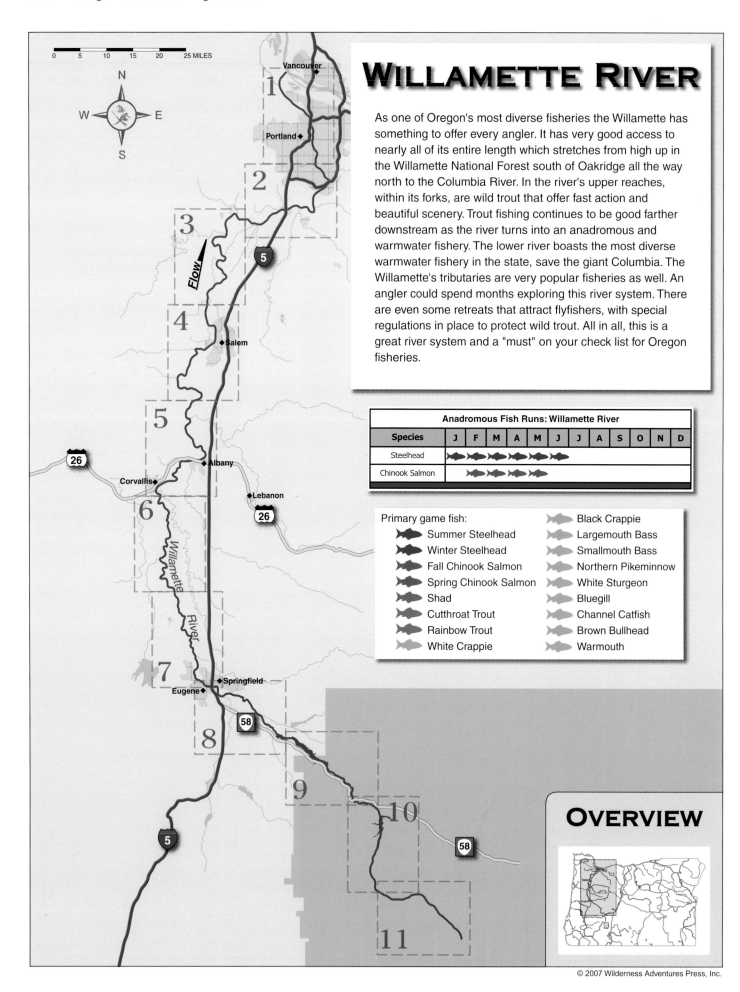

WILLAMETTE RIVER

As one of Oregon's most diverse fisheries the Willamette has something to offer every angler. It has very good access to nearly all of its entire length which stretches from high up in the Willamette National Forest south of Oakridge all the way north to the Columbia River. In the river's upper reaches, within its forks, are wild trout that offer fast action and beautiful scenery. Trout fishing continues to be good farther downstream as the river turns into an anadromous and warmwater fishery. The lower river boasts the most diverse warmwater fishery in the state, save the giant Columbia. The Willamette's tributaries are very popular fisheries as well. An angler could spend months exploring this river system. There are even some retreats that attract flyfishers, with special regulations in place to protect wild trout. All in all, this is a great river system and a "must" on your check list for Oregon fisheries.

Anadromous Fish Runs: Willamette River												
Species	J	F	M	A	M	J	J	A	S	O	N	D
Steelhead												
Chinook Salmon												

Primary game fish:

- Summer Steelhead
- Winter Steelhead
- Fall Chinook Salmon
- Spring Chinook Salmon
- Shad
- Cutthroat Trout
- Rainbow Trout
- White Crappie
- Black Crappie
- Largemouth Bass
- Smallmouth Bass
- Northern Pikeminnow
- White Sturgeon
- Bluegill
- Channel Catfish
- Brown Bullhead
- Warmouth

OVERVIEW

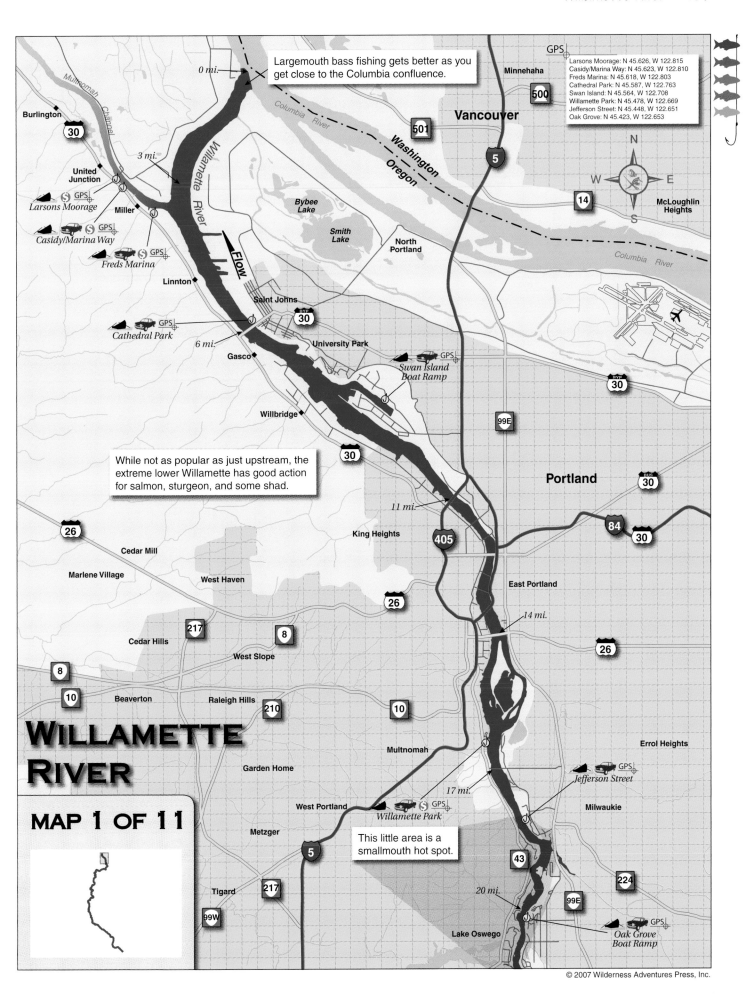

Largemouth bass fishing gets better as you get close to the Columbia confluence.

Larsons Moorage: N 45.626, W 122.815
Casidy/Marina Way: N 45.623, W 122.810
Freds Marina: N 45.618, W 122.803
Cathedral Park: N 45.587, W 122.763
Swan Island: N 45.564, W 122.708
Willamette Park: N 45.478, W 122.669
Jefferson Street: N 45.448, W 122.651
Oak Grove: N 45.423, W 122.653

While not as popular as just upstream, the extreme lower Willamette has good action for salmon, sturgeon, and some shad.

This little area is a smallmouth hot spot.

WILLAMETTE RIVER

MAP 1 OF 11

© 2007 Wilderness Adventures Press, Inc.

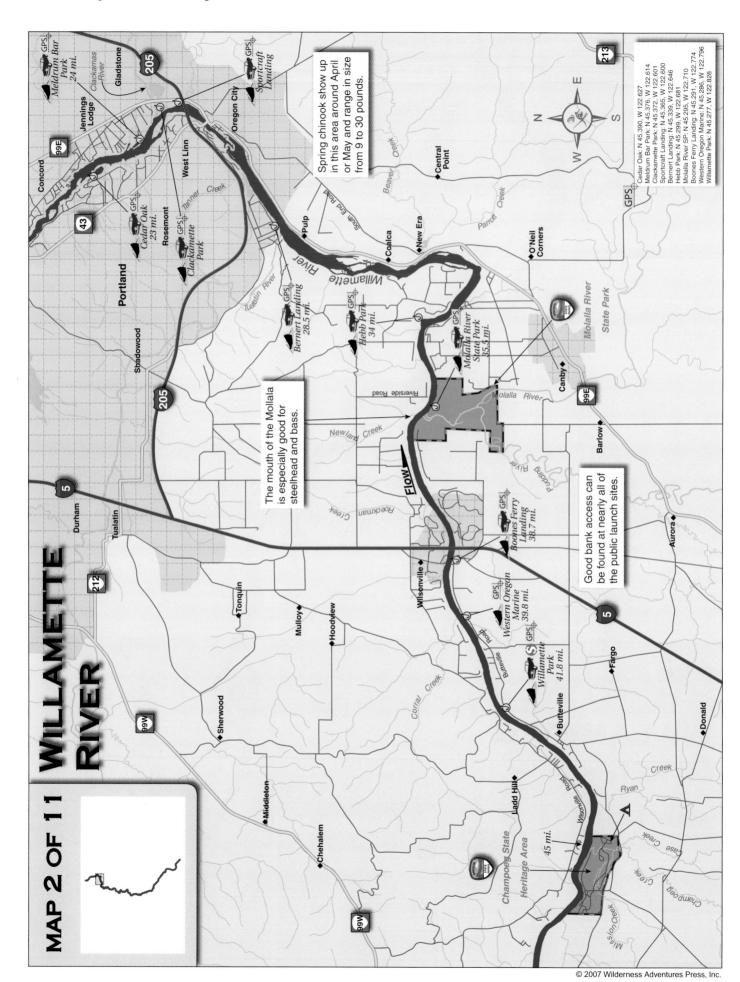

MAP 2 OF 11

WILLAMETTE
RIVER

Spring chinook show up in this area around April or May and range in size from 9 to 30 pounds.

The mouth of the Mollala is especially good for steelhead and bass.

Good bank access can be found at nearly all of the public launch sites.

Cedar Oak: N 45.390, W 122.627
Meldrum Bar Park: N 45.376, W 122.614
Clackamette Park: N 45.372, W 122.601
Sportcraft Landing: N 45.365, W 122.600
Bernert Landing: N 45.339, W 122.646
Hebb Park: N 45.299, W 122.681
Molalla River SP: N 45.295, W 122.710
Boones Ferry Landing: N 45.291, W 122.774
Western Oregon Marine: N 45.286, W 122.796
Willamette Park: N 45.277, W 122.828

Meldrum Bar Park 24 mi.
Jennings Lodge
Gladstone
Clackamas River
Sportcraft Landing
Oregon City
West Linn
Concord
Portland
Cedar Oak 23 mi.
Rosemont
Clackamette Park
Shadowood
Tualatin River
Bernert Landing 28.5 mi.
Hebb Park 34 mi.
Willamette River
Pulp
Coalca
New Era
Central Point
Beaver Creek
South End Road
Parrott Creek
O'Neil Corners
Molalla River State Park
Molalla River State Park 35.5 mi.
Riverside Road
Newland Creek
Molalla River
Canby
Barlow
Pudding River
Rockman Creek
FLOW
Boones Ferry Landing 38.7 mi.
Wilsonville
Western Oregon Marine 39.8 mi.
Aurora
Fargo
Donald
Willamette Park 41.8 mi.
Butteville
Corral Creek
Road
Durham
Tualatin
Tonquin
Mulloy
Hoodview
Sherwood
Middleton
Chehalem
Ladd Hill
45 mi.
Champoeg State Heritage Area
Ryan Creek
Wilsonville Road
Champoeg Creek
Case Creek
Mission Creek

© 2007 Wilderness Adventures Press, Inc.

MAP 3 OF 11 WILLAMETTE RIVER

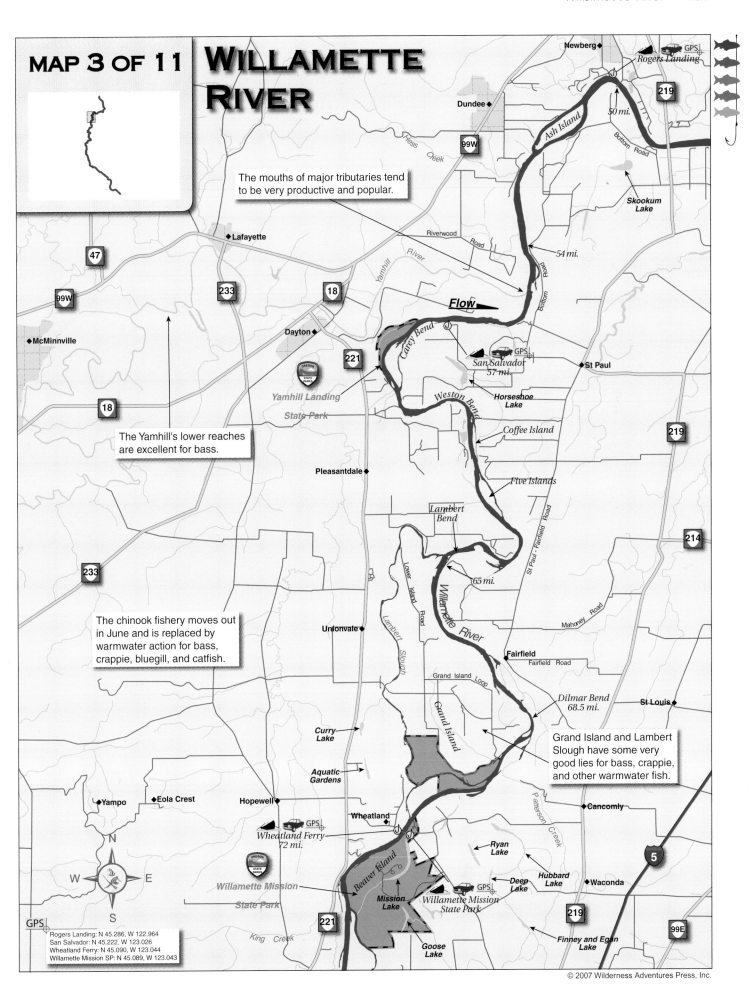

Newberg

Rogers Landing

GPS

219

Dundee

99W

Hess Creek

Ash Island

Bottom Road

50 mi.

Skookum Lake

Riverwood Road

54 mi.

The mouths of major tributaries tend to be very productive and popular.

Lafayette

47

99W

233

18

Yamhill River

Flow

Bottom Road

Carey Bend

San Salvador
57 mi.

GPS

St Paul

McMinnville

Dayton

221

Weston Bend

Horseshoe Lake

OREGON STATE PARKS

Yamhill Landing
State Park

Coffee Island

219

The Yamhill's lower reaches are excellent for bass.

18

Pleasantdale

Five Islands

St Paul - Fairfield Road

214

Lambert Bend

65 mi.

233

Willamette River

Lower Island Road

Mahoney Road

The chinook fishery moves out in June and is replaced by warmwater action for bass, crappie, bluegill, and catfish.

Unionvale

Lambert Slough

Fairfield

Fairfield Road

Grand Island Loop

Dilmar Bend
68.5 mi.

St Louis

Curry Lake

Grand Island

Grand Island and Lambert Slough have some very good lies for bass, crappie, and other warmwater fish.

Aquatic Gardens

Yampo

Eola Crest

Hopewell

Wheatland

Patterson Creek

Cancomly

5

Wheatland Ferry
72 mi.

GPS

Ryan Lake

Hubbard Lake

Waconda

OREGON STATE PARKS

Beaver Island

Deep Lake

Willamette Mission
State Park

Willamette Mission
State Park

Mission Lake

GPS

219

99E

221

King Creek

Goose Lake

Finney and Egan Lake

GPS

Rogers Landing: N 45.286, W 122.964
San Salvador: N 45.222, W 123.026
Wheatland Ferry: N 45.090, W 123.044
Willamette Mission SP: N 45.089, W 123.043

© 2007 Wilderness Adventures Press, Inc.

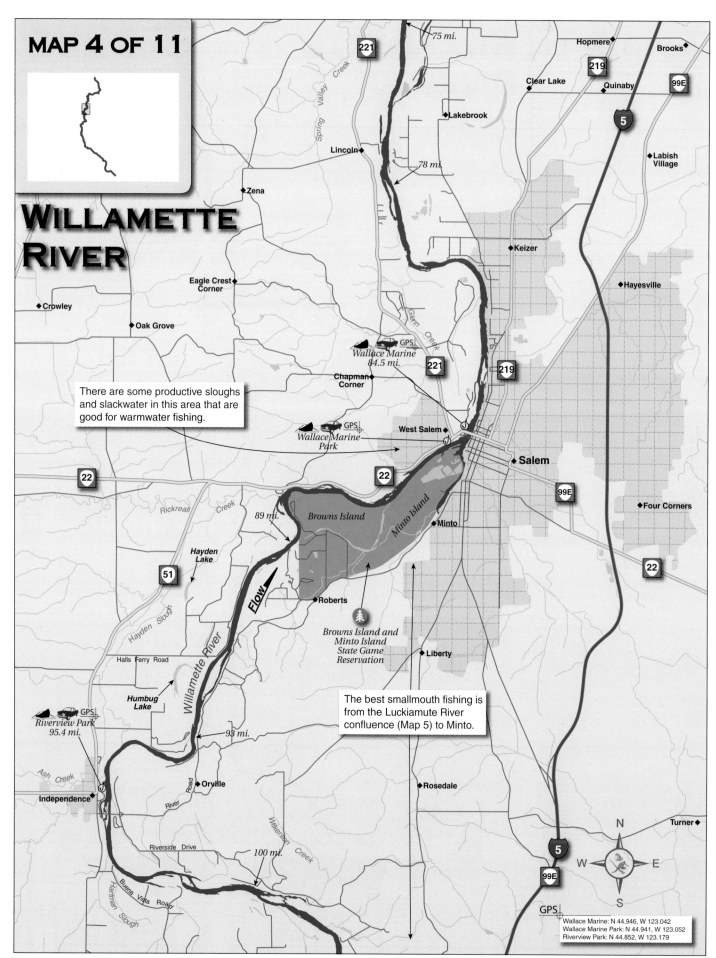

MAP 4 OF 11

WILLAMETTE RIVER

There are some productive sloughs and slackwater in this area that are good for warmwater fishing.

The best smallmouth fishing is from the Luckiamute River confluence (Map 5) to Minto.

Wallace Marine
84.5 mi.

Wallace Marine Park

Riverview Park
95.4 mi.

Browns Island

Minto Island

Browns Island and Minto Island State Game Reservation

Hayden Lake

Humbug Lake

Flow

Willamette River

Wallace Marine: N 44.946, W 123.042
Wallace Marine Park: N 44.941, W 123.052
Riverview Park: N 44.852, W 123.179

75 mi.

78 mi.

89 mi.

93 mi.

100 mi.

Spring Valley Creek

Glen Creek

Rickreall Creek

Hayden Slough

Halls Ferry Road

Ash Creek

River Road

Orville

Riverside Drive

Buena Vista Road

Hartman Slough

Wilkerson Creek

Crowley

Oak Grove

Eagle Crest Corner

Zena

Lincoln

Lakebrook

Hopmere

Brooks

Clear Lake

Quinaby

Labish Village

Keizer

Hayesville

Chapman Corner

West Salem

Salem

Four Corners

Minto

Liberty

Roberts

Rosedale

Independence

Turner

Crowley

221

219

99E

5

221

219

22

22

51

99E

5

99E

GPS

GPS

GPS

GPS

N
W   E
S

© 2007 Wilderness Adventures Press, Inc.

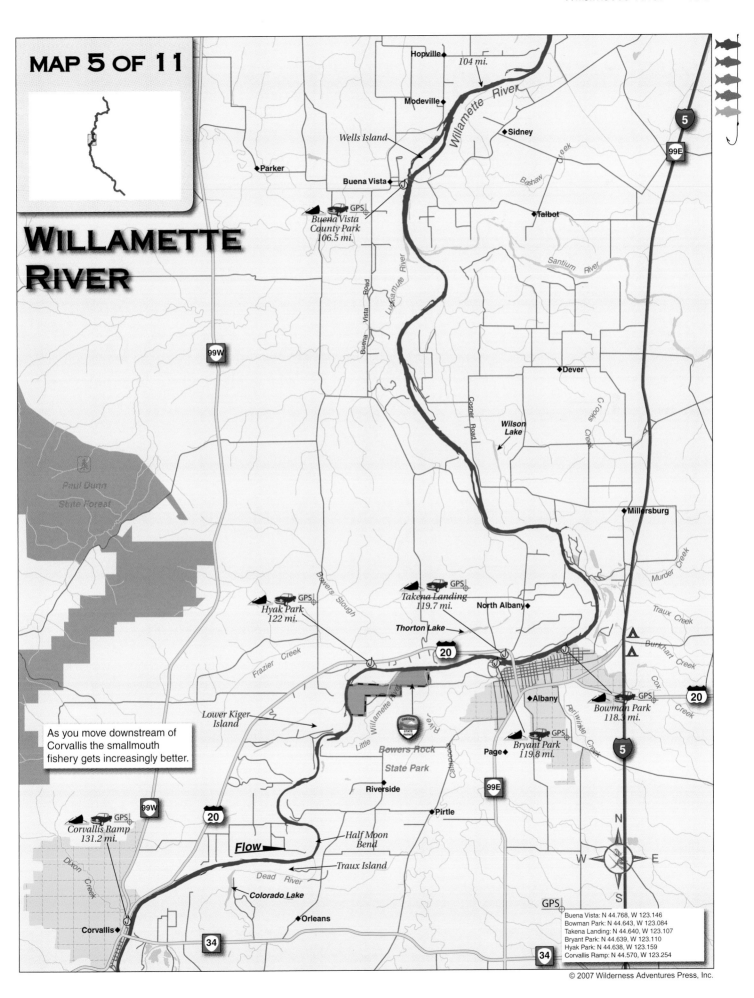

MAP 5 OF 11

WILLAMETTE RIVER

Hopville

104 mi.

Modeville

Sidney

Wells Island

Parker

Buena Vista

Talbot

Buena Vista
County Park
106.5 mi.

GPS

Dever

Wilson
Lake

Millersburg

Takena Landing
119.7 mi.

Hyak Park
122 mi.

North Albany

Thorton Lake

Bowman Park
118.3 mi.

Lower Kiger
Island

Albany

Bryant Park
119.8 mi.

Page

Bowers Rock
State Park

As you move downstream of
Corvallis the smallmouth
fishery gets increasingly better.

Riverside

Pirtle

Corvallis Ramp
131.2 mi.

Flow

Half Moon
Bend

Traux Island

Colorado Lake

Orleans

Corvallis

Buena Vista: N 44.768, W 123.146
Bowman Park: N 44.643, W 123.084
Takena Landing: N 44.640, W 123.107
Bryant Park: N 44.639, W 123.110
Hyak Park: N 44.638, W 123.159
Corvallis Ramp: N 44.570, W 123.254

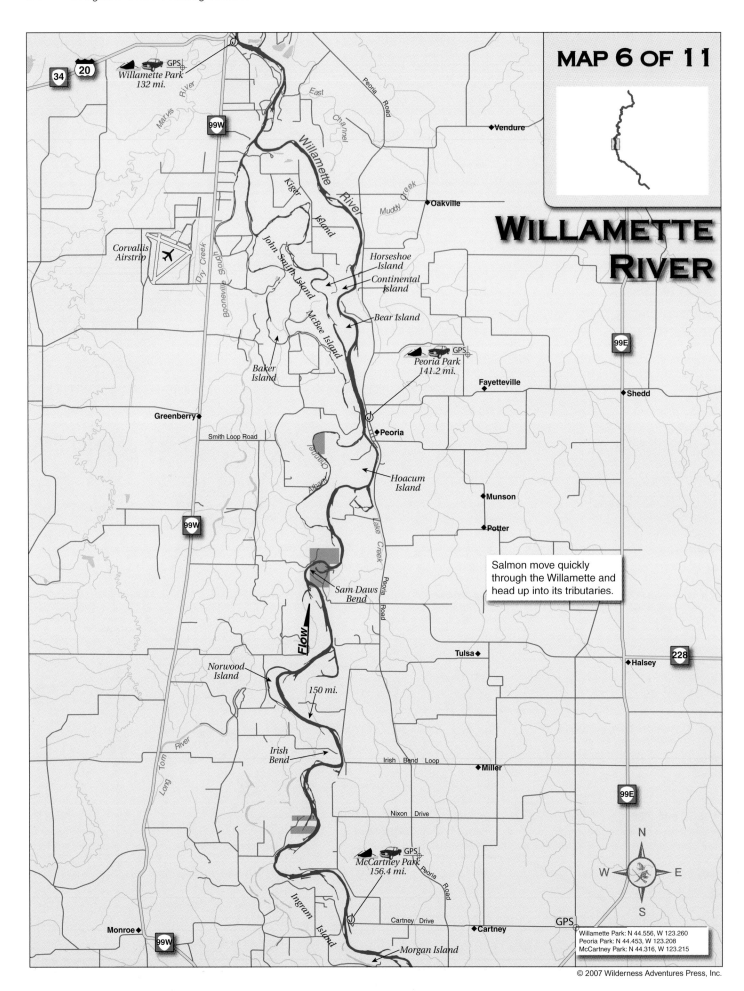

MAP **6** OF **11**

WILLAMETTE RIVER

34 20
Willamette Park
132 mi. GPS

99W

Marvis River

Willamette River

East Channel

Peoria Road

◆ Vendure

◆ Oakville

Muddy Creek

99E

Corvallis Airstrip

Kiger Island

John Smith Island

Horseshoe Island

Continental Island

Bear Island

McBee Island

Baker Island

Peoria Park
141.2 mi. GPS

Fayetteville

◆ Shedd

Dry Creek

Booneville Slough

Greenberry ◆

Smith Loop Road

Peoria

◆ Peoria

Hoacum Island

◆ Munson

◆ Potter

99W

Channel

Albany

Lake Creek

Salmon move quickly
through the Willamette and
head up into its tributaries.

Sam Daws Bend

Flow

Tulsa ◆

228

◆ Halsey

Norwood Island

150 mi.

Long Tom River

Irish Bend

Irish Bend Loop

◆ Miller

Peoria Road

Nixon Drive

99E

McCartney Park
156.4 mi. GPS

N

W   E

S

Ingram Island

Monroe ◆

99W

Cartney Drive

◆ Cartney

GPS

Morgan Island

Willamette Park: N 44.556, W 123.260
Peoria Park: N 44.453, W 123.208
McCartney Park: N 44.316, W 123.215

© 2007 Wilderness Adventures Press, Inc.

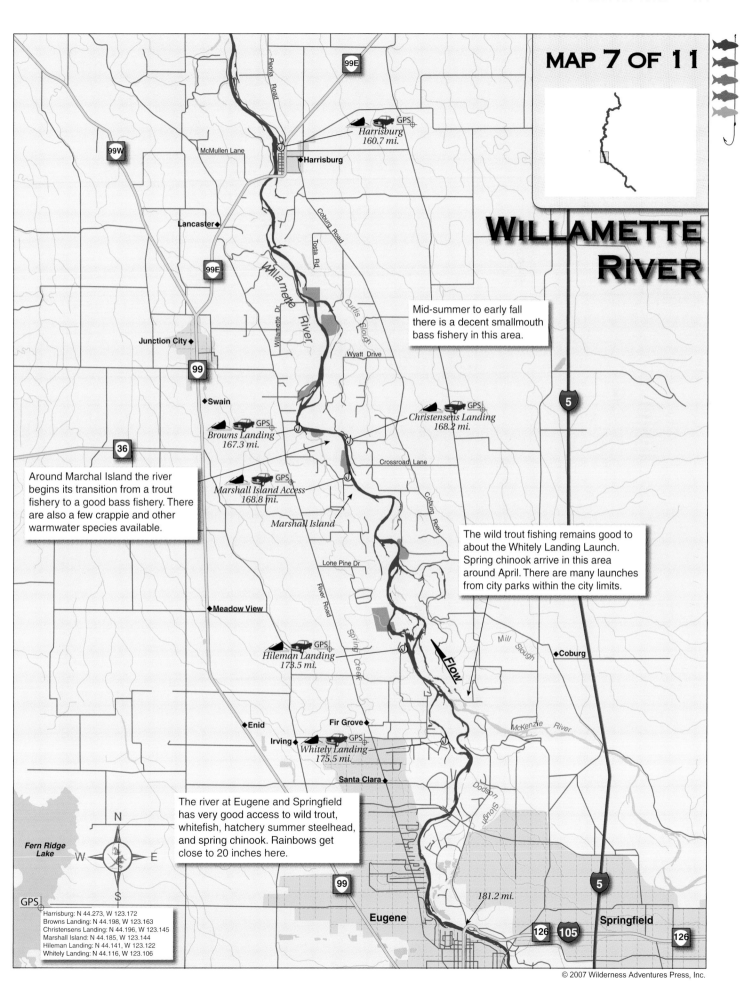

MAP **7** OF **11**

WILLAMETTE RIVER

Mid-summer to early fall there is a decent smallmouth bass fishery in this area.

Around Marchal Island the river begins its transition from a trout fishery to a good bass fishery. There are also a few crappie and other warmwater species available.

The wild trout fishing remains good to about the Whitely Landing Launch. Spring chinook arrive in this area around April. There are many launches from city parks within the city limits.

The river at Eugene and Springfield has very good access to wild trout, whitefish, hatchery summer steelhead, and spring chinook. Rainbows get close to 20 inches here.

Harrisburg
160.7 mi.

Christensens Landing
168.2 mi.

Browns Landing
167.3 mi.

Marshall Island Access
168.8 mi.

Marshall Island

Hileman Landing
173.5 mi.

Whitely Landing
175.5 mi.

Flow

181.2 mi.

Fern Ridge Lake

Harrisburg: N 44.273, W 123.172
Browns Landing: N 44.198, W 123.163
Christensens Landing: N 44.196, W 123.145
Marshall Island: N 44.185, W 123.144
Hileman Landing: N 44.141, W 123.122
Whitely Landing: N 44.116, W 123.106

© 2007 Wilderness Adventures Press, Inc.

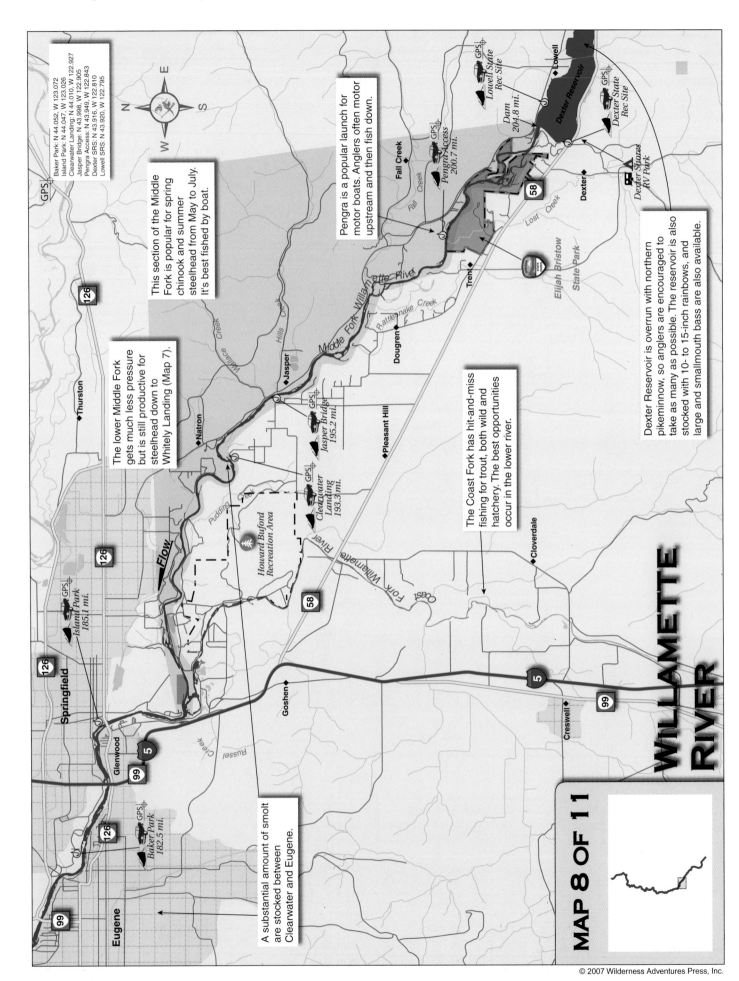

Baker Park: N 44.052, W 123.072
Island Park: N 44.047, W 123.026
Clearwater Landing: N 44.010, W 122.927
Jasper Bridge: N 43.998, W 122.905
Pengra Access: N 43.949, W 122.843
Dexter SRS: N 43.916, W 122.810
Lowell SRS: N 43.920, W 122.795

This section of the Middle Fork is popular for spring chinook and summer steelhead from May to July. It's best fished by boat.

Pengra is a popular launch for motor boats. Anglers often motor upstream and then fish down.

The lower Middle Fork gets much less pressure but is still productive for steelhead down to Whitely Landing (Map 7).

Dexter Reservoir is overrun with northern pikeminnow, so anglers are encouraged to take as many as possible. The reservoir is also stocked with 10- to 15-inch rainbows, and large and smallmouth bass are also available.

The Coast Fork has hit-and-miss fishing for trout, both wild and hatchery. The best opportunities occur in the lower river.

A substantial amount of smolt are stocked between Clearwater and Eugene.

Lowell State Rec Site

Dexter State Rec Site

Dexter Shores RV Park

Dam 204.8 mi.

Pengra Access 200.7 mi.

Jasper Bridge 195.2 mi.

Clearwater Landing 193.3 mi.

Island Park 185.1 mi.

Baker Park 182.5 mi.

Lowell

Dexter

Trent

Fall Creek

Dougren

Pleasant Hill

Cloverdale

Goshen

Creswell

Natron

Jasper

Thurston

Springfield

Glenwood

Eugene

Elijah Bristow State Park

Howard Buford Recreation Area

Middle Fork Willamette River

Coast Fork Willamette River

Fall Creek

Lost Creek

Rattlesnake Creek

Pudding

Russel Creek

Hills Creek

Wallace Creek

Flow

WILLAMETTE RIVER

MAP 8 OF 11

© 2007 Wilderness Adventures Press, Inc.

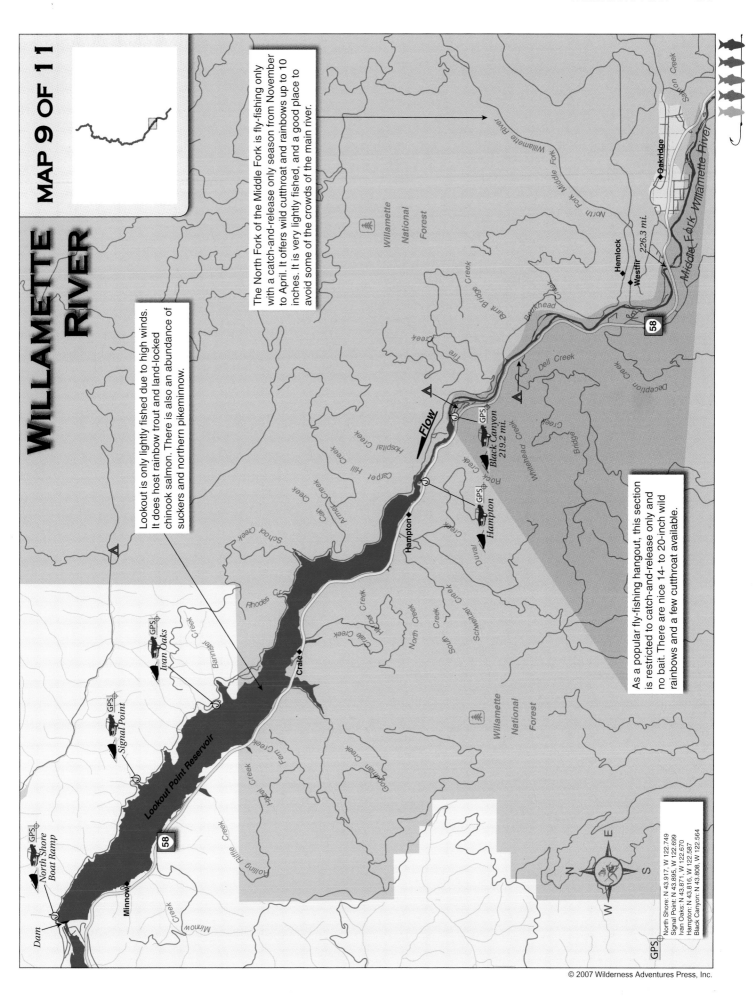

WILLAMETTE RIVER

MAP 9 OF 11

The North Fork of the Middle Fork is fly-fishing only with a catch-and-release only season from November to April. It offers wild cutthroat and rainbows up to 10 inches. It is very lightly fished, and a good place to avoid some of the crowds of the main river.

Lookout is only lightly fished due to high winds. It does host rainbow trout and land-locked chinook salmon. There is also an abundance of suckers and northern pikeminnow.

As a popular fly-fishing hangout, this section is restricted to catch-and-release only and no bait. There are nice 14- to 20-inch wild rainbows and a few cutthroat available.

Willamette National Forest

Oakridge

Hemlock

Westfir

226.3 mi.

58

North Fork Middle Fork Willamette River

Middle Fork Willamette River

Salmon Creek

Deception Creek

Dell Creek

Whitehead Creek

Beckhead

Burnt Bridge Creek

Tire Creek

Black Canyon
219.2 mi.

Rock Creek

Hampton

Duval Creek

Schneider Creek

South Creek

North Creek

Hope Creek

Craig Creek

Willamette National Forest

GPS

Flow

Hospital Creek

Carpet Hill Creek

Ammer Creek

Can Creek

School Creek

Rhodes Creek

Banister Creek

Craig

Fern Creek

Hazel Creek

Goodman Creek

Rolling Rifle Creek

58

Lookout Point Reservoir

Minnow

Minnow Creek

Dam

North Shore
Boat Ramp

GPS

Signal Point

GPS

Ivan Oaks

GPS

N
E
S
W

GPS

North Shore: N 43.917, W 122.749
Signal Point: N 43.895, W 122.699
Ivan Oaks: N 43.871, W 122.670
Hampton: N 43.816, W 122.587
Black Canyon: N 43.808, W 122.564

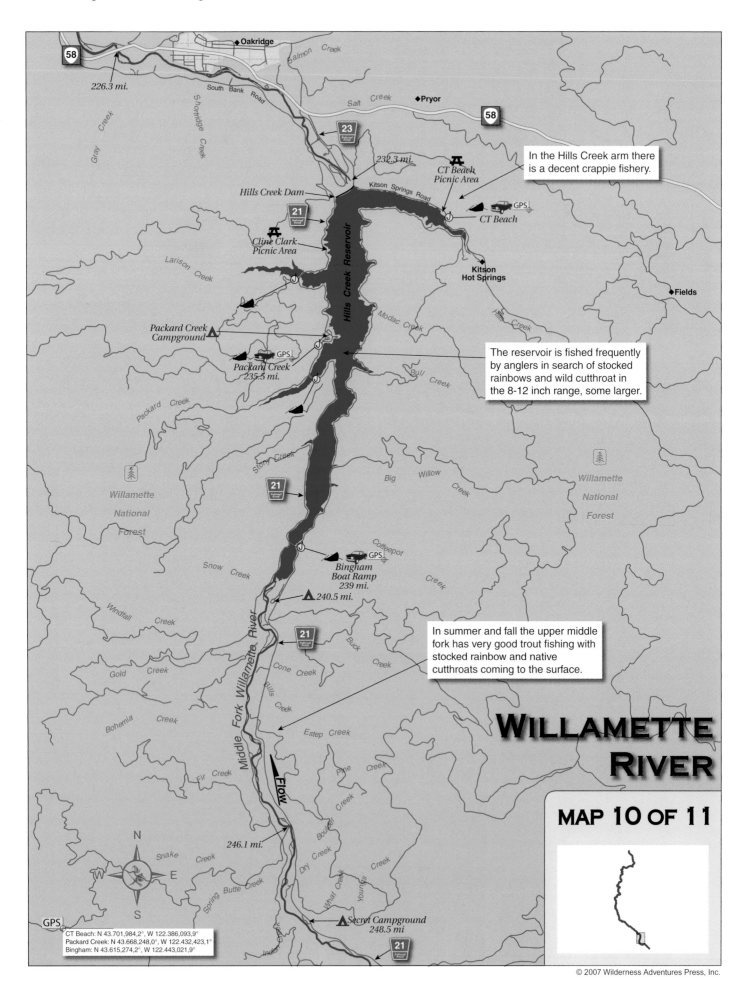

In the Hills Creek arm there is a decent crappie fishery.

The reservoir is fished frequently by anglers in search of stocked rainbows and wild cutthroat in the 8-12 inch range, some larger.

In summer and fall the upper middle fork has very good trout fishing with stocked rainbow and native cutthroats coming to the surface.

Oakridge

226.3 mi.

Pryor

58

23

232.3 mi.

CT Beach Picnic Area

GPS

CT Beach

Hills Creek Dam

Kitson Springs Road

21

Cline Clark Picnic Area

Kitson Hot Springs

Fields

Larison Creek

Hills Creek Reservoir

Modac Creek

Packard Creek Campground

GPS

Packard Creek 235.5 mi.

Gray Creek

Shortridge Creek

South Bank Road

Salmon Creek

Salt Creek

Bull Creek

Packard Creek

Stony Creek

Big Willow Creek

Willamette National Forest

21

Willamette National Forest

Snow Creek

Bingham Boat Ramp 239 mi.

GPS

Coffeepot Creek

240.5 mi.

Windfall Creek

Gold Creek

Buck Creek

Cone Creek

Ellis Creek

21

Bohemia Creek

Middle Fork Willamette River

Fir Creek

Estep Creek

Pine Creek

WILLAMETTE RIVER

MAP 10 OF 11

Flow

246.1 mi.

Snake Creek

Spring Butte Creek

Boulder Creek

Dry Creek

What Creek

Youngs Creek

Indian

Secret Campground 248.5 mi

21

N
W E
S

GPS

CT Beach: N 43.701,984,2°, W 122.386,093,9°
Packard Creek: N 43.668,248,0°, W 122.432,423,1°
Bingham: N 43.615,274,2°, W 122.443,021,9°

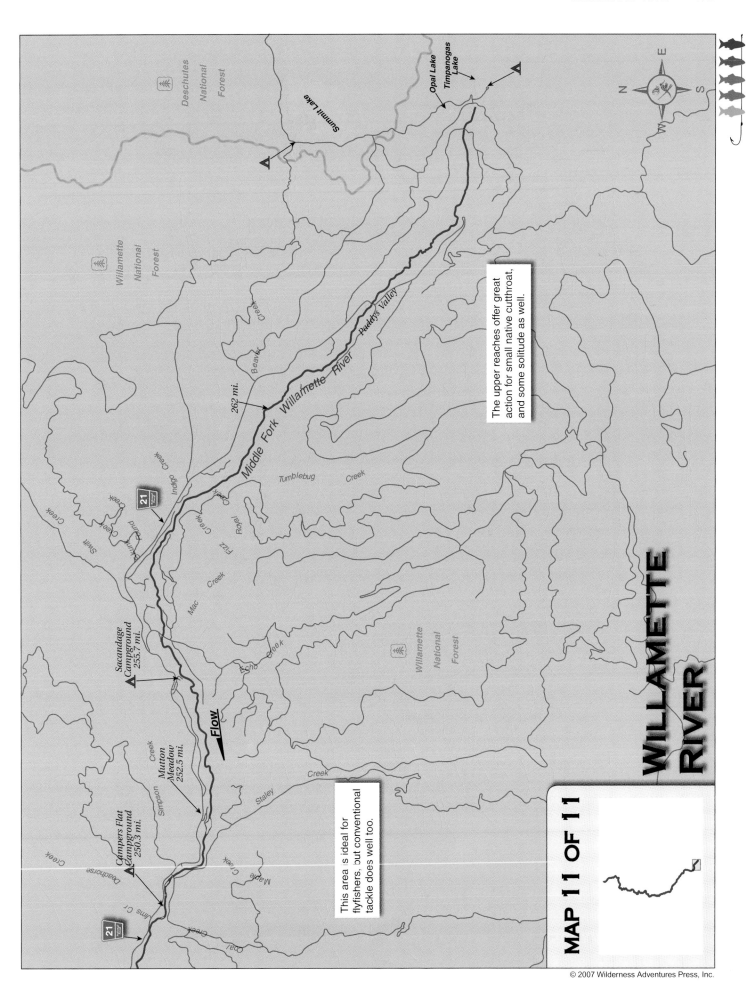

The upper reaches offer great action for small native cutthroat, and some solitude as well.

Opal Lake

Timpanogas Lake

Summit Lake

Deschutes National Forest

Willamette National Forest

Paddys Valley

Beal Creek

Middle Fork Willamette River

262 mi.

Tumblebug Creek

Indigo Creek

Skunray Creek

Swift Creek

Royal Creek

Fizz Creek

Mac Creek

Echo Creek

Willamette National Forest

Sacandage Campground 255.7 mi.

Flow

Mutton Meadow 252.5 mi.

Simpson Creek

Staley Creek

Campers Flat Campground 250.3 mi.

Deadhorse Creek

Jims Cr.

Maple Creek

Opal Creek

This area is ideal for flyfishers, but conventional tackle does well too.

MAP 11 OF 11

WILLAMETTE RIVER

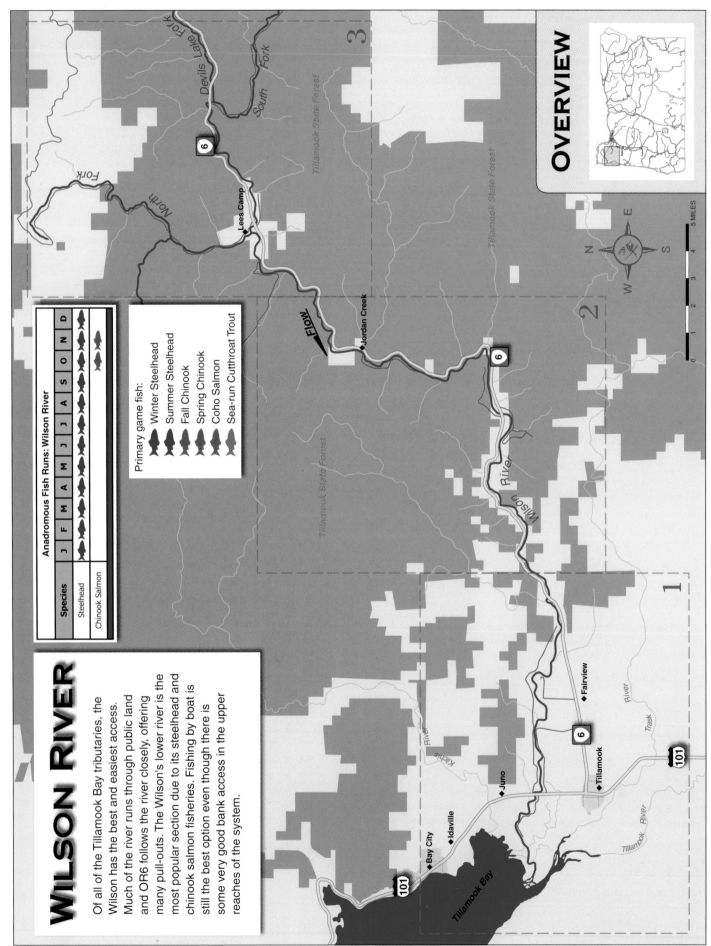

OVERVIEW

WILSON RIVER

Of all of the Tillamook Bay tributaries, the Wilson has the best and easiest access. Much of the river runs through public land and OR6 follows the river closely, offering many pull-outs. The Wilson's lower river is the most popular section due to its steelhead and chinook salmon fisheries. Fishing by boat is still the best option even though there is some very good bank access in the upper reaches of the system.

Anadromous Fish Runs: Wilson River

Species	J	F	M	A	M	J	J	A	S	O	N	D
Steelhead	🐟	🐟	🐟	🐟	🐟	🐟	🐟	🐟	🐟	🐟	🐟	🐟
Chinook Salmon									🐟	🐟	🐟	🐟

Primary game fish:

Winter Steelhead
Summer Steelhead
Fall Chinook
Spring Chinook
Coho Salmon
Sea-run Cutthroat Trout

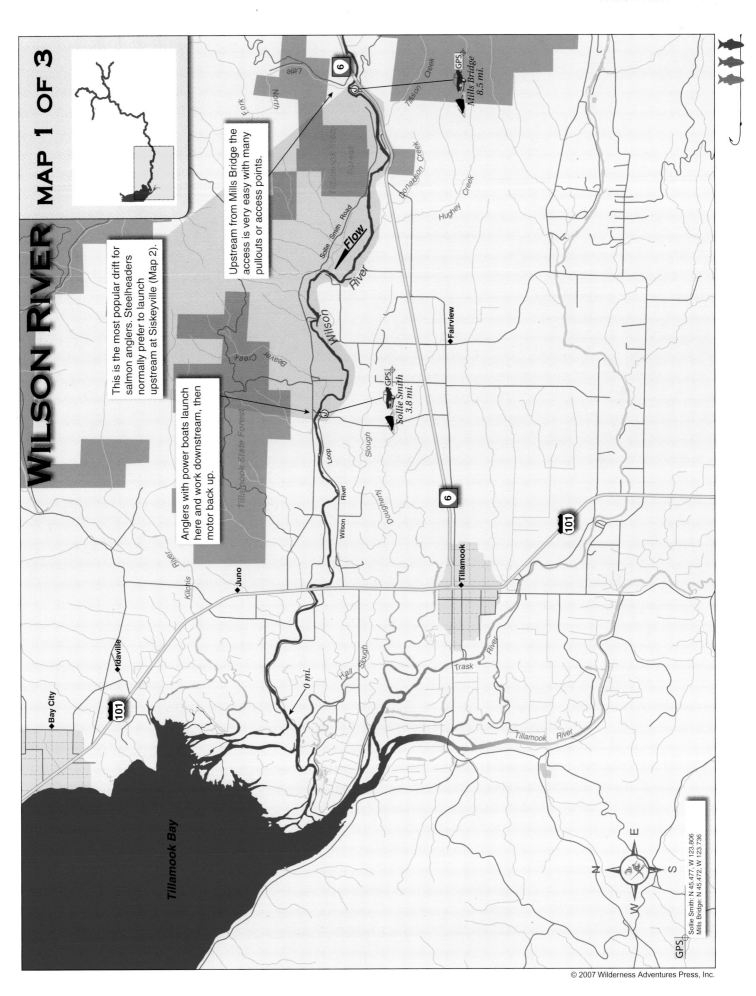

This is the most popular drift for salmon anglers. Steelheaders normally prefer to launch upstream at Siskeyville (Map 2).

Upstream from Mills Bridge the access is very easy with many pullouts or access points.

Anglers with power boats launch here and work downstream, then motor back up.

Flow

Mills Bridge 8.5 mi.

GPS

Sollie Smith 3.8 mi.

GPS

Wilson River

Sollie Smith Road

Little North Fork

Tillamook State Forest

Beaver Creek

Tillson Creek

Donaldson Creek

Hughey Creek

Fairview

Loop

Slough

Wilson River

Dougherty

Tillamook

0 mi.

Hall Slough

Trask River

Tillamook River

Tillamook Bay

Juno

Idaville

Bay City

GPS
Sollie Smith: N 45.477, W 123.806
Mills Bridge: N 45.472, W 123.736

© 2007 Wilderness Adventures Press, Inc.

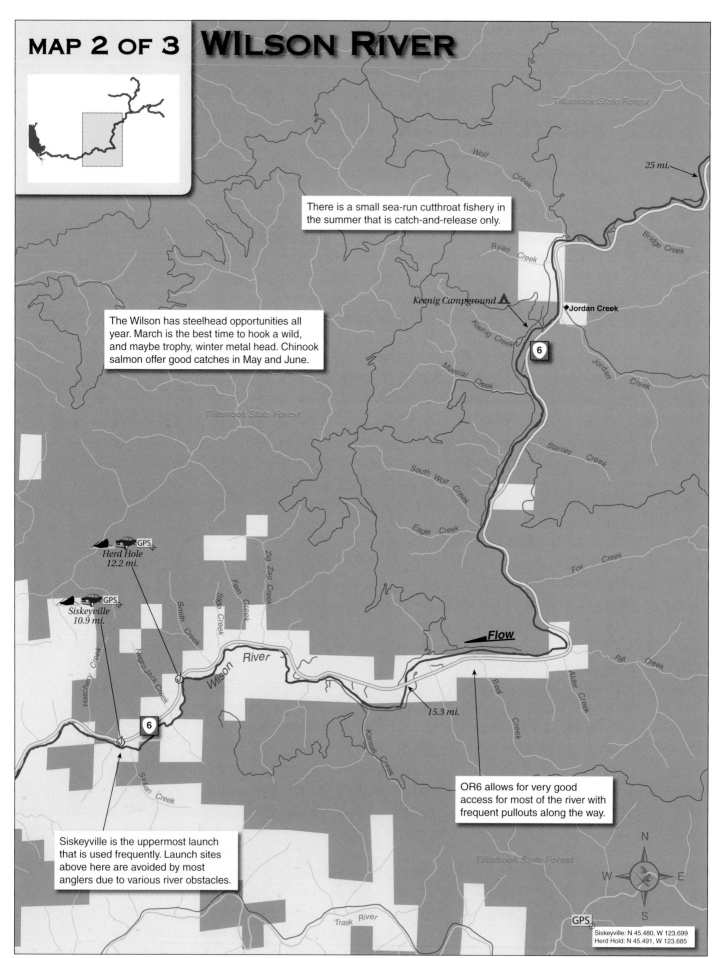

MAP 2 OF 3 WILSON RIVER

25 mi.

Tillamook State Forest

Wolf Creek

Bridge Creek

Ryan Creek

There is a small sea-run cutthroat fishery in the summer that is catch-and-release only.

Keenig Campground

Keenig Creek

◆ Jordan Creek

6

Jordan Creek

The Wilson has steelhead opportunities all year. March is the best time to hook a wild, and maybe trophy, winter metal head. Chinook salmon offer good catches in May and June.

Muesial Creek

Stanley Creek

Tillamook State Forest

South Wolf Creek

Eagle Creek

Fox Creek

Herd Hole
12.2 mi.
GPS

Siskeyville
10.9 mi.
GPS

Zig Zag Creek

Fern Creek

Slide Creek

Smith Creek

Flow

Fall Creek

Alder Creek

Bear Creek

Hatchery Creek

Negro Jack Creek

Wilson River

15.3 mi.

Kansas Creek

OR6 allows for very good access for most of the river with frequent pullouts along the way.

6

Siskeyville is the uppermost launch that is used frequently. Launch sites above here are avoided by most anglers due to various river obstacles.

Sylvan Creek

Tillamook State Forest

N

W   E

S

Trask River

GPS
Siskeyville: N 45.480, W 123.699
Herd Hold: N 45.491, W 123.685

© 2007 Wilderness Adventures Press, Inc.

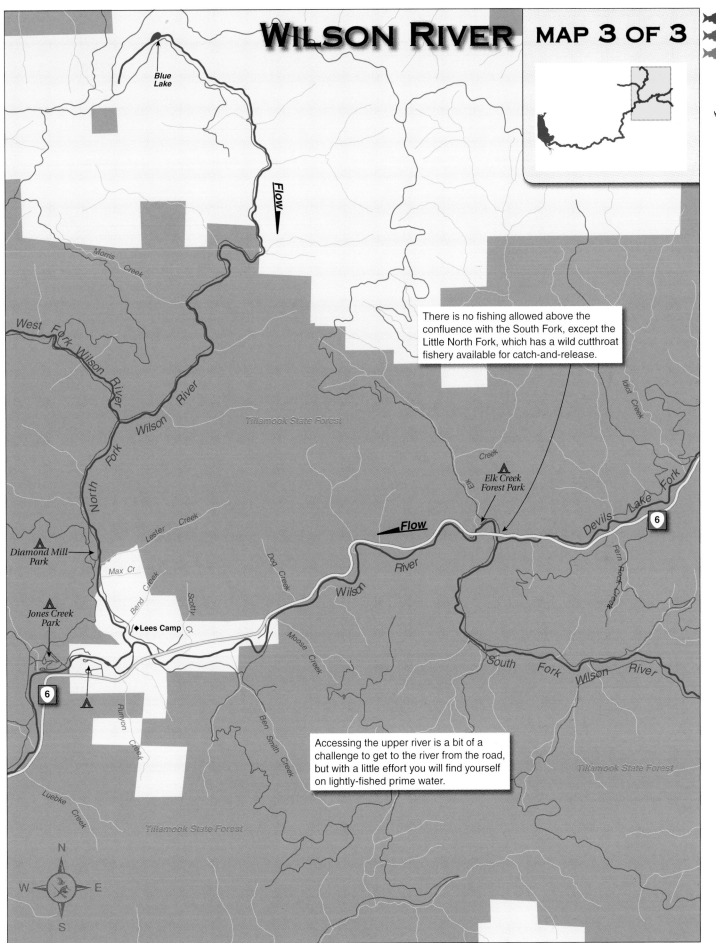

WILSON RIVER

MAP 3 OF 3

Blue Lake

Flow

Morris Creek

West Fork Wilson River

Tillamook State Forest

There is no fishing allowed above the confluence with the South Fork, except the Little North Fork, which has a wild cutthroat fishery available for catch-and-release.

Idiot Creek

Elk Creek

Elk Creek Forest Park

Devils Lake Fork

6

Flow

Wilson River

Lester Creek

Diamond Mill Park

North Fork Wilson River

Max Cr

Bend Creek

Scotty

Dog Creek

Fern Rock Creek

Jones Creek Park

◆Lees Camp

6

Runyon Creek

Moose Creek

South Fork Wilson River

Ben Smith Creek

Accessing the upper river is a bit of a challenge to get to the river from the road, but with a little effort you will find yourself on lightly-fished prime water.

Tillamook State Forest

Luebke Creek

Tillamook State Forest

N
W E
S

NOTES

NOTES

NOTES

NOTES

NOTES

NOTES

Other Fishing Titles Available From Wilderness Adventures Press™

California's Best Fishing Waters

Colorado's Best Fishing Waters

Montana's Best Fishing Waters

Washington's Best Fishing Waters

Flyfisher's Guide to Alaska

Flyfisher's Guide to Chesapeake Bay

Flyfisher's Guide to Colorado

Flyfisher's Guide to the Florida Keys

Flyfisher's Guide to Freshwater Florida

Flyfisher's Guide to Saltwater Florida: Includes Light Tackle

Flyfisher's Guide to Idaho

Flyfisher's Guide to Montana

Flyfisher's Guide to Michigan

Flyfisher's Guide to Minnesota

Flyfisher's Guide to Missouri and Arkansas

Flyfisher's Guide to New Mexico

Flyfisher's Guide to New York

Flyfisher's Guide to Northern California

Flyfisher's Guide to Northern New England

Flyfisher's Guide to Oregon

Flyfisher's Guide to Pennsylvania

Flyfisher's Guide to Texas

Flyfisher's Guide to Utah

Flyfisher's Guide to Virginia

Flyfisher's Guide to Washington

Flyfisher's Guide to Wisconsin & Iowa

Flyfisher's Guide to Wyoming

Flyfisher's Guide to Yellowstone National Park

On the Fly Guide to the Northwest

On the Fly Guide to the Northern Rockies

Saltwater Angler's Guide to the Southeast

Saltwater Angler's Guide to Southern California

Field Guide to Fishing Knots

Go-To Flies: 101 Patterns the Pros Use When All Else Fails